## The Best Test Preparation for the

# SAT Subject Test

# Chemistry

## 6<sup>th</sup> EDITION

**With REA's TEST*ware*® on CD-ROM**

**Updated and Edited by**
## Kevin Reel
Head of School
The Colorado Springs School
Colorado Springs, CO

*Research & Education Association*
*Visit our website at*
**www.rea.com**

**Research & Education Association**
61 Ethel Road West
Piscataway, New Jersey 08854
E-mail: info@rea.com

The Best Test Preparation for the
**SAT SUBJECT TEST IN CHEMISTRY**
With TEST*ware*® on CD-ROM

**Published 2009**

Copyright © 2007 by Research & Education Association, Inc. Prior
edition copyright © 2000, 1998, 1996, 1991, 1987 by Research &
Education Association, Inc. All rights reserved. No part of this
book may be reproduced in any form without permission of the
publisher.

Printed in the United States of America

Library of Congress Control Number 2006927457

ISBN-13: 978-0-7386-0273-8
ISBN-10: 0-7386-0273-6

# CONTENTS

## About Our Editor

Kevin R. Reel has been in science education for over 25 years. He is currently the high school principal at the Westminster Schools in Atlanta, Georgia. Mr. Reel is also the former head of the science department and has taught courses in biology, chemistry, environmental science, and earth science. He has written numerous articles for academic journals and has contributed to many textbooks in chemistry, health, and environmental science. He earned his B.A. and M.S. from Stanford University.

## About Research & Education Association

Founded in 1959, Research & Education Association is dedicated to publishing the finest and most effective educational materials—including software, study guides, and test preps—for students in middle school, high school, college, graduate school, and beyond.

REA's Test Preparation series includes books and software for all academic levels in almost all disciplines. Research & Education Association publishes test preps for students who have not yet entered high school, as well as high school students preparing to enter college. Students from countries around the world seeking to attend college in the United States will find the assistance they need in REA's publications. For college students seeking advanced degrees, REA publishes test preps for many major graduate school admission examinations in a wide variety of disciplines, including engineering, law, and medicine. Students at every level, in every field, with every ambition can find what they are looking for among REA's publications.

REA's publications and educational materials are highly regarded and continually receive an unprecedented amount of praise from professionals, instructors, librarians, parents, and students. Our authors are as diverse as the fields represented in the books we publish. They are well-known in their respective disciplines and serve on the faculties of prestigious high schools, colleges, and universities throughout the United States and Canada.

Today, REA's wide-ranging catalog is a leading resource for teachers, students, and professionals.

We invite you to visit us at *www.rea.com* to find out how "REA is making the world smarter."

# Acknowledgments

We wish to thank William Uhland, Research Scientist, for developing our original course review material.

In addition we would like to thank Larry B. Kling, Vice President, Editorial, for his overall guidance, which brought this publication to completion; Pam Weston, Vice President, Publishing, for setting the quality standards for production integrity and managing the publication to completion; John Cording, Vice President, Technology, for coordinating the design and development of REA's TEST*ware*® software; Diane Goldschmidt, Senior Editor, for project management; Christine Reilley and Anne Winthrop Esposito, Senior Editors, for preflight editorial review; and Heena Patel and Michelle Boykins, Technology Project Managers, for their design contributions and software testing efforts. Our cover was designed by Senior Graphic Designer Christine Saul.

We also wish to thank Patricia Van Arnum for her technical and editorial review; Kathy Caratozzolo of Caragraphics for page composition; and Jeff LoBalbo, Senior Graphic Artist, for post-production file-mapping.

# SAT Chemistry Subject Test
# Independent Study Schedule

The following study schedule allows for thorough preparation for the SAT Chemistry Subject Test. Although it is designed for eight weeks, it can be condensed into a four-week course by condensing each two-week period into one. Be sure to set aside enough time—at least two hours each day—to study. But no matter which study schedule works best for you, the more time you spend studying, the more prepared and relaxed you will feel on the day of the exam.

| Week | Activity |
|------|----------|
| 1 | Read Chapter 1, which will introduce you to the SAT Chemistry Subject Test. Then take Practice Test 1 on CD-ROM to determine your strengths and weaknesses. You can then determine the areas in which you need to focus more study efforts. |
| 2 | Carefully read and study the Course Review included in this book. Familiarize yourself with all the material, especially the areas you had trouble with in Practice Test 1. Go through each of the problems you answered incorrectly and make sure you understand how to arrive at the right answer. Recognizing where you went wrong will help you avoid the same mistakes in other problems. |
| 3 & 4 | Take Practice Test 2 on CD-ROM and Practice Test 3 in this book, and after scoring each exam, carefully review all explanations for your incorrect responses. If there are any types of questions or particular subjects that seem difficult to you, review those subjects by studying again the appropriate section of the Course Review. |
| 5 & 6 | Take Practice Test 4 and Practice Test 5 in this book, and after scoring each exam, carefully review all explanations for your incorrect responses. If there are any types of questions or particular subjects that seem difficult to you, review those subjects by studying again the appropriate section of the Course Review. |

| Week | Activity |
|:---:|:---|
| 7 | Take Practice Test 6 in this book, and after scoring your exam, carefully review all explanations for your incorrect responses. If there are any types of questions or particular subjects that seem difficult to you, review those subjects by studying again the appropriate section of the Course Review. |
| 8 | Retake all of the practice tests either on CD-ROM or in this book. Pay particular attention to the questions you had difficulty with the first time you encountered them. By going through the tests again, you not only strengthen areas of weakness, but you also reinforce your overall grasp of the topics found on the SAT Chemistry Subject Test. |

# INSTALLING REA's TEST*ware*®

## SYSTEM REQUIREMENTS

Pentium 75 MHz (300 MHz recommended), or a higher or compatible processor; Microsoft Windows 98, NT 4 (SP6), ME, 2000, or XP; 64 MB Available RAM; Internet Explorer 5.5 or higher (Internet Explorer 5.5 is included on the CD); minimum 60 MB available hard-disk space; VGA or higher-resolution monitor, 800x600 resolution setting; Microsoft Mouse, Microsoft Intellimouse, or compatible pointing device.

## INSTALLATION

1. Insert the SAT Chemistry Subject Test TEST*ware*® CD-ROM into the CD-ROM drive.
2. If the installation doesn't begin automatically, from the Start Menu, choose the RUN command. When the RUN dialog box appears, type d:\setup (where *d* is the letter of your CD-ROM drive) at the prompt and click OK.
3. The installation process will begin. A dialog box proposing the directory "Program Files\REA\SATChemistry" will appear. If the name and location are suitable, click OK. If you wish to specify a different name or location, type it in and click OK.
4. Start the SAT Chemistry Subject Test TEST*ware*® application by double-clicking on the icon.

REA's SAT Chemistry Subject Test TEST*ware*® is **EASY** to **LEARN AND USE**. To achieve maximum benefits, we recommend that you take a few minutes to go through the on-screen tutorial on your computer. The "screen buttons" are also explained there to familiarize you with the program.

## SSD ACCOMMODATIONS FOR STUDENTS WITH DISABILITIES

Many students qualify for extra time to take the SAT Chemistry Subject Test, and our TEST*ware*® can be adapted to accommodate your time extension. This allows you to practice under the same extended time accommodations that you will receive on the actual test day. To customize your TEST*ware*® to suit the most common extensions, visit our website at *www.rea.com/ssd*.

## TECHNICAL SUPPORT

REA's TEST*ware*® is backed by customer and technical support. For questions about **installation or operation of your software**, contact us at:

**Research & Education Association**
Phone: (732) 819-8880 (9 a.m. to 5 p.m. ET, Monday–Friday)
Fax: (732) 819-8808
Website: www.rea.com
E-mail: info@rea.com

**Note to Windows XP Users:** In order for the TEST*ware*® to function properly, please install and run the application under the same computer-administrator level user account. Installing the TEST*ware*® as one user and running it as another could cause file access path conflicts.

# Excelling on the SAT Chemistry Subject Test

# Chapter 1

# EXCELLING ON THE SAT CHEMISTRY SUBJECT TEST

## ABOUT THIS BOOK AND TEST*ware*®

This book, along with REA's exclusive TEST*ware*® software, provides you with an accurate and complete representation of the SAT Chemistry Subject Test. Inside you will find a complete review designed to provide you with the information and strategies needed to do well on the exam, as well as six practice tests based on the actual exam. The practice tests contain every type of question that you can expect to appear on the SAT Chemistry Subject Test. Following each test you will find an answer key with detailed explanations designed to help you master the test material.

Practice Tests 1 and 2 are included in two formats: in printed form in this book and in TEST*ware*® format on the enclosed CD. **We recommend that you begin your preparation by first taking the computerized version of your test.** The software provides timed conditions and instantaneous, accurate scoring, which make it all the easier to pinpoint your strengths and weaknesses.

## ABOUT THE TEST

### Who Takes the Test and What Is It Used For?

Students planning to attend college take the SAT Chemistry Subject Test for one of two reasons:

(1) Because it is an admission requirement of the college or university to which they are applying

*OR*

(2) To demonstrate proficiency in chemistry.

The SAT Chemistry test is designed for students who have taken a one-year introductory course in chemistry.

## Who Administers the Test?

The SAT Chemistry Subject Test is developed by the College Board and administered by Educational Testing Service (ETS). The test development process involves the assistance of educators throughout the country, and is designed and implemented to ensure that the content and difficulty level of the test are appropriate.

## When Should the SAT Chemistry Subject Test Be Taken?

If you are applying to a college that requires Subject Test scores as part of the admissions process, you should take the SAT Chemistry Subject Test by November or January of your senior year. If your scores are being used only for placement purposes, you may be able to take the test in the spring. Make sure to contact the colleges to which you are applying for more specific information.

## When and Where Is the Test Given?

The SAT Chemistry Subject Test is administered six times a year at many locations throughout the country, mostly high schools. The test is given in October, November, December, January, May, and June.

To receive information on upcoming administrations of the exam, consult the publication *Taking the SAT Subject Tests,* which may be obtained from your guidance counselor or by contacting:

College Board SAT Program
P.O. Box 025505
Miami, FL 33102
Phone: (866) 756-7346
Website: *www.collegeboard.com*

## Is There a Registration Fee?

You must pay a registration fee to take the SAT Chemistry Subject Test. Consult the College Board's Website (*www.collegeboard.com*) for information on the fee structure. Financial assistance may be granted in certain situations. To find out if you qualify and to register for assistance, contact your academic advisor.

# HOW TO USE THIS BOOK AND TEST*ware*®

## What Do I Study First?

Remember that the SAT Chemistry Subject Test is designed to test knowledge that has been acquired throughout your education. Therefore, the best way to prepare for the exam is to refresh yourself by thoroughly studying our review material and taking the sample tests provided in this book. They will familiarize you with the types of questions, directions, and format of the SAT Chemistry Subject Test.

To begin your studies, read the suggestions for test taking and take Practice Test 1 on CD-ROM to determine your strengths and weaknesses. Next, study the course review material focusing on your specific problem areas. The course review includes the information you need to know when taking the exam. Then take Practice Test 2 on CD-ROM and the remaining practice tests in this book to become familiar with the format and feel of the SAT Chemistry Subject Test.

To best utilize your study time, follow our Independent Study Schedule, which you will find in the front of this book.

## SSD Accommodations for Students with Disabilities

Many students qualify for extra time to take the SAT Subject Tests. For information, contact:

> College Board Services for Students with Disabilities
> PO Box 6226
> Princeton, NJ 08541-6226
> Phone: (609) 771-7137 Monday through Friday,
>     8 a.m. to 6 p.m. (Eastern time)
> TTY: (609) 882-4118
> Fax: (609) 771-7944
> E-mail: ssd@info.collegeboard.org

Our TEST*ware*® can be adapted to accommodate your time extension. This allows you to practice under the same extended time accommodations that you will receive on the actual test day. To customize your TEST*ware*® to suit the most common extensions, visit our website at *www.rea.com/ssd*.

## When Should I Start Studying?

It is never too early to start studying for the SAT Chemistry test. The earlier you begin, the more time you will have to sharpen your skills. Do not procrastinate! Cramming is *not* an effective way to study, since it does not allow you the time needed to learn the test material. The sooner you learn the format of the exam, the more comfortable you will be when you take it.

# FORMAT OF THE SAT CHEMISTRY SUBJECT TEST

The SAT Chemistry test is a one-hour exam consisting of 85 multiple-choice questions.

The first part of the exam consists of *classification* questions. This question type presents a list of statements or questions that you must match up with a group of choices lettered (A) through (E). Each choice may be used once, more than once, or not at all.

The exam then shifts to *relationship analysis* questions which you will answer in a specially numbered section of your answer sheet. You will have to determine if each of two statements is true or false *and* if the second statement is a correct explanation of the first.

The last section is composed strictly of multiple-choice questions with choices lettered (A) through (E).

> *Note:* The relationship analysis questions on the SAT Chemistry exam must be answered on a special section of your answer sheet labeled "Chemistry." These questions will be numbered beginning with 101 and must be answered according to the special instructions given at the beginning of the section.

## Material Tested

The following chart summarizes the approximate distribution of topics covered on the SAT Chemistry Subject Test.

| Topic | Percentage | Number of Questions |
|---|---|---|
| Structure of Matter | 25 | 21 |
| States of Matter | 15 | 13 |
| Reaction Types | 14 | 12 |
| Stoichiometry | 12 | 10 |
| Equilibrium & Reaction Times | 7 | 6 |
| Thermodynamics | 6 | 5 |
| Descriptive Chemistry | 13 | 11 |
| Laboratory | 8 | 7 |

Each test will have approximately five questions based on the balancing of equations and predicting products of chemical reactions.

The questions on the SAT Chemistry test are also grouped into three larger categories according to how they test your understanding of the subject material.

| Category | Definition | Approximate Percentage of Test |
|---|---|---|
| Factual Recall | Demonstrating a knowledge and understanding of important concepts and specific information. | 20 |
| Application | Taking a specific principle and applying it to a practical situation. | 45 |
| Integration | Inferring information and drawing conclusions from particular relationships. | 35 |

Other information regarding the SAT Chemistry test:

- A periodic table including atomic number and masses of elements is provided to all test takers

- Calculator use is not allowed

- Problem solving requires simple calculations

- The metric system of units is used

## SCORING THE SAT CHEMISTRY SUBJECT TEST

The SAT Chemistry test, like all other Subject Tests, is scored on a 200-800 scale.

### How Do I Score My Practice Test?

Your exam is scored by crediting one point for each correct answer and deducting one-fourth of a point for each incorrect answer. There is no deduction for answers that are omitted. Use the worksheet below to calculate your raw score and to record your scores for the six practice tests. Once you have calculated your raw score, consult the conversion table on page 11 to find your scaled score.

## Scoring Worksheet

_____    −    (_____ x 1/4)    =    _____

number correct          number incorrect          Raw Score
                        (do not include           (round to nearest
                        unanswered questions)     whole point)

| | Raw Score | Scaled Score |
|---|---|---|
| Test 1 | _____ | _____ |
| Test 2 | _____ | _____ |
| Test 3 | _____ | _____ |
| Test 4 | _____ | _____ |
| Test 5 | _____ | _____ |
| Test 6 | _____ | _____ |

## STUDYING FOR THE SAT CHEMISTRY TEST

It is very important to choose the time and place for studying that works best for you. Some students may set aside a certain number of hours every morning to study, while others may choose to study at night before going to sleep. Other students may study during the day, while waiting on a line, or even while eating lunch. Only you can determine when and where your study time will be most effective. Be consistent and use your time wisely. Work out a study routine and stick to it!

When you take the practice tests, try to make your testing conditions as much like the actual test as possible. Turn your television and radio off, and sit down at a quiet table free from distraction. Make sure to time yourself with a timer.

As you complete each practice test, score your test and thoroughly review the explanations to the questions you answered incorrectly; however, do not review too much at any one time. Concentrate on one problem area at a time by reviewing the questions and explanations, and by studying our review until you are confident you completely understand the material.

Keep track of your scores. By doing so, you will be able to gauge your progress and discover general weaknesses in particular sections. You should carefully study the reviews that cover your areas of difficulty, as this will build your skills in those areas.

## TEST-TAKING TIPS

Although you may be unfamiliar with standardized tests such as the SAT Chemistry Subject Test, there are many ways to acquaint yourself with this type of examination and help alleviate your test-taking anxieties. Listed below are ways to help you become accustomed to the SAT Chemistry Subject Test, some of which may apply to other standardized tests as well.

**Become comfortable with the format of the exam.** When you are practicing to take the SAT Chemistry Subject Test, simulate the conditions under which you will be taking the actual test. Stay calm and pace yourself. After simulating the test only a couple of times, you will boost your chances of doing well, and you will be able to sit down for the actual exam with much more confidence.

**Know the directions and format for each section of the test.** Familiarizing yourself with the directions and format of the exam will not only save you time, but will also ensure that you are familiar enough with the SAT Chemistry Subject Test to avoid nervousness (and the mistakes caused by being nervous).

**Do your scratchwork in the margins of the test booklet.** You will not be given scrap paper during the exam, and you may not perform scratchwork on your answer sheet. Space is provided in your test booklet to do any necessary work or draw diagrams.

**If you are unsure of an answer, and can eliminate three answer choices, guess.** Use the process of elimination by going through each answer to a question and ruling out as many of the answer choices as possible. By eliminating three answer choices, you give yourself a fifty-fifty chance of answering correctly since there will only be two choices left from which to make your guess.

**Mark your answers in the appropriate spaces on the answer sheet.** Each numbered row will contain five ovals corresponding to each answer choice for that question. Fill in the circle that corresponds to your answer darkly, completely, and neatly. You can change your answer, but remember to completely erase your old answer. Any stray lines or unnecessary marks may cause the machine to score your answer incorrectly. When you have finished working on a section, you may want to go back and check to make sure your answers correspond to the correct questions. Marking one answer in the wrong space will throw off the rest of your test, whether it is graded by machine or by hand.

**You don't have to answer every question.** You are not penalized if you do not answer every question. The only penalty you receive is if you answer a question incorrectly. Try to use the guessing strategy, but if you are truly stumped by a question, you do not have to answer it.

**Work quickly and steadily.** You have a limited amount of time to work on each section, so you need to work quickly and steadily. Avoid focusing on one problem for too long. Taking the practice tests in this book will help you to learn how to budget your time.

## Before the Test

Make sure you know where your test center is well in advance of your test day so you do not get lost on the day of the test. On the night before the test, gather together the materials you will need the next day:

- Your admission ticket
- Two forms of identification (*e.g.,* driver's license, student identification card, or current alien registration card)
- Two No. 2 pencils with erasers
- Directions to the test center
- A watch (if you wish) but not one that makes noise, as it may disturb other test-takers

On the day of the test, you should wake up early (it is hoped after a decent night's rest) and have a good breakfast. Dress comfortably, so that you are not distracted by being too hot or too cold while taking the test. Also, plan to arrive at the test center early. This will allow you to collect your thoughts and relax before the test, and will also spare you the stress of being late. If you arrive after the test begins, you will not be admitted and you will not receive a refund.

## During the Test

When you arrive at the test center, try to find a seat where you feel you will be comfortable. Follow all the rules and instructions given by the test supervisor. If you do not, you risk being dismissed from the test and having your scores canceled.

Once all the test materials are passed out, the test instructor will give you directions for filling out your answer sheet. Fill this sheet out carefully since this information will appear on your score report.

## After the Test

When you have completed the SAT Chemistry Subject Test, you may hand in your test materials and leave. Then, go home and relax!

### When Will I Receive My Score Report and What Will It Look Like?

You should receive your score report about three weeks after you take the test. This report will include your scores, percentile ranks, and interpretive information.

# SAT Chemistry Score Conversion Table*

| Raw Score | Scaled Score | Raw Score | Scaled Score | Raw Score | Scaled Score |
|---|---|---|---|---|---|
| 85 | 800 | 50 | 650 | 15 | 450 |
| 84 | 800 | 49 | 640 | 14 | 450 |
| 83 | 800 | 48 | 640 | 13 | 440 |
| 82 | 800 | 47 | 630 | 12 | 440 |
| 81 | 800 | 46 | 620 | 11 | 430 |
| 80 | 800 | 45 | 620 | 10 | 430 |
| 79 | 800 | 44 | 610 | 9 | 420 |
| 78 | 800 | 43 | 610 | 8 | 420 |
| 77 | 790 | 42 | 600 | 7 | 410 |
| 76 | 790 | 41 | 600 | 6 | 410 |
| 75 | 780 | 40 | 590 | 5 | 400 |
| 74 | 780 | 39 | 590 | 4 | 390 |
| 73 | 770 | 38 | 580 | 3 | 390 |
| 72 | 770 | 37 | 580 | 2 | 380 |
| 71 | 760 | 36 | 570 | 1 | 380 |
| 70 | 760 | 35 | 560 | 0 | 370 |
| 69 | 750 | 34 | 560 | -1 | 370 |
| 68 | 750 | 33 | 550 | -2 | 360 |
| 67 | 740 | 32 | 550 | -3 | 360 |
| 66 | 730 | 31 | 540 | -4 | 350 |
| 65 | 730 | 30 | 540 | -5 | 340 |
| 64 | 720 | 29 | 530 | -6 | 340 |
| 63 | 720 | 28 | 530 | -7 | 330 |
| 62 | 710 | 27 | 520 | -8 | 330 |
| 61 | 710 | 26 | 510 | -9 | 320 |
| 60 | 700 | 25 | 510 | -10 | 320 |
| 59 | 700 | 24 | 500 | -11 | 310 |
| 58 | 690 | 23 | 500 | -12 | 310 |
| 57 | 690 | 22 | 490 | -13 | 300 |
| 56 | 680 | 21 | 490 | -14 | 300 |
| 55 | 670 | 20 | 480 | -15 | 290 |
| 54 | 670 | 19 | 480 | -16 | 280 |
| 53 | 660 | 18 | 470 | -17 | 280 |
| 52 | 660 | 17 | 470 | -18 | 270 |
| 51 | 650 | 16 | 460 | -19 | 270 |

*Scoring for REA's practice tests strongly approximates that for the actual test. Bear in mind that scaled scores for different editions of the SAT Chemistry test are adjusted to take into account small shifts in content and in the overall performance of the test-taker population.

# SAT CHEMISTRY
# COURSE REVIEW

# CHAPTER 2

# COURSE REVIEW

## ATOMIC THEORY

### Origins of Atomic Theory

*Dalton*

John Dalton performed chemical reactions and carefully measured the masses of reactants and products. He proposed that all matter is composed of subunits call **atoms**. Atoms had different identities, called **elements.** Elements combined together in definite ratios to form **compounds**. He showed that atoms are never created or destroyed during chemical reactions.

*Thompson*

J.J. Thompson observed the deflection of particles in a cathode ray tube. He concluded that atoms are composed of positive and negative charges. He called negative charges **electrons**, and he suggested that the positive charges were distributed in islands throughout the atom, like raisins in raisin bread. Some people at the time called this the "plum pudding" model of the atom.

*Rutherford*

Ernest Rutherford fired alpha particles (that he knew to be positively charged) through thin gold foil. When he measured the resulting scatter patterns of the alpha particles after they hit the foil, he found that most of the alpha particles moved right through the foil, or were deflected slightly. However, some alpha particles were deflected at large angles, as though they had collided with a heavier object and bounced back. Rutherford concluded that the positive charge and mass of the atom was concentrated at the center of the atom, and that the rest of the atom is mostly empty space. This directly countered Thompson's "plum pudding" model.

## Bohr

Niels Bohr applied the idea of quantized energy to show that electrons exist around the nucleus at a fixed radius, and that electrons with higher energy exist farther from the nucleus. The Bohr model is only accurate for atoms and ions with one electron. It was clear that a more complex model was needed to explain atoms with multiple electrons. He also showed that electrons give off energy in the form of electromagnetic radiation when they move from a higher level, or excited state, to a lower level. The energy represented by the light, using Plank's equation, represents the difference between the two energy levels of the electron.

## Schrödinger

Erwin Schrödinger attributed a wave function to electrons. The wave function describes the probability of where an electron might exist. The regions of high probability are called **orbitals**, even though they are more like clouds than orbits. These orbitals can be described as *s*, *p*, *d*, or *f* orbitals, as used in electron configurations.

## Components of Atomic Structure

The combined number of protons and neutrons in the nucleus is represented by the mass number, which corresponds to the isotopic atomic weight. The atomic number is the number of protons found in the nucleus.

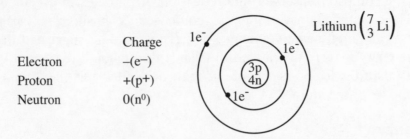

|  | Charge |
|---|---|
| Electron | $-(e^-)$ |
| Proton | $+(p^+)$ |
| Neutron | $0(n^0)$ |

The electrons found in the outermost shell are called valence electrons. When these electrons are lost or partially lost (through sharing), the oxidation state is assigned a positive value for the element. If valence electrons are gained or partially gained by an atom, its oxidation number is taken to be negative.

## Atomic Weight

Atomic weight is the average number of nucleons (protons and neutrons) present in the nucleus of an atom of a specific element. The number of protons (represented by the atomic number) determines the element. For example, hydrogen will always have one proton in its nucleus, carbon will always have six, and lead will always have 82. The number of neutrons in an element can vary. Atoms that have the same number of protons, but different number of neutrons are called isotopes. The atomic weights listed on the periodic table are average of all of the naturally occurring isotopes. All atoms of lead have 82 protons, however, in nature lead atoms can exist with 122, 124, 125, and 126 neutrons, resulting in atoms with atomic weights of 204, 206, 207, and 208. Hence, we could say that in nature we find four isotopes of lead. To determine a value to place on a chart of atomic weights, we take a weighted average, based upon the natural abundance of each lead isotope. The abundances are as follows:

Pb-204    1.42% abundant

Pb-206    24.1%

Pb-207    22.1%

Pb-208    52.4%

Using this data we can calculate the average atomic weight of lead as:

$$(0.0142)(204) + (0.241)(206) + (0.221)(207) + (0.524)(208)$$

$$= 207.2$$

Some elements, such as gold, all exist as one isotope. All gold has 79 protons and 118 neutrons, and hence an atomic weight of 197. Other elements, such as lead can have two or more isotopes of differing abundances. (Tin is the "winner," with 10 different isotopes, with abundances ranging from 0.38% up to 32.4%, giving an average atomic weight of 118.679.) As can be seen, atomic weights need not be whole numbers.

## The Wave Mechanical Model

Each wave function corresponds to a certain electronic energy and describes a region about the nucleus (called an orbital) where an electron having that energy may be found. The square of the wave function, $|y|^2$, is called a probability density, and equals the probability per unit volume of finding the electron in a given region of space.

## Electron Configuration and Quantum Numbers

**The principal quantum number ($n$)** represents the principal energy level of the atom in which the electron is located and is related to the average distance of the electron from the nucleus. The principal quantum number is a positive integer starting with 1 and ranges up to 7 (this corresponds to the number of rows in the periodic table) or the number of energy levels associated with the known elements.

**The azimuthal number ($l$)** designates the subshells of the principal energy level. The azimuthal number ($l$) may be 0, 1, 2, and 3. The azimuthal number for a given element will range from 0 up to 1 less the principal quantum number; thus $l = n - 1$

**The magnetic quantum number $m_l$** designates the orientation of the orbital in space. The magnetic quantum number $m_l$ may be any integer ranging from $-l$ to 0 to $+l$.

**The spin quantum number $m_s$** represents the spin of the electron and may be either $-\frac{1}{2}$ or $+\frac{1}{2}$. For electrons to pair up in an orbital, they must have opposite spins. So in a given orbital, one electron will be $m_s = -\frac{1}{2}$, and the other will be $m_s = +\frac{1}{2}$.

The spin quantum number is not needed for the wave equation but is needed to meet the Pauli exclusion principle (see below).

Table I (below) summarizes the quantum numbers n, $l$ and $m_l$ for the first four principal energy levels.

## Summary of Quantum Numbers

| Principal Quantum Number, $n$ (Shell) | Azimuthal Quantum Number, $l$ (Subshell) | Subshell Designation | Magnetic Quantum Number, $m$ (Orbital) | Number of Orbitals in Subshell |
|---|---|---|---|---|
| 1 | 0 | $1s$ | 0 | 1 |
| 2 | 0 | $2s$ | 0 | 1 |
|   | 1 | $2p$ | $-1, 0, +1$ | 3 |
| 3 | 0 | $3s$ | 0 | 1 |
|   | 1 | $3p$ | $-1, 0, +1$ | 3 |
|   | 2 | $3d$ | $-2, -1, 0, +1, +2$ | 5 |
| 4 | 0 | $4s$ | 0 | 1 |
|   | 1 | $4p$ | $-1, 0, +1$ | 3 |
|   | 2 | $4d$ | $-2, -1, 0, +1, +2$ | 5 |
|   | 3 | $4f$ | $-3, -2, -1, 0, +1, +2, +3$ | 7 |

## Subshells and Electron Configuration

The Pauli exclusion principle states that no two electrons within the same atom may have the same four quantum numbers.

## Subdivision of Main Energy Levels

| main energy level | 1 | 2 | | 3 | | | 4 | | | |
|---|---|---|---|---|---|---|---|---|---|---|
| number of sublevels (n) | 1 | 2 | | 3 | | | 4 | | | |
| total number of orbitals ($n^2$) | 1 | 4 | | 9 | | | 16 | | | |
| type of orbitals | s | s | p | s | p | d | s | p | d | f |
| number of orbitals per sublevel | 1 | 1 | 3 | 1 | 3 | 5 | 1 | 3 | 5 | 7 |
| maximum number of electrons per sublevel | 2 | 2 | 6 | 2 | 6 | 10 | 2 | 6 | 10 | 14 |
| maximum number of electrons per main level ($2n^2$) | 2 | 8 | | 18 | | | 32 | | | |

## Electron Arrangements

| Main Levels | 1 | 2 | | | | 3 | Summary |
|---|---|---|---|---|---|---|---|
| Sublevels | s | s | p | | | s | |
| H | ↑ | | | | | | $1s^1$ |
| He | ↑↓ | | | | | | $1s^2$ |
| Li | ↑↓ | ↑ | | | | | $1s^22s^1$ |
| Be | ↑↓ | ↑↓ | | | | | $1s^22s^2$ |
| B | ↑↓ | ↑↓ | ↑ | ○ | ○ | | $1s^22s^22p^1$ |
| C | ↑↓ | ↑↓ | ↑ | ↑ | ○ | | $1s^22s^22p^2$ |
| N | ↑↓ | ↑↓ | ↑ | ↑ | ↑ | | $1s^22s^22p^3$ |
| O | ↑↓ | ↑↓ | ↑↓ | ↑ | ↑ | | $1s^22s^22p^4$ |
| F | ↑↓ | ↑↓ | ↑↓ | ↑↓ | ↑ | | $1s^22s^22p^5$ |
| Ne | ↑↓ | ↑↓ | ↑↓ | ↑↓ | ↑↓ | | $1s^22s^22p^6$ |
| Na | ↑↓ | ↑↓ | ↑↓ | ↑↓ | ↑↓ | ↑ | $1s^22s^22p^63s^1$ |
| Mg | ↑↓ | ↑↓ | ↑↓ | ↑↓ | ↑↓ | ↑↓ | $1s^22s^22p^63s^2$ |

Hund's rule states that for a set of orbitals at the same sublevel, each orbital is occupied by one electron before any orbital has two. Therefore, the first electrons to occupy orbitals within a sublevel have parallel spins. The rule is shown in the table above.

Transition elements are elements whose highest energy electrons occupy the d sublevel.

Transition elements can exhibit various oxidation numbers. An example of this is manganese, with possible oxidation numbers of +2, +3, +4, +6 and +7.

Groups IB through VIIB and Group VIII constitute the transition elements.

## Periodic Trends

### *Ionization Energy*

In the manner that the periodic table is set up, many trends appear. Ionization energy is one such trend. Ionization energy is the energy required to remove the highest energy electron from the ground state of an atom in the gas phase. The first ionization energy always refers to the electron that is most easily removed from the intact gas phase atom. The first ionization energy always refers to the electron that is most easily removed from the intact gas phase atom. Each subsequent electron becomes more and more difficult to remove from the cation formed. Ionization energies increase as you move from left to right across a row or period on the periodic table and increase as you move from bottom to top of a group or column on the periodic table.

### *Electron Affinity*

Electron affinity is defined as the energy needed to add an electron to a gaseous atom or ion.

Some atoms readily attract electrons, and their electron affinity has a negative value, meaning that energy is released.

For example, the halogens (the elements in Group VIIA of the periodic table) have seven electrons in their outer shell and are looking to add another electron to achieve noble gas configuration. It is much easier for chlorine, for example, to gain one electron than to lose seven. Electrons that are strongly held by an element, such as with the halogens, have a large negative value for electron affinity.

Other atoms, do not accept electrons readily, and their electron affinity is a positive value, indicating that energy must be used to add the electron. This is the case with the noble gases such as neon (Group VIIA on the periodic table).

The electron affinity of atoms generally follows the same trend as ionization energy.

Atomic radius is another trend in the periodic table. As atomic number increases across the table, atomic radius decreases. Each time one returns to the alkali metals, atomic radius increases and then decreases as you move across the table.

### Electronegativity

The electronegativity of an element is a number that measures the relative strength with which the atoms of the element attract valence electrons in a chemical bond. This electronegativity number is based on an arbitrary scale from 0 to 4. Metals have electronegativities less than 2. Electronegativity increases from left to right in a period and decreases as you go down a group.

If we neglect the row of inert gases on the periodic table, the further to the right and up an element is, the greater its electronegativity. (Electronegativity is the ability of an atom to pull electrons off of another atom.) Looking at the periodic chart, one can easily see that fluorine is the most electronegative element, while cesium is the least. Elements with very great differences in electronegativity (*i.e.,* from opposite sides of the periodic table) are more likely to combine by an ionic bond, *e.g.,* CsF. Elements with *no* difference in electronegativity will combine by a non-polar covalent board, *e.g.,* $Cl_2$. Elements with slight differences in electronegativity (usually from the same side of the periodic table) will combine by a polar covalent bond, *e.g.,* HCl, BrCl, $SO_2$.

## Types of Bonds

An ionic bond occurs when one or more electrons are transferred from the valence shell of one atom to the valence shell of another.

The atom that loses electrons becomes a positively charged ion (cation), while the atom that acquires electrons becomes a negatively charged ion (anion). The ionic bond results from the coulombic attraction between the oppositely charged ions.

The octet rule states that atoms tend to gain or lose electrons until there are eight electrons in their valence shell.

A covalent bond results from the sharing of a pair of electrons between atoms to satisfy each other's octet.

In a nonpolar covalent bond, the electrons are shared equally.

Nonpolar covalent bonds are characteristic of homonuclear diatomic molecules. For example, the fluorine molecule:

$$\cdot \ddot{\underset{\cdot\cdot}{F}} : \quad \cdot \ddot{\underset{\cdot\cdot}{F}} : \longrightarrow : \ddot{\underset{\cdot\cdot}{F}} : \ddot{\underset{\cdot\cdot}{F}} :$$

Fluorine atoms → Fluorine molecule

Where there is an unequal sharing of electrons between the atoms involved, the bond is called a polar covalent bond. An example:

$$H \; \overset{..}{\underset{..}{\overset{\times}{\bullet}}Cl:} \qquad \times \text{ hydrogen electron}$$
$$\bullet \text{ chlorine electrons}$$

$$H \; \overset{..}{\underset{\times\bullet}{\overset{\times}{\bullet}}O:} \qquad \times \text{ hydrogen electrons}$$
$$H \qquad \qquad \bullet \text{ oxygen electrons}$$

Because of the unequal sharing, the bonds shown are said to be polar bonds (dipoles). The more electronegative element in the bond is the negative end of the bond dipole. In each of the molecules shown here, there is also a non-zero molecular dipole moment, given by the vector sum of the bond dipoles.

A dipole consists of a positive and negative charge separated by a distance. A dipole is described by its dipole moment, which is equal to the charge times the distance between the positive and negative charges:

net dipole moment = charge × distance

In polar molecular substances, the positive pole of one molecule attracts the negative pole of another. The force of attraction between polar molecules is called a dipolar force.

When a hydrogen atom is bonded to a highly electronegative atom, it will become partially positively-charged, and will be attracted to neighboring electron pairs. This creates a hydrogen bond. The more polar the molecule, the more effective the hydrogen bond is in binding the molecules into a larger unit.

The relatively weak attractive forces between molecules are called Van der Waals forces. These forces become apparent only when the molecules approach one another closely (usually at low temperatures and high pressure). This is due to the way the positive charges of one molecule attract the negative charges of another molecule. Compounds of the solid state that are bound mainly by this type of attraction have soft crystals, are easily deformed, and vaporize easily. Because of the low intermolecular forces, the melting points are low and evaporation takes place so easily that it may occur at room temperature. Examples of substances with this last characteristic are iodine crystals and napthalene crystals.

**Metallic Bonds** — In a metal the atoms all share their outer electrons in a manner that might be thought of as an electron "atmosphere." The electrons hop freely from one atom to another, and it is this property that make metals good conductors of electricity and heat.

Ionic substances are characterized by the following properties:

1.  Ionic crystals have large lattice energies because the electro-static forces between them are strong.

2.  In the solid phase, they are poor electrical conductors.

3.  In the liquid phase, they are relatively good conductors of electric current; the mobile charges are the ions (in contrast to metallic conduction, where the electrons constitute the mobile charges).

4.  They have relatively high melting and boiling points.

5.  They are relatively non-volatile and have low vapor pressure.

6.  They are brittle.

7.  Those that are soluble in water form electrolytic solutions that are good conductors of electricity.

The following are general properties of molecular crystals and/or liquids:

1.  Molecular crystals tend to have small lattice energies and are easily deformed because their constituent molecules have rela-tively weak forces between them.

2.  Both the solids and liquids are poor electrical conductors.

3.  Many exist as gases at room temperature and atmospheric pressure; those that are solid or liquid at room temperature are relatively volatile.

4.  Both the solids and liquids have low melting and boiling points.

5.  The solids are generally soft and have a waxy consistency.

6.  A large amount of energy is often required to chemically de-compose the solids and liquids into simpler substances.

## Hybridization

### *Summary of Hybridization*

| Number of Bonds | Number of Unused Electron Pairs | Type of Hybrid Orbital | Angle between Bonded Atoms | Geometry | Example |
|---|---|---|---|---|---|
| 2 | 0 | $sp$ | 180° | Linear | $BeF_2$ |
| 3 | 0 | $sp^2$ | 120° | Trigonal planar | $BF_3$ |
| 4 | 0 | $sp^3$ | 109.5° | Tetrahedral | $CH_4$ |
| 3 | 1 | $sp^3$ | 90° to 109.5° | Pyramidal | $NH_3$ |
| 2 | 2 | $sp^3$ | 90° to 109.5° | Angular | $H_2O$ |
| 5 | 0 | $sp^3d$ | 90°, 120° | Trigonal bipyramidal | $PCL_5$ |
| 6 | 0 | $sp^3d^2$ | 90° | Octahedral | $SF_6$ |

From the geometry of these hybridized bonds we can predict the shape of the resultant molecule.

### *Example:*

Methane hybridizes the *s* orbitals from hydrogen with 3 *p* orbital from carbon, the resulting bond is referred to as "$sp^3$." Its shape is tetrahedral, as is the shape of the resulting methane molecule. Note also that the slight difference in electronegativity causes a polar covalent bond to be formed between the carbon and each hydrogen. Each such bond has its associated dipole moment, but as shown below, each dipole cancels:

methane:no net dipole

$$H \rightleftharpoons C \rightleftharpoons H$$

Hence, a molecule that contains polar bonds may not be polar. One must check to see whether or not the dipoles cancel.

## Double and Triple Bonds

Sharing two pairs of electrons produces a double bond. An example:

$$O:\ \ C\ :O \quad \text{or,} \quad O = C = O$$

The sharing of three electron pairs results in a triple bond. An example:

$$H\ C\ C\ H \quad \text{or,} \quad H - C \equiv C - H$$

Greater energy is required to break double bonds than single bonds, and triple bonds are harder to break than double bonds. Molecules which contain double and triple bonds have smaller interatomic distances and greater bond strength than molecules with only single bonds. Thus, in the series

$$H_3C - CH_3, \quad H_2C = CH_2, \quad HC \equiv CH,$$

the carbon-carbon distance decreases, and the C-C bond energy increases because of increased bonding.

### Sigma and Pi Bonds

A molecular orbital that is symmetrical around the line passing through two nuclei is called a *sigma* ($\sigma$) orbital, which is made from hybrid electrons. When the electron density in this orbital is concentrated in the bonding region between two nuclei, the bond is called a *sigma* bond.

The bond that is formed by the sideways overlap of two unhybridized *p* orbitals, and that provides electron density above and below the line connecting the bound nuclei, is called a *Pi* ($\pi$) bond.

*Pi* bonds are present in molecules containing double or triple bonds.

Of the sigma and *pi* bonds, the former has greater orbital overlap and is generally the stronger bond.

## Nuclear Reactions

### Alpha Decay

Alpha decay occurs when a nucleus emits a package of two protons and two neutrons, called an alpha particle ($\alpha$), which is equivalent to the nucleus of a helium atom. It usually occurs with elements that have a mass number greater than 60. Alpha decay causes the mass number to decrease by four and the atomic number to decrease by two.

### Beta Decay

Beta decay occurs when a nucleus emits a beta particle ($\beta$-) that degrades into an electron as it passes out of the atom. It usually occurs with elements that have a mass number greater than its atomic weight. Beta decay causes the mass number to remain the same, but increases the atomic number by one by converting a neutron into a proton.

### Rate of Decay

The rate of nuclear decay is proportional to the decay rate constant which, when multiplied by the half-life, equals 0.693. The half-life of the material is the length of time that it takes for half of the material to decompose.

# CHEMICAL COMPOUNDS AND FORMULAS

## Mole Concept

The gram-atomic weight of any element is defined as the mass, in grams, which contains one mole of atoms of that element.

For example, approximately 12.0 g of carbon, 16.0 g oxygen, and 32.1 g sulfur, each contain 1 mole of atoms. The term "one mole" in the above definition is a certain number of atoms. Just as a dozen always means 12, and a gross is always 144, a mole is always $6.02 \times 10^{23}$. The value $6.02 \times 10^{23}$ is also known as Avogadro's number, which by definition is the number of atoms in one gram of pure hydrogen.

### *Example:*

What is the atomic weight of lead if 207.2 grams of the metal are found to have as many atoms as 1 gram of hydrogen (Avogadro's number)?

If we have Avogadro's number of atoms present, that is $6.02 \times 10^{23}$, we then have 1 mole of atoms present. This gives us 207.2 g/mol, which satisfies the above definition of atomic weight, the answer is 207.2 Daltons, or 207.2 a.m.u. (atomic mass units). Note the types of units used.

The atoms that make up matter can be subdivided into outer layers containing negatively charged electrons. These outer layers are a great distance from the central nucleus, which is quite dense. The nucleus is made up of two types of particles—protons, which are positively charged, and neutrons, which have no charge. The general term for a particle in a nucleus is "nucleon." The atomic weight tells how many nucleons are in the nucleus of that type of atom. For example, carbon has an atomic weight of 12; thus, it has 12 nucleons in its nucleus. (Remember, the atomic weight also tells us that 12 grams of carbon would contain 1 mole ($6.02 \times 10^{23}$) of atoms.)

## Molecular Weight and Formula Weight

The formula weight of a molecule or compound is determined by the addition of its component atomic weights. The formula weight for covalently-bonded molecules is called the molecular weight.

Some people argue that crystaline substances do not occur in molecular units, hence cannot have a molecular weight. Instead, the term "Formula Weight" is used with the same meaning as molecular weight. Hence, one can state that sodium chloride has a formula weight of 58.44 g/mole rather than molecular weight of 58.44 g/mole. In either case the numerical value is the same.

### Example:

$$\text{F.W. of } CaCO_3 = 1(40) + 1(12) + 3(16)$$

$$= 100 \frac{g}{mol}$$

## Equivalent Weight

Equivalent weights are the amounts of substances that react completely with one another in chemical reactions.

For oxidation–reduction reactions, an equivalent is defined as the quantity of a substance that either gains or loses 1 mole of electrons.

In acid-base reactions, an equivalent of an acid is defined as the quantity of an acid that supplies 1 mole of $H^+$. An equivalent of a base supplies 1 mole of $OH^-$.

## Chemical Composition

**Weight Percent** — Percent composition is the same in chemistry as it is anywhere else. Percent simply means parts-per-hundred. The most common method of percent composition in chemistry is by weight. For example, if 15.789 grams (g) of magnesium metal is allowed to combine with an unlimited supply of oxygen, magnesium oxide is formed. The magnesium oxide formed has a weight of 26.182 g. Assuming that no magnesium was lost in the reaction, a simple subtraction (26.182 – 15.789) tells us that 10.393 g of oxygen combined with the magnesium. To find the percent of oxygen in magnesium oxide, one then divides the weight of oxygen by the total weight of magnesium oxide, and multiplies by 100:

$$\frac{10.393}{26.182} \times 100 = 39.695\% \text{ oxygen}.$$

Since we are dealing with a *binary* compound (a compound composed of only two elements), we can find the percent of magnesium by subtracting the percent of oxygen from one hundred (since the total of all percents must equal one hundred): $100 - 39.695 = 60.305\%$ magnesium. When working with compounds made up of more than two elements, the percentage of each element must be determined by dividing the weight of each element present by the total weight of the material it is in. To check your work, remember the total of all of the percentages must add up to one hundred. Using the example above to find the percent of magnesium, we get

$$\frac{15.789}{26.182} \times 100 = 60.305\% \text{ magnesium},$$

the same answer as before, $60.305 + 39.695 = 100$; therefore, the method works.

The percent composition of a compound can be used to determine its empirical formula (the empirical formula is the *simplest,* not necessarily the actual, ratio of atoms found in a compound).

## *Example:*

Ortho-phosphoric acid is composed of 3.1% hydrogen, 31.6% phosphorus, and 65.3% oxygen by weight. What is its empirical formula?

The easiest way to solve this is to assume we have 100 grams of ortho phosphoric acid. From this it is easy to conclude we will have 3.1 grams of hydrogen, 31.6 grams of phosphorus and 65.3 grams of oxygen. Let us then determine the number of moles of each element present, by dividing by the molecular weight:

$$\frac{3.1 \text{ g}}{1.0079 \text{ g/mol}} = 3.1 \text{ moles of hydrogen,}$$

$$\frac{31.6 \text{ g}}{30.9738 \text{ g/mol}} = 1.02 \text{ moles of phosphorus,}$$

$$\frac{65.3 \text{ g}}{15.9994 \text{ g/mol}} = 4.08 \text{ moles of oxygen,}$$

This gives us a molar ratio of

H : P : O of 3.1 : 1.02 : 4.08 (respectively).

To find the smallest ratio we will divide each number by the smallest of the three:

$$\frac{3.1}{1.02} : \frac{1.02}{1.02} : \frac{4.08}{1.02} = 3.0 : 1.00 : 4.00$$

for H:P:O, hence we can write the empirical formula: $H_3PO_4$ for ortho-phosphoric acid.

# STATES OF MATTER

## The Kinetic-Molecular Theory

The kinetic-molecular theory states the following:

1.  Gases are composed of tiny particles that are separated from each other by otherwise empty space. The distance between particles is very large compared with the size of the particles.

2. Gas molecules are in constant, continuous, random, and straight-line motion.

3. The molecules collide with one another in perfectly elastic collisions (no net loss in energy).

4. The attractive forces between the particles (i.e., atoms or molecules) is negligible. The particles move independently of each other.

5. The average kinetic energy of all the molecules of gas is directly proportional to the absolute temperature of the gas.

6. All gases at the same temperature will have the same kinetic energy.

## Gas Laws

The molecules of an ideal gas would have zero volume, and their collisions would be totally elastic. Real gases behave very much like ideal gases under low pressures and high temperatures.

A gas has no shape of its own; rather, it takes the shape of the container. It has no fixed volume, but is compressed or expanded as its container changes in size. The volume of a gas is the volume of the container in which it is held.

Pressure is defined as force per unit area. Atmospheric pressure is measured using a barometer.

Atmospheric pressure is directly related to the length (h) of the column of mercury in a barometer and is expressed in mm or cm of mercury (Hg).

Standard atmospheric pressure is expressed in several ways: 14.7 pounds per square inch (psi), 760 mm of mercury, 760 torr or simply 1 "atmosphere" (1 atm).

### *Boyle's Law*

Boyle's law states that, at a constant temperature, the volume of a gas is inversely proportional to the pressure:

$$v \propto \frac{1}{P} \quad \text{or} \quad V = \text{constant} \times \frac{1}{P} \quad \text{or} \quad PV = \text{constant}.$$

$P_i V_i = P_f V_f \leftarrow$ Units Must Agree, where $(i)$ = initial and $(f)$ = final

$$V_f = V_i \left( \frac{P_i}{P_f} \right)$$

## Charles' Law

Charles' law states that at constant pressure, the volume of a given quantity of a gas varies directly with the temperature:

$$\frac{V_1}{T_1} = \frac{V_2}{T_2} \text{ or } \frac{V_1}{V_2} = \frac{T_1}{T_2} \leftarrow \text{ Units Must Agree}$$

If Charles' law was strictly obeyed, gases would not condense when they are cooled. This means that gases behave in an ideal fashion only at relatively high temperatures and low pressures.

## Law of Gay-Lussac

The law of Gay-Lussac states that at constant volume, the pressure exerted by a given mass of gas varies directly with the absolute temperature:

$P \propto T$ (where volume and mass of gas are constant).

$$\frac{P_1}{T_1} = \frac{P_2}{T_2} \leftarrow \text{ Units Must Agree}$$

Gay-Lussac's law of combining volumes states that when reactions take place in the gaseous state, under conditions of constant temperature and pressure, the volumes of reactants and products can be expressed as ratios of small whole numbers.

## Ideal Gas Law

$$V \propto \frac{1}{P}, \quad V \propto T, \quad V \propto n$$

then $\quad V \propto \frac{nT}{P}$

$$PV = nRT$$

The hypothetical ideal gas obeys the ideal gas law. This statement is also called the equation of state of an ideal gas because it relates the variables ($P$, $V$, $n$, $T$) that specify properties of the gas. Molecules of ideal gases have no attraction for one another and have no intrinsic volume; they are "point particles." Real gases act in a less than ideal way, especially under conditions of increased pressure and/or decreased temperature. Real gas behavior approaches that of ideal gases as the gas pressure becomes very low.

When using the ideal gas law, the term "R" is always a constant. The volume is in liters, the temperature in Kelvin, and pressure is in atmospheres. $R$ has a value of 0.082 and units of liter · atm/mole Kelvin. Remember, this value of $R$ can only be used under the stated conditions. Be sure the units of variables $(P, V, n, T)$ are the same as the units in the constant $R$. $P$ = atm, $V$ = liters, $n$ = moles, $T$ = Kelvin.

## Combined Gas Law

The combined gas law states that for a given mass of gas, the volume is inversely proportional to the pressure and directly proportional to the absolute temperature. This law can be written

$$\frac{P_1 V_1}{T_1} = \frac{P_2 V_2}{T_2}$$

where $P_1$ is the original pressure, $V_1$ is the original volume, $T_1$ is the original absolute temperature, $P_2$ is the new pressure, $V_2$ is the new volume and $T_2$ is the new absolute temperature.

## Dalton's Law of Partial Pressures

The pressure exerted by each gas in a mixture is called its partial pressure. The total pressure exerted by a mixture of gases is equal to the sum of the partial pressures of the gases in the mixture. This statement, known as Dalton's law of partial pressures, can be expressed

$$P_T = P_a + P_b + P_c + \ldots$$

Therefore, in order to obtain $P_{gas}$, the $P_{H_2O}$ must be known. $P_{H_2O}$ values depend on atmospheric conditions temperature and pressure, and vary accordingly. When a gas is collected over water (a typical laboratory method), some water vapor mixes with the gas. The total gas pressure then is given by

$$P_T = P_{gas} + P_{H_2O}$$

where $P_{gas}$ = pressure of dry gas and $P_{H_2O}$ = vapor pressure of water at the temperature of the system.

## Avogadro's Law

Avogadro's law states that under conditions of constant temperature and pressure, equal volumes of different gases contain equal numbers of molecules.

If the initial and final pressure and temperature are the same, then the relationship between the number of molecules, $N$, and the volume, $V$, is,

$$\frac{V_f}{V_i} = \frac{N_f}{N_i}$$

### Graham's Law

Graham's law is a result of the kinetic theory of matter, since two different gases at the same temperature and pressure will both have the same kinetic energy. Therefore, when two gases effuse out of a small hole in a container, each gas will migrate out of the container at a rate that is inversely proportional to the square of the molar mass. For two gases, *gas a* and *gas b*, the following equation would hold true.

$$\frac{\text{rate}_a^{\,2}}{\text{rate}_b^{\,2}} = \frac{\text{Mass}_b}{\text{Mass}_a}$$

## Solids

Properties of solids are as follows:

1.  They retain their shape and volume when transferred from one container to another.

2.  They are virtually incompressible.

3.  They exhibit extremely slow rates of diffusion.

In a solid, the attractive forces between the atoms, molecules, or ions are relatively strong. The particles are held in a rigid structural array, wherein they exhibit only vibrational motion.

There are two types of solids, amorphous and crystalline. Crystalline solids are species composed of structural units bounded by specific (regular) geometric patterns. They are characterized by sharp melting points.

Amorphous substances do not display geometric regularity in the solid; glass is an example of an amorphous solid. Amorphous substances have no sharp melting point, but melt over a wide range of temperatures.

When solids are heated at certain pressures, some solids vaporize directly without passing through the liquid phase. This is called sublimation. The heat required to change 1 mole of solid $A$ completely to vapor is called the molar heat of sublimation, $\Delta H_{\text{sub}}$.

Note that $\Delta H_{\text{sublimation}} = \Delta H_{\text{fusion}} + \Delta H_{\text{vaporization}}$ where the molar heat of sublimation is equal to the molar heat of fusion plus the molar heat of vaporization. The molar heat of fusion ($\Delta H_{\text{fusion}}$) is the amount of heat needed to convert 1 mole of a solid to a liquid. The molar heat of vaporization ($\Delta H_{\text{vaporization}}$) is the amount of heat required to convert 1 mole of liquid to a gas.

## Phase Diagram

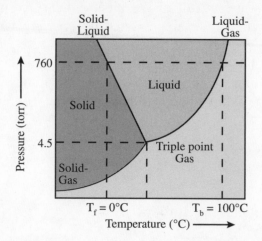

Phase diagram for water (somewhat distorted).

In a closed system, when the rates of evaporation and condensation are equal, the system is in phase equilibrium.

In a closed system, when opposing changes are taking place at equal rates, the system is said to be in dynamic equilibrium. Virtually all of the equilibria considered in this review are dynamic equilibria.

## Properties of Liquids

### Density

### *Example:*

If a solution has a volume of 532 mL and a mass of 438 g, what is its density?

$$\frac{438 \text{ g}}{532 \text{ mL}} = 0.823 \text{ g/mL}$$

Note that since the density is less than 1 (the density of water), it is lighter than water.

## The Solution Process

**Solvation** is the interaction of solvent molecules with solute molecules (or ions) to form loosely bonded aggregates of both solvent and solute. The attraction between solute and solvent must be greater than the force that holds the solute together in order for the solute to dissolve.

Solubility is affected by concentration, temperature, and in some cases pressure. When the concentration exceeds the saturation point of the solution, the dissolved solute is in equilibrium with the solid or gas solute. Increasing the temperature will increase the solubility with solutions that have an endothermic heat of solution, and decrease the solubility with solutions that have an exothermic heat of solution. Pressure only affects solutions where gases are involved in liquid; the solubility of a gas is proportional to the pressure of the gas above the solution (Henry's Law).

## Solution Chemistry

### Concentration Units

**Mole fraction** is the number of moles of a particular component of a solution divided by the total number of moles of all of the substances present in the solution:

$$X_A = \frac{n_A}{n_A + n_B + n_c + \ldots}$$

$$\sum_{i=1}^{N} x_i = 1$$

Mole percent is equal to 100% × mole fraction. Weight fraction specifies the fraction of the total weight of a solution that is contributed by a particular component. Weight percent is equal to 100% × weight fraction.

**Molarity (*M*)** of a solution is the number of moles of solute per liter of solution:

$$\text{Molarity } (M) = \frac{\text{moles of solute}}{\text{liters of solution}}$$

**Molality (*m*)** of a solution is the number of moles of solute per kilogram (1000 g) of solvent.

$$\text{Molality } (m) = \frac{\text{moles of solute}}{\text{kilograms of solvent}}$$

When using water as a solvent, the molality (m) of a dilute solution is equal to the molarity (M).

**Normality (*N*)** of a solution is the number of equivalents of solute per liter of solution:

$$\text{Normality } (N) = \frac{\text{equivalents of solute}}{\text{liter of solvent}}$$

The number of equivalents present depends on what species is used in the reaction. If we are looking at hydrogen ions ($H^+$), then hydrochloric acid in the reaction

$$HCl \rightarrow H^+ + Cl^-$$

produces 1 equivalent per 1 mole, hence a 1 molar solution of HCl is also 1 normal. For sulfuric acid, the reaction

$$H_2SO_4 \rightarrow 2H^+ + SO_4^{2-}$$

gives two equivalents per mole, hence a 1-molar solution of $H_2SO_4$ is 2 normal. Ortho-phosphoric acid can give up 3 hydrogen atoms

$$H_3PO_4 \rightarrow 3H^+ + PO_4^{-3},$$

hence a 1 molar solution of $H_3PO_4$ is 3 normal. The same can be done for the production of hydroxide ions ($OH^-$). One mole of radium hydroxide would produce two equivalents of hydroxide ions

$$Ra(OH)_2 \rightarrow Ra^{++} + 2OH^-$$

hence a solution that is 0.02 molar of $Ra(OH)_2$ would be 0.04 normal with respect to $OH^-$. Electrons can also be expressed in equivalence.

$$Hg_2^{++} \rightarrow 2Hg^{++} + 2e^-$$

is an example of such a reaction, and a solution 0.5 molar of $Hg_2^{++}$ would be 1.0 normal, since two equivalents of electrons are produced for every mole of $Hg_2^{++}$. In chemistry today normality is only used in classroom experiments and standardized examination.

## Neutralization

A neutralization occurs when an equal amount of an acid and a base are mixed together. The resulting product of a neutralization is a salt and water.

### *Example:*

What volume of a 0.163 $M$ sulfuric acid solution is needed to neutralize 45.3 mL of a 5.06 $M$ solution of potassium hydroxide?

First we need to write the equation. We start with

$$H_2SO_4 + KOH \rightarrow ?$$

Knowing that the results will be a salt and water, we can write the products as potassium sulfate and water.

$$H_2SO_4 + KOH \rightarrow K_2SO_4 + H_2O$$

We now balance the equation

$$H_2SO_4 + 2KOH \rightarrow K_2SO_4 + 2H_2O$$

Notice that each mole of sulfuric acid require two moles of potassium hydroxide. We do *not* need to calculate molecular weights for this type of problem,

45.3 mL of KOH = 0.0453 L of KOH,

0.0453 L $\times$ 5.06 mol/L = 0.229 mol

of KOH present. Using the above balanced equation, we can see that we will need $^1/_2 \times 0.229 = 0.115$ moles of $H_2SO_4$ to neutralize the KOH. Using the given concentration of $H_2SO_4$, we get

$$\frac{0.115 \text{ mol}}{0.163 \text{ mol/L}} = 0.703 \text{ L} = 703 \text{ mL}$$

of the $H_2SO_4$ solution, needed to neutralize 45.3 mL of the KOH solution. Note: make sure you obtain like units or the answer will turn out wrong.

### Example:

What volume of an unknown acid, $X$ that is 2.04$N$ is needed to neutralize 15.6 mL of a base, $Y$ that is 10.1$N$? We know that one equivalent of $X$ will neutralize one equivalent of $Y$. To find the equivalent of $Y$, we multiply

(15.6 mL = 0.0156 L) 0.0156 L $\times$ 10.1 eq/L = 0.158 eq

of $Y$ present. We know that we need 0.158 equivalent of $X$ present. To calculate the volume of $X$ containing this amount, we divided by the concentration

$$\frac{0.158 \text{ eq}}{2.04 \text{ eq/L}} = 0.0772 \text{ L} = 77.2 \text{ mL}$$

needed of acid $X$ to neutralize 15.6 mL of base $Y$.

When using units of normality, the balanced equation does *not* need to be written, nor do formulas.

### Raoult's Law and Vapor Pressure

When the rate of evaporation equals the rate of condensation, the system is in equilibrium.

The vapor pressure is the pressure exerted by the gas molecules when they are in equilibrium with the liquid.

The vapor pressure increases with increasing temperature.

Raoult's law states that the vapor pressure of a solution at a particular temperature is equal to the mole fraction of the solvent in the liquid phase multiplied by the vapor pressure of the pure solvent at the same temperature:

$$P_{solution} = X_{solvent} P^0_{solvent}$$

and

$$P_A = X_A P^0_{A,}$$

where $P_A$ is the vapor pressure of $A$ with solute added, $P^0_A$ is the vapor pressure of pure $A$, and $X_A$ is the mole fraction of $A$ in the solution. The solute is assumed here to be nonvolatile (e.g., NaCl or sucrose in water).

## Colligative Properties of Solutions

**Colligative properties** are those properties that are affected by the number of particles dissolved in solution. Freezing point, boiling point, vapor pressure, and osmotic pressure are all colligative properties.

For ideal solutions, the vapor pressure of an aqueous solution is always lowered by the addition of more solute, which causes the boiling point to be raised (boiling point elevation).

Freezing-point depression is the difference between the freezing points of a pure solvent and a solution mixed with a solute. It is directly proportional to the molal concentration concentration of the solution, or more precisely, to the solute activity, according to the equation:

$$\Delta T_f = i \cdot K_f \cdot activity$$

- activity is in units of mol/kg, and is equal to an activity coefficient times the molality

- $\Delta T_f$, the freezing point depression is defined as $T - T_f$, where T is the freezing point of the solution and $T_f$ is the freezing point of the pure solvent.

- $K_f$, the freezing-point, is a colligative property, given by $RT_f^2/\Delta H_f$, where $R$ is the gas constant, and $T_f$ is the normal freezing point of the solvent and $\Delta H_f$ is the heat of fusion per kilogram of the solvent

○ $K_f$ for water is 1.858 K·kg/mol (or more commonly used, 1.858 C/m) which means that per mole of solute dissolved in a kilogram of water the freezing point depression is 1.858 K

- $i$ is the *i factor* or the *van't Hoff factor*; $i$ is the factor that takes into account the presence of ions in a solution. It indicates the number of particles formed.

Freezing point depression can be used to measure the degree of dissociation of a solute or to measure its activity.

$$\Delta T = T_{solution} - T_{pure\ solvent}$$

The above rule is only accurate for dilute solutions.

When using water as a solvent, the boiling point elevation is 0.512 °C per mole of solute per kilogram of solution. The freezing point depression is −1.86°C per mole of solute per kilogram of solution. Remember, these values apply only to water, and are only accurate for dilute solutions. When dissolving salts which tend to dissociate in some solvents (e.g. water), the total number of moles of *ions* formed must be used.

### Example:

One mole of $Na_3PO_4$ would produce a total of 4 moles of ions when dissolved in water

$$Na_3PO_4 \rightarrow 3Na^+ + PO_4^{3-}$$

If 5.00 grams of sodium chloride are dissolved in 520 grams of water, what is the boiling point and freezing point of the solution? Sodium chloride (NaCl) has a molecular weight of 58.44 g/mol, hence we have

$$\frac{5.00\ g}{58.44\ g/mol} = 0.856\ mol$$

Since sodium chloride ionizes in water to give us two ions (NaCl $\rightarrow$ Na$^+$ + Cl$^-$), we have $2 \times 0.0856 = 0.171$ moles of ions present. The total mass of the solution is 0.520 kg + 0.00500 kg = 0.525 kg (note change from grams to kilograms) this gives us

$$\frac{0.171\ mol}{0.525\ kg} = 0.326\ moles\ of\ ion/kg.$$

Multiplying this by the boiling point elevation of water we get

$$0.326\ mol/kg \times 0.512\ °C/mol/kg = 0.167\ °C.$$

Since water normally boils at 100.00 °C we can add this amount to the normal boiling point and get 100.00 + 0.167 = 100.17 °C for the new boiling point (notice the significant figures). In the same manner, the freezing point can be calculated. We have already calculated the number of ions per kg of solution, and we multiply the freezing point depression of water by this factor to get 1.86 °C/mol/kg × 0.326 mol/kg = 0.606 °C. Since water normally freezes at 0.00 °C, we subtract our value from the normal freezing point to obtain 0.00 – 0.606 = – 0.61 °C (Notice sign and significant figures).

## Osmotic Pressure

Osmosis is the diffusion of a solvent through a semipermeable membrane into a more concentrated solution.

The osmotic pressure of a solution is the minimum pressure that must be applied to the solution to prevent the flow of solvent from pure solvent into the solution.

The osmotic pressure for a solution is:

$$\pi = CRT$$

where $\pi$ is the osmotic pressure, $C$ is the concentration in molality or molarity, $R$ is the gas constant from ideal gas law, and $T$ is the temperature (K). (Note the formal similarity of the osmotic pressure equation to the ideal gas law, $C = n/v$.)

Solutions that have the same osmotic pressure are called isotonic solutions.

Reverse osmosis is a method for recovering pure solvent from a solution by applying pressure on the solution, forcing more water through the semipermeable membrane.

# STOICHIOMETRY

## Balancing Chemical Equations

When balancing chemical equations, one must make sure that there are the same number of atoms of each element on both the left and right side of the arrow.

## Example:

$$2\,NaOH + H_2SO_4 \rightarrow Na_2SO_4 + 2H_2O.$$

$$\left(\begin{array}{l} \text{Na : 2 atoms} \\ \text{O: 6 atoms} \\ \text{H: 4 atoms} \\ \text{S: 1 atom} \end{array}\right) \quad \begin{array}{ll} \text{Na:} & 2 \\ \text{O:} & 6 \\ \text{H:} & 4 \\ \text{S:} & 1 \end{array}$$

## Calculations Based on Chemical Equations

The coefficients in a chemical equation provide the ratio in which moles of one substance react with moles of another.

## Example:

$C_2H_4 + 3O_2 \rightarrow 2CO_2 + 2H_2O$ represents

1 mol of $C_2H_4$ + 3 mol $O_2 \rightarrow$ 2 mol $CO_2$ + 2 mol $H_2O$.

In this equation, the number of moles of $O_2$ consumed is always equal to three times the number of moles of $C_2H_4$ that react.

## Limiting-Reactant Calculations

The reactant that is used up first in a chemical reaction is called the limiting reactant, and the amount of product is determined (or limited) by the limiting reactant.

The following examples will show how the above information can be used: Sulfuric Acid ($H_2SO_4$) will react with Sodium Bicarbonate ($NaHCO_3$) to form Sodium Sulfate ($Na_2SO_4$), water ($H_2O$) and Carbon Dioxide ($CO_2$). If 2.45 grams of sulfuric acid are reacted with 5.42 grams of sodium bicarbonate, assuming the reaction is 100%, find:

1) The amount of reactants left over

2) The grams of sodium sulfate produced

3) The volume of carbon dioxide produced at STP

To start these calculations, we first need to balance the equation. First, we shall write the reactant, followed by the product:

$$H_2SO_4 + NaHCO_3 \rightarrow Na_2SO_4 + H_2O + CO_2\uparrow$$

We will note on the left side of the arrow there are a total of:

| 3 H's and on the right side: | 2 H's |
|---|---|
| 1 S | 1 S |
| 7 O's | 7 O's |
| 1 Na | 2 Na's |
| 1 C | 1 C |

It is obvious that we need more sodiums (Na) on the left side, and more hydrogens (H) on the right. If we place a "2" before the sodium bicarbonate we get:

$$H_2SO_4 + 2\,NaHCO_3 \rightarrow Na_2SO_4 + H_2O + CO_2 \uparrow, \text{ or}$$

| left: | right: |
|---|---|
| 4 H's | 2 H's |
| 1 S | 1 S |
| 10 O's | 7 O's |
| 2 Na's | 2 Na's |
| 2 C's | 1 C |

Note that although we now have two sodiums on each side, other elements have changed as well. Since we have also doubled the number of carbons (C) on the left, let us next place a "2" before carbon dioxide to have the same number of carbons on the right:

$$H_2SO_4 + 2NaHCO_3 \rightarrow Na_2SO_4 + H_2O + 2CO_2 \uparrow$$

| left: | right: |
|---|---|
| 4 H's | 2 H's |
| 1 S | 1 S |
| 10 O's | 9 O's |
| 2 Na's | 2 Na's |
| 2 C's | 2 C's |

Things are beginning to look better. If we put a "2" before the water, the hydrogens should balance:

$$H_2SO_4 + 2NaHCO_3 \rightarrow Na_2SO_4 + 2H_2O + 2CO_2\uparrow$$

| left: | right: |
|-------|--------|
| 4 H's | 4 H's |
| 1 S | 1 S |
| 10 O's | 10 O's |
| 2 Na's | 2 Na's |
| 2 C's | 2 C's |

Notice that by balancing the hydrogens, we also balance the oxygens. (Balancing equations becomes easier with practice.) We know that one mole of sulfuric acid reacts with two moles of sodium bicarbonate to yield one mole of sodium sulfate, and two moles each of water and carbon dioxide. Unfortunately, we were given the number of grams of starting material, not moles, hence a conversion must be made. The atomic weights for sulfuric acid and sodium bicarbonate are 98.7 g/mol and 84.00 g/mol, respectively. To find the number of moles, the mass of the material is divided by its atomic weight:

$$\frac{2.45 \text{ g of } H_2SO_4}{98.7 \text{ g / mol}} = 0.0248 \text{ mol of } H_2SO_4,$$

$$\frac{5.42 \text{ g of } NaHCO_3}{84.0 \text{ g/mol}} = 0.0645 \text{ mol of } NaHCO_3$$

Since twice as much sodium bicarbonate is needed as sulfuric acid, it can be calculated that 0.0496 ($2 \times 0.0248$) moles of sodium bicarbonate will react with the 0.0248 moles of sulfuric acid present, leaving 0.0149 moles (0.0645 – 0.0496) of sodium bicarbonate left over, un-reacted. Since the sulfuric acid is used up, it is called the "limiting reagent." To answer question one, there would be zero grams of sulfuric acid left over, and

$$0.0149 \text{ mol} \times 100.0 \text{ g/mol} = 1.49 \text{ g}$$

of sodium bicarbonate left over.

To answer question number two we must first calculate the formula weight of sodium sulfate, which is 142.0. Next, by looking at the stoichiometric ratios of the balanced equation, it can be seen that the 0.0248 moles of sulfuric acid (start with the limiting reagent) will produce 0.0248 moles of sodium sulfate. Converting to grams gives us

$$0.0248 \text{ mol} \times 142.0 \text{ g/mol} = 3.52 \text{ g}$$

of sodium sulfate produced.

The third question can be answered *without* finding the molecular weight of carbon-dioxide. First, by stoichiometry, and starting with the limiting reagent, 0.0248 moles of sulfuric acid will produce 2 × 0.0496 moles of carbon-dioxide. At STP one mole gas will have a volume 22.4 liters, hence

$$22.4 \text{ L/mol} \times 0.0496 \text{ mol} = 1.11 \text{ L of } CO_2.$$

As a rule, always write down your units to be sure they cancel out and leave your answer in the desired units.

# REACTION TYPES

## Acid-Base Reactions

### *Definitions of Acids and Bases*

1.  **Arrhenius Theory** states that acids are substances that ionize in water to donate protons ($H^+$), and bases produce hydroxide ions ($OH^-$) when put into water.

2.  **Brønsted-Lowry Theory** states that acids donate protons, like an Arrhenius acid, and bases accept protons. Simply put, a proton moves from one compound to another. Each compound in a conjugate acid-base pair are different from each other by the existence of a proton.

3.  **Lewis Theory** defines an acid as an electron-pair acceptor and a base is an electron-pair donor. The Lewis definition of acid-base reactions allow the inclusion of reactions that may not involve protons, such as the formation of coordination complexes.

### *Types of Acid-Base Reactions*

### 1. A strong acid neutralizes a strong base

The net ionic reaction for this type of acid-base neutralization is always the same. Students should memorize the strong acids and bases.

$$H^+ + OH^- \rightarrow H_2O$$

## 2. A strong acid neutralizes a weak base

The net ionic equation should depict a proton combining with the basic molecule.

$$H^+ + NH_3 \rightarrow NH_4^+$$

## 3. A strong base reacts with a weak acid

A proton from the weak acid combines with the hydroxide ion to form an anion and water.

$$HC_2H_3O_2 + OH^- \rightarrow C_2H_3O_2^- + H_2O$$

## 4. A weak acid reacts with a weak base

Keep any eye out for Lewis acid-base reactions, in which the acid accepts an electron pair from and combines with a weak base.

$$BF_3 + NH_3 \rightarrow BF_3NH_3$$

## 5. A coordination-complex formed

This is another example of a Lewis acid-base reaction, where the metal serves as an electron-acceptor. You would recognize this if a transition metal is placed in a solution with soluble ammonia, cyanide, hydroxide, or thiocyanate ions. You may combine the metal with as many polyatomic anions as you wish; just be sure that the total charge on the ion is correct. The oxidation state of the metallic atom does not change.

$$Fe^{3+} + SCN^- \rightarrow FeSCN^{2+}$$

## Precipitation Reactions

Precipitation reactions occur when soluble reactants are mixed together to form an insoluble product. Precipitation reactions are best written as **net ionic reactions**, where only the ions that combine to form the precipitate are shown. All other ions that remain dissolved in solution are **spectator ions**.

Full equation: $Pb(NO_3)_2\ (aq) + 2\ KI\ (aq) \rightarrow PbI_2\ (s) + 2\ KNO_3\ (aq)$

Net ionic reaction: $Pb^{2+}\ (aq) + 2\ I^-\ (aq) \rightarrow PbI_2\ (s)$

### Solubility Rules

1. All compounds with IA metals and ammonium are **soluble**.

2. All **nitrates are soluble**.

3. All **chlorates and perchlorates are soluble**.

4. All **acetates are soluble**.

5. All **halides are soluble**, EXCEPT those that combine with $Ag^+$, $Pb^{2+}$, and $Hg_2^{2+}$

6. All **sulfates are soluble**, EXCEPT those that combine with $Ag^+$, $Pb^{2+}$, and $Hg_2^{2+}$, $Ca^{2+}$, $Sr^{2+}$, $Ba^{2+}$.

7. All **hydroxides are insoluble**, EXCEPT those with IA metals, ammonium, $Ca^{2+}$, $Sr^{2+}$, $Ba^{2+}$.

8. All **carbonates are insoluble**, EXCEPT those that contain IA metals and ammonium.

9. All **phosphates are insoluble**, EXCEPT those that contain IA metals and ammonium.

10. All **sulfites are insoluble**, EXCEPT those that contain IA metals and ammonium.

11. All **chromates are insoluble**, EXCEPT those that contain IA metals and ammonium.

12. All **sulfides are insoluble**, EXCEPT those that contain IA metals, IIA metals, and ammonium.

# ELECTROCHEMISTRY

## Oxidation and Reduction

**Oxidation** is defined as a reaction in which atoms or ions undergo an increase in oxidation state. The agent that caused oxidation to occur is called the oxidizing agent and is itself reduced in the process.

**Reduction** is defined as a reaction in which atoms or ions undergo decrease in oxidation state. The agent that caused reduction to occur is called the reducing agent and is itself oxidized in the process.

An **oxidation number** can be defined as the charge that an atom would have if both of the electrons in each bond were assigned to the more electronegative element. The term "oxidation state" is used interchangeably with the term "oxidation number."

The following are the basic rules for assigning oxidation numbers:

1. The oxidation number of any element in its elemental form is zero.

2. The oxidation number of any simple ion (one atom) is equal to the charge on the ion.

3.  The sum of all of the oxidation numbers of all of the atoms in a neutral compound is zero.

(More generally, the sum of the oxidation numbers of all of the atoms in a given species is equal to the net charge on that species.)

## Balancing Oxidation-Reduction Reactions Using the Oxidation Number Method

### The Oxidation-Number-Change Method:

1.  Assign oxidation numbers to each atom in the equation.

2.  Note which atoms change oxidation number, and calculate the number of electrons transferred, per atom, during oxidation and reduction.

3.  When more than one atom of an element that changes oxidation number is present in a formula, calculate the number of electrons transferred per formula unit.

4.  Make the number of electrons gained equal to the number lost.

5.  Once the coefficients from step 4 have been obtained, the remainder of the equation is balanced by inspection, adding $H^+$ (in acid solution), $OH^-$ (in basic solution), and $H_2O$, as required.

## Balancing Redox Equations: The Ion-Electron Method

### The Ion-Electron Method:

1.  Determine which of the substances present are involved in the oxidation-reduction.

2.  Break the overall reaction into two half-reactions, one for the oxidation step and one for the reduction step.

3.  Balance for mass (*i.e.*, make sure there is the same number of each kind of atom on each side of the equation) for all species except H and O.

4.  Add $H^+$ and $H_2O$ as required (in acidic solutions), or $OH^-$ and $H_2O$ as required (in basic solutions) to balance O first, then H.

5.  Balance these reactions electrically by adding electrons to either side so that the total electric charge is the same on the left and right sides.

6.    Multiply the two balanced half-reactions by the appropriate factors so that the same number of electrons is transferred in each.

7.    Add these half-reactions to obtain the balanced overall reaction. (The electrons should cancel from both sides of the final equation.)

## Voltaic or Galvanic Cells

Following the example below is a table of standard electrode potentials. Under these conditions all concentrations are 1 molar, all gases are at 1 atmosphere, and the temperature is 25 °C. The first reaction on the table is the reduction of a lithium ion to a lithium:

$$Li^+ + e^- \rightarrow Li$$

with a potential listed of –3.045 volts. Were we to reverse reaction (*e.g.*, oxidize a lithium atom to an ion):

$$Li \rightarrow Li^+ + e^-$$

the potential would be +3.045 volts. The potentials (voltages) for each of these half reactions are summed up. If the sum of the potentials are positive, the reaction is spontaneous, and will run on its own. If it is negative, the energy has to be supplied to make the reaction go.

### *Example:*

If iron metal is placed in a copper (II) sulfate solution, will the copper displace the iron spontaneously, or will no reaction occur?

We know that copper (II) sulfate, $CuSO_4$, when in water exists as ions (*e.g.*, $Cu^{++} + SO_4^{2-}$). To reduce copper (II) ions to copper metal would require the copper ions to each gain 2 electrons, and would be written as:

$$Cu^{++} + 2e^- \rightarrow Cu^\circ.$$

Looking at our table, we can see the potential for this half-reaction is +0.337 volts. If the copper is replacing the iron, then the iron is being oxidized to ferrous (iron II) ions, e.g.,

$$Fe^\circ \rightarrow Fe^{++} + 2e^-.$$

The potential for this half reaction is +0.440 volts (remember to change the sign when reversing a reaction!). Summing the potentials for the two half-reactions we get:

$$+ 0.337 + 0.440 = + 0.777 \text{ volts.}$$

Since the voltage is positive, it means the reaction will run by itself and give off energy. If we were to simply place an iron bar in a copper (II) sulfate solution, this energy would be given up as heat, but with a proper arrangement of the material we would be able to use this energy as electric current (with a potential of 0.777 volts under standard conditions). When the reaction reaches equilibrium (in this case we will have copper metal and iron (II) sulfate) we say the battery is dead. The two half-reactions above can be summed to give us the total reaction:

$$Cu^{++} + 2e^- \rightarrow Cu^\circ$$

$$+ Fe^\circ \rightarrow Fe^{++} + 2e^-$$

$$\overline{Cu^{++} + Fe^\circ + 2e^- \rightarrow 2e^- + Fe^{++} + Cu^\circ}$$

The two electrons on each side of the arrow can be cancelled out to give us:

$$Cu^{++} + Fe^\circ \rightarrow Cu^\circ + Fe^{++}$$

Notice that in a redox equation, the number of charges on each side of the arrow are equal.

What about the reaction of aluminum chloride in water ($AlCl_3$) with the formation of chlorine gas ($Cl_2$) to give us metallic aluminum? Will that reaction go spontaneously? Again, we know that $AlCl_3$ in water exists as $Al^{3+} + Cl^-$. To reduce the aluminum ions to aluminum metal would require the reaction

$$Al^{3+} + 3e^- \rightarrow Al^\circ,$$

and from the table it can be seen that the potential for this reaction is –1.66 volts. The only donor for electrons would be the chloride ions, by the reaction:

$$2\ Cl^- \rightarrow 2e^- + Cl_2.$$

The potential for this reaction is – 1.3595 volts. Summing these potentials we get –3.02 volts. Because this value is negative, we know that the reaction will not go on its own (in other words, aluminum chloride will *not* spontaneously break down into aluminum metal and chlorine gas).

## STANDARD ELECTRODE POTENTIAL IN AQUEOUS SOLUTIONS AT 25°C

| Electrode | Electrode Reaction | $E°_{red}(V)$ |
|---|---|---|
| **Acid Solutions** | | |
| Li I Li$^+$ | Li$^+$ + e$^-$ $\rightleftharpoons$ Li | −3.045 |
| K I K$^+$ | K$^+$ + e$^-$ $\rightleftharpoons$ K | −2.925 |
| Ba I Ba$^{2+}$ | Ba$^{2+}$ + 2e$^-$ $\rightleftharpoons$ Ba | −2.906 |
| Ca I Ca$^{2+}$ | Ca$^{2+}$ + 2e$^-$ $\rightleftharpoons$ Ca | −2.87 |
| Na I Na$^+$ | Na$^+$ + e$^-$ $\rightleftharpoons$ Na | −2.714 |
| La I La$^{3+}$ | La$^{3+}$ + 3e$^-$ $\rightleftharpoons$ La | −2.52 |
| Mg I Mg$^{2+}$ | Mg$^{2+}$ + 2e$^-$ $\rightleftharpoons$ Mg | −2.363 |
| Th I Th$^{4+}$ | Th$^{4+}$ + 4e$^-$ $\rightleftharpoons$ Th | −1.90 |
| U I U$^{3+}$ | U$^{3+}$ + 3e$^-$ $\rightleftharpoons$ U | −1.80 |
| Al I Al$^{3+}$ | Al$^{3+}$ + 3e$^-$ $\rightleftharpoons$ Al | −1.66 |
| Mn I Mn$^{2+}$ | Mn$^{2+}$ + 2e$^-$ $\rightleftharpoons$ Mn | −1.180 |
| V I V$^{2+}$ | V$^{2+}$ + 2e$^-$ $\rightleftharpoons$ V | −1.18 |
| Zn I Zn$^{2+}$ | Zn$^{2+}$ + 2e$^-$ $\rightleftharpoons$ Zn | −0.763 |
| Tl I Tl I I I$^-$ | Tl I (s) + e$^-$ $\rightleftharpoons$ Tl + I$^-$ | −0.753 |
| Cr I Cr$^{3+}$ | Cr$^{3+}$ + 3e$^-$ $\rightleftharpoons$ Cr | −0.744 |
| Tl I TlBr I Br$^-$ | TlBr(s) + e$^-$ $\rightleftharpoons$ Tl + Br$^-$ | −0.658 |
| Pt I U$^{3+}$, U$^{4+}$ | U$^{4+}$ + e$^-$ $\rightleftharpoons$ U3$^+$ | −0.61 |
| Fe I Fe$^{2+}$ | Fe$^{2+}$ + 2e$^-$ $\rightleftharpoons$ Fe | −0.440 |
| Cd I Cd$^{2+}$ | Cd$^{2+}$ + 2e$^-$ $\rightleftharpoons$ Cd | −0.403 |
| Pb I PbSO$_4$ I So$_4^{2-}$ | PbSO$_4$ + 2e$^-$ $\rightleftharpoons$ Pb + SO$_4^{2-}$ | −0.359 |
| Tl I Tl$^+$ | Tl$^+$ + e$^-$ $\rightleftharpoons$ Tl | −0.3363 |
| Ag I AgI I I$^-$ | Ag I + e$^-$ $\rightleftharpoons$ Ag + I$^-$ | 0.152 |
| Pb I Pb$^{2+}$ | Pb$^{2+}$ + 2e$^-$ $\rightleftharpoons$ Pb | −0.126 |
| Pt I D$_2$ I D$^+$ | 2D$^+$ + 2e$^-$ $\rightleftharpoons$ D$_2$ | −0.0034 |
| Pt I H$_2$ I H$^+$ | 2H+ + 2e$^-$ $\rightleftharpoons$ H$_2$ | −0.0000 |
| Ag I AgBr I Br$^-$ | AgBr + e$^-$ $\rightleftharpoons$ Ag + Br$^-$ | +0.071 |
| Ag I AgCl I Cl$^-$ | AgCl + e$^-$ $\rightleftharpoons$ Ag + Cl$^-$ | +0.2225 |
| Pt I Hg I Hg$_2$Cl$_2$ I Cl$^-$ | Hg$_2$Cl$_2$ + 2e$^-$ $\rightleftharpoons$ 2Cl$^-$ + 2Hg(l) | +0.2676 |
| Cu I Cu$^{2+}$ | Cu$^{2+}$ + 2e$^-$ $\rightleftharpoons$ Cu | +0.337 |
| Pt I I$_2$ I I$^-$ | I$_2^-$ + 2e$^-$ $\rightleftharpoons$ 3I$^-$ | +0.536 |
| Pt I O$_2$ I H$_2$O$_2$ | O$_2$ + 2H$^+$ + 2e$^-$ $\rightleftharpoons$ H$_2$O$_2$ | +0.682 |
| Pt I Fe$^{2+}$, Fe$^{3+}$ | Fe$^{3+}$ + e$^-$ $\rightleftharpoons$ Fe$^{2+}$ | +0.771 |
| Ag I Ag$^+$ | Ag$^+$ + e$^-$ $\rightleftharpoons$ Ag | +0.7991 |
| Au I AuCl$_4^-$, Cl$^-$ | AuCl$_4^-$ + 3e$^-$ $\rightleftharpoons$ Au + 4Cl$^-$ | +1.00 |
| Pt I Br$_2$ I Br$^-$ | Br$_2$ + 2e$^-$ $\rightleftharpoons$ 2Br$^-$ | +1.065 |
| Pt I Tl$^+$, Tl$^{3+}$ | Tl$^{3+}$ + 2e$^-$ $\rightleftharpoons$ Tl$^+$ | +1.25 |
| Pt I H$^+$, Cr$_2$O$_7^{2-}$, Cr$^{3+}$ | Cr$_2$O$_7^{2-}$ + 14H$^+$ + 6e$^-$ $\rightleftharpoons$ 2Cr$^{3+}$ + 7H$_2$O | +1.33 |
| Pt I Cl$_2$ I Cl$^-$ | Cl$_2$ + 2e$^-$ $\rightleftharpoons$ 2Cl$^-$ | +1.3595 |
| Pt I Ce$^{4+}$, Ce$^{3+}$ | Ce$^{4+}$ + e$^-$ $\rightleftharpoons$ Ce$^{3+}$ | +1.45 |
| Au I Au$^{3+}$ | Au$^{3+}$ + 3e$^-$ $\rightleftharpoons$ Au | +1.50 |
| Pt I Mn$^{2+}$, MnO$_4^-$ | MnO$^{4-}$ + 8H$^+$ + 5e$^-$ $\rightleftharpoons$ Mn$^{2+}$ + 4H$_2$O | +1.51 |
| Au I Au$^+$ | Au$^+$ + e$^-$ $\rightleftharpoons$ Au | +1.68 |
| PbSO$_4$ I PbO$_2$ I H$_2$SO$_4$ | PbO$_2$ + SO$_4$ + 4H$^+$ + 2e$^-$ $\rightleftharpoons$ PbSO$_4$ + 2H$_2$O | +1.685 |
| Pt I F$_2$ I F$^-$ | F$_2$(g) + 2e$^-$ $\rightleftharpoons$ 2F$^-$ | +2.87 |
| | | |
| **Basic Solutions** | | |
| Pt I SO$_3^{2-}$, SO$_4^{2-}$ | SO$_4^{2-}$ + H$_2$O + 2e$^-$ $\rightleftharpoons$ SO$_3^{2-}$ + 2OH$^-$ | −0.93 |
| Pt I H$_2$ I OH$^-$ | 2H$_2$O + 2e$^-$ $\rightleftharpoons$ H$_2$ + 2OH$^-$ | −0.828 |
| Ag I Ag(NH$_3$)$_2^+$, NH$_3$(aq) | Ag(NH$_3$)$_2^+$ + e$^-$ $\rightleftharpoons$ Ag + 2NH$_3$ (aq) | +0.373 |
| Pt I O$_2$ I OH$^-$ | O$_2$ + 2H$_2$O + 4e$^-$ $\rightleftharpoons$ 4OH$^-$ | +0.401 |
| Pt I MnO$_2$ I MnO$_4^-$ | MnO$_4^-$ + 2H$_2$O + 3e$^-$ $\rightleftharpoons$ MnO$_2$ + 4OH$^-$ | +0.588 |

One of the most common voltaic cells is the ordinary "dry cell" used in flashlights. It is shown in the drawing below, along with the reactions occurring during the cell's discharge:

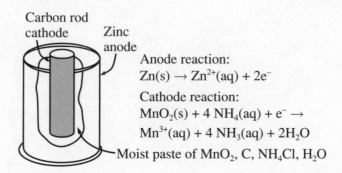

Carbon rod cathode  Zinc anode

Anode reaction:
$$Zn(s) \rightarrow Zn^{2+}(aq) + 2e^-$$

Cathode reaction:
$$MnO_2(s) + 4\ NH_4(aq) + e^- \rightarrow$$
$$Mn^{3+}(aq) + 4\ NH_3(aq) + 2H_2O$$

Moist paste of $MnO_2$, C, $NH_4Cl$, $H_2O$

In galvanic or voltaic cells, the chemical energy is converted into electrical energy.

In galvanic cells, the anode is negative and the cathode is positive (the opposite is true in electrolytic cells).

The force with which the electrons flow from the negative electrode to the positive electrode through an external wire is called the electromotive force, or emf, and is measured in volts (*V*):

$$1V = \frac{1\ \text{Joule}}{\text{coulomb}}$$

The greater the tendency or potential of the two half-reactions to occur spontaneously, the greater will be the emf of the cell. The emf of the cell is also called the cell potential, $E_{cell}$. The cell potential for the Zn/Cu cell can be written

$$E^0_{cell} = E^0_{Cu} - E^0_{Zn}$$

where the $E^0$s are standard reduction potentials.

The overall standard cell potential is obtained by subtracting the smaller reduction potential from the larger one. A positive emf corresponds to a negative $\Delta G$ and therefore to a spontaneous process.

## Electrolytic Cells

Reactions that do not occur spontaneously can be forced to take place by supplying energy with an external current. These reactions are called electrolytic reactions.

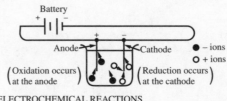

ELECTROCHEMICAL REACTIONS
In electrolytic cells, electrical energy is converted into chemical energy.

## *Faraday's Law*

One faraday is one mole of electrons.

(1F = 1 mole of electrons; F is the "faraday.")

1 F ~ 96,500 coul; the charge on 1 F is approximately 96,500 coulombs.

One coulomb is the amount of charge that moves past any given point in a circuit when a current of 1 ampere (amp) is supplied for one second. (Alternatively, one ampere is equivalent to 1 coulomb/second.)

Faraday's law states that during electrolysis, the passage of 1 faraday through the circuit brings about the oxidation of one equivalent weight of a substance at one electrode (anode) and reduction of one equivalent weight at the other electrode (cathode). Note that in all cells, oxidation occurs at the anode and reduction at the cathode.

## Non-Standard-State Cell Potentials

For a cell at concentrations and conditions other than standard, a potential can be calculated using the following Nernst equation:

$$E_{cell} = E_{cell}^0 - \frac{.059}{n} \log Q$$

where $E^0{}_{cell}$ is the standard-state cell voltage, $n$ is the number of electrons exchanged in the equations for the reaction, and $Q$ is the mass action quotient (which is similar in form to an equilibrium constant).

For the cell reaction

$Zn + Cu^{2+} \rightarrow Cu + Zn^{2+}$, the term $Q = [Zn^{2+}]/Cu^{2+}$

the Nernst equation takes the form:

$$E = E^0 - \frac{.059}{n} \log \frac{[Zn^{2+}]}{[Cu^{2+}]}$$

$$\Delta G = -nFE$$

is the Nernst equation. Also,

$$E = E^0 - \frac{RT}{nF} \ln Q$$

and $\qquad E = E^0 - \frac{.059}{n} \log Q$

which is analogous to

$$\Delta G = \Delta G^\circ + RT \ln Q.$$

# EQUILIBRIUM

## The Law of Mass Action

At equilibrium, both the forward and reverse reactions take place at the same rate, and thus the concentrations of reactants and products no longer change with time.

For a reversible reaction at equilibrium and a constant temperature, a certain ratio of reactant and product concentrations has a constant value, $K$ (equilibrium constant).

For the reaction $aA + bB \rightleftharpoons eE + fF$, at constant temperature,

$$K_c = \frac{[E]^e[F]^f}{[A]^a[B]^b} = \frac{\text{Products}}{\text{Reactants}}$$

where the [...] denotes equilibrium molar concentrations, and $K_c$ is the equilibrium constant.

The entire relationship is known as the law of mass action.

$$\frac{[E]^e[F]^f}{[A]^a[B]^b} = K_c$$

is known as the mass action expression. Note that if any of the species (*A, B, E, F*) is a pure solid or pure liquid, it does not appear in the expression for $K_c$.

For the reaction

$$N_2(g) + 3H_2(g) \rightleftharpoons 2NH_3(g),$$

$$K_p = \frac{(P_{NH_3})^2}{P_{N_2}(P_{H_2})^3}$$

where $K_p$ is the equilibrium constant derived from partial pressures.

## Le Chatelier's Principle

Le Chatelier's principle states that when a system at equilibrium is disturbed by a change in pressure, temperature, or amount of product or reactant, the reaction will shift to minimize the change and establish a new equilibrium.

Concentration changes can shift the equilibrium to use up the compound whose concentration increases, or produce the compound whose concentration decreases. Adding products to a reaction at equilibrium will shift the reaction to produce reactants; adding reactants to a reaction at equilibrium will shift the reaction to produce products.

An increase in temperature causes the equilibrium to shift to use up the added heat. For example, when heat is added to an exothermic reaction, it will shift to the left to use up the heat. An endothermic reaction will shift to the right to use up heat when heat is added.

An increase in pressure causes an equilibrium to shift in the direction that produces the fewest number of gas moles. For example, in a reaction that dissolves a gas in a liquid, increasing the pressure on the system will cause the equilibrium to shift to produce more dissolved gas.

Addition of a catalyst or an inert gas will not cause an equilibrium to shift; the amounts of reactants and products would remain unchanged.

## Kinetics and Equilibrium

The rate of an elementary chemical reaction is proportional to the concentrations of the reactants raised to powers equal to their coefficients in the balanced equation.

For $a$A + $b$B $\rightleftharpoons$ $e$E + $f$F,

$$\text{rate}_f = k_f [A]^a [B]^b,$$

$$\text{rate}_r = k_r [E]^e [F]^f$$

and

$$\frac{k_f}{k_r} = \frac{[E]^e [F]^f}{[A]^a [B]^b} = K_c$$

where $k_f$ and $k_r$ are rate constants for the forward and reverse reactions, respectively.

## Example:

The aluminum fluoride ion complex ($[AlF_6]^{3-}$) can dissociate to form aluminum and fluoride ions

$$[AlF_6]^{3-} \rightarrow Al^{3+} + 6F^-,$$

with a $K_c$ of $2 \times 10^{-24}$ at 25 °C. If 1.25 moles of $[AlF_6]^{3-}$ are dissolved in 2.25 liters of water at 25 °C, what will be the concentration of fluoride ions at equilibrium? We first set up our equation:

$$\frac{[Al^{+++}] [F^-]^6}{[AlF_6^{-3}]} = K_c$$

We know the value of $K_c$. We also know the initial value of $[AlF_6]^{-3}$ to be

$$\frac{1.25 \text{ moles}}{2.25 \text{ L}} = 0.556 \, M$$

at equilibrium a certain amount of $[AlF_6]$ will be gone, call it $X$, and the new concentration will be

$$\frac{1.25 - X}{2.25 \text{ L}}$$

(Remember, we must divide by volume to get units of concentration for the above formula to work!) Using the stoichiometric relationship, we can see that at equilibrium $X$ moles of $Al^{3+}$ will be formed and $6X$ moles of $F^-$. Converting these into units of concentration and plugging into the equilibrium formula yields:

$$\frac{\left(\dfrac{X}{2.25}\right)\left(\dfrac{6X}{2.25}\right)^6}{\left(\dfrac{1.25 - X}{2.25}\right)} = 2 \times 10^{-24}$$

Since the $K_c$ is very small, the amount of $[AlF_6]$ dissociating is very small, hence, the "$1.25 - X$" term in the denominator can be simplified to "$1.25$" ($X$ is very close to 0).

This gives:

$$\frac{\left(\dfrac{X}{2.25}\right)\left(\dfrac{6X}{2.25}\right)^6}{\left(\dfrac{1.25}{2.25}\right)} = 2 \times 10^{-24}$$

$$\frac{\left(\dfrac{X}{2.25}\right)\left(\dfrac{6X}{2.25}\right)^6}{0.556} = 2 \times 10^{-24}$$

$$\frac{36X^2}{5.06} = 1.11^{-24}$$

$$36X^2 = 5.61 \times 10^{-24}$$

$$X^2 = 1.56 \times 10^{-25}$$

$$X = 3.95 \times 10^{-13} \text{ moles}$$

However, the number of moles of fluorine is equal to $6X$, so we have $2.37 \times 10^{-12}$ moles of F⁻, in a volume of 2.25 liters, which gives a concentration of

$$\frac{2.37 \times 10^{-12}}{2.25 \text{ L}} = 1.05 \times 10^{-12} \, M$$

for [F⁻] at equilibrium.

## Equilibrium Constants

1.  Equilibrium constants are ratios. For the reaction, $aA + bB \leftrightarrow cC + dD$, The ratio of the product concentrations, raised to their stoichiometric coefficients, to the reactant concentrations, raised to their stoichiometric coefficients, is the equilibrium constant, $K_{eq}$. This is also called the law of mass action.

$$K_{eq} = \frac{[C]^c[D]^d}{[A]^a[B]^b}$$

2.  Pure substances, such as water or solids, do not show up in the equilibrium expression; only molar solutions or, as with $K_p$, gaseous pressures.

3.  The equilibrium constant for a multi-step process is equal to the product of the equilibrium constants for each step.

4.  The equilibrium constant for a reverse reaction is the inverse of the equilibrium constant for a forward reaction.

| Type of Reaction | Equilibrium Constant |
|---|---|
| Reaction in solution; reactants and products expressed as a concentration in moles/liter. | $K_c$ |
| Gaseous reaction, reactants and products expressed in units of pressure. <br> $N_2\,(g) + 3\,H_2\,(g) \leftrightarrow 2\,NH_3\,(g)$ | $K_p$ |
| The dissociation of water <br> $H_2O \leftrightarrow H^+\,(aq) + OH^-\,(aq)$ | $K_w$ |
| Reactions that produce a proton ($H^+$) from a Brønsted-Lowry acid. <br> *eg*: $HC_2H_3O_2\,(aq) \leftrightarrow H^+\,(aq) + C_2H_3O_2^-\,(aq)$ | $K_a$ |
| Reactions that produce a hydroxide ion ($OH^-$) from a Bronsted-Lowry base. <br> *eg*: $H_2O + C_2H_3O_2^-\,(aq) \leftrightarrow HC_2H_3O_2\,(aq) + OH^-\,(aq)$ | $K_b$ |
| Reactions that produce dissolved ions in aqueous solution from a solid. <br> *eg*: $PbI_2\,(s) \leftrightarrow Pb^{2+}\,(aq) + 2\,I^-\,(aq)$ | $K_{sp}$ |

## Le Chatelier's Principle and Chemical Equilibrium

Le Chatelier's principle states that when a system at equilibrium is disturbed by the application of a stress (change in temperature, pressure, or concentration) it reacts to minimize the stress and attain a new equilibrium position.

### *Effect of Changing the Concentrations of Equilibrium*

When a system at equilibrium is disturbed by adding or removing one of the substances, all the concentrations will change until a new equilibrium point is reached with the same value of $K_{eq}$.

An increase in the concentrations of reactants shifts the equilibrium to the right, thus increasing the amount of products formed. Decreasing the concentrations of reactants does the opposite.

## Ionization of Water, pH

For the equation

$$H_2O + H_2O \rightleftharpoons H_3O^+ + OH^-, \quad K_w = [H_3O^+][OH^-]$$

$$(\text{or } K_w = [H^+][OH^-]) = 1.0 \times 10^{-14} \text{ at } 25\ °C,$$

where $[H_3O^+][OH^-]$ is the product of ionic concentrations, and $K_w$ is the ion product constant for water (or simply the ionization constant or dissociation constant).

$$pH = -\log[H^+]$$

$$pOH = -\log[OH^-]$$

$$pK_w = pH + pOH = 14.0$$

In a neutral solution, pH = 7.0. In an acidic solution pH is less than 7.0. In basic solutions, pH is greater than 7.0. The smaller the pH, the more acidic is the solution. Note that since $pK_w$ (like all equilibrium constants) varies with temperature, neutral pH is less than (or greater than) 7.0 when the temperature is higher than (or lower than) 25 °C.

## Dissociation of Weak Electrolytes

For the equation

$$A^- + H_2O \rightleftharpoons HA + OH^-,$$

$$K_b = \frac{[HA][OH^-]}{[HA]}$$

where $K_b$ is the base ionization constant.

$$K_a = \frac{[H^+][A^-]}{[HA]}$$

where $K_a$ is the acid ionization constant.

$$K_b = \frac{K_w}{K_a}$$

for any **conjugate** acid/base pair, and therefore,

$$K_w = [H^+][OH^-].$$

## Dissociation of Polyprotic Acids

For $H_2S \rightleftharpoons H^+ + HS^-$,

$$K_{a_1} = \frac{[H^+][HS^-]}{[H_2S]}$$

For $HS^- \rightleftharpoons H^+ + S^{2-}$,

$$K_{a_2} = \frac{[H^+][S^{2-}]}{[HS^-]}$$

$K_{a_1}$ is much greater than $K_{a_2}$

Also,

$$K_a = K_{a_1} \times K_{a_2} = \frac{[H^+][HS^-]}{[H_2S]} \times \frac{[H^+][S^{2-}]}{[HS^-]}$$

$$= \frac{[H^+]^2[S^{2-}]}{[H_2S]}$$

This last equation is useful only in situations where two of the three concentrations are given and you wish to calculate the third.

## Buffers

Buffer solutions are equilibrium systems that resist changes in acidity and maintain constant pH when acids or bases are added to them.

The most effective pH range for any buffer is at or near the pH where the acid and salt concentrations are equal (that is, $pK_a$).

The pH for a buffer is given by

$$\text{pH} = pK_a + \log\frac{[A^-]}{[HA]} = pK_a + \log\frac{[\text{base}]}{[\text{acid}]}$$

which is obtained very simply from the equation for weak acid equilibrium,

$$K_a = \frac{[H^+][A^-]}{[HA]}.$$

## Hydrolysis

Hydrolysis refers to the action of salts of weak acids or bases with water to form acidic or basic solutions.

### Salts of Weak Acids and Strong Bases: Anion Hydrolysis

For $C_2H_3O_2^- + H_2O \rightleftharpoons HC_2H_3O_2 + OH^-$,

$$K_h = \frac{[HC_2H_3O_2][OH^-]}{[C_2H_3O_2^-]},$$

where $K_h$ is the hydrolysis constant for the acetate ion, which is just $K_b$ for acetate.

Also,

$$K_a = \frac{[H^+][C_2H_3O_2^-]}{[HC_2H_3O_2]}$$

and $\quad K_h = \dfrac{K_w}{K_a}$

### Salts of Strong Acids and Weak Bases: Cation Hydrolysis

For $NH_4^+ + H_2O \rightleftharpoons H_3O^+ + NH_3$,

$$K_h = \frac{[H_3O^+][NH_3]}{[NH_4^+]}$$

($K_h = K_a$ for $NH_4^+$). Also, $K_h = \dfrac{K_w}{K_b}$

and $\quad K_b = \dfrac{[NH_4^+][OH^-]}{[NH_3]}$

### Hydrolysis of Salts of Polyprotic Acids

For $S^{2-} + H_2O \rightleftharpoons HS^- + OH^-$,

$$K_{h_1} = \frac{K_w}{K_{a_2}} = \frac{[HS^-][OH^-]}{[S^{2-}]},$$

where $K_{a_2}$ is the acid dissociation constant for the weak acid $HS^-$.

For $HS^- + H_2O \rightleftharpoons H_2S + OH^-$,

$$K_{h2} = \frac{K_w}{K_{a_1}} = \frac{[H_2S][OH^-]}{[HS^-]},$$

where $K_{a_1}$ is the dissociation constant for the weak acid $H_2S$.

For accurate acid/base reactions, molarity should be carried out to four significant figures. This is also the convention in laboratory experiments.

Tables giving the values of $K_a$ and $K_b$ for various acids and bases at different temperatures are readily available. These can be used to calculate the degree of ionization.

### *Example:*

Formic acid has a $K_a$ of $1.8 \times 10^{-4}$. What is the pH of a $0.0400\ M$ solution? We know that formic acid dissociates to give us a hydrogen in:

$$HCOOH \rightleftharpoons HCOO^- + H^+.$$

First, we set up the equilibrium equation:

$$\frac{[H^+][HCOO^-]}{[HCOOH]} = K_a$$

We know that the equilibrium concentration of HCOOH is $0.0400\ M$ minus the amount that dissociates to $HCOO^-$ and $H^+$. If we term this amount $X$, then $[HCOOH] = 0.0400 - X$. We also know from stoichiometry that $[H^+] = [HCOO^-] = X$. Substituting this into the equation, we get:

$$\frac{(X)(X)}{(0.0400 - X)} = 1.8 \times 10^{-4}$$

$$\frac{X^2}{(0.0400 - X)} = 1.8 \times 10^{-4}$$

$$X^2 = (0.0400)(1.8 \times 10^{-4}) - X(1.8 \times 10^{-4})$$

$$X^2 + (1.8 \times 10^{-4})X - 7.2 \times 10^{-6} = 0$$

which can be solved as a quadratic. However, an even simpler solution is possible. Since we know from the $K_a$ very little of the acid will dissociate, we can assume $X$ is very small in terms of the 0.0400 molar concentration we subtract it from, and hence, can be ignored. This then gives us:

$$\frac{X^2}{0.0400} = 1.8 \times 10^{-4}$$

$$X^2 = 7.2 \times 10^{-6}$$

If the $[H+] = 2.7 \times 10^{-3}$, then the pH $(-\log [H^+]) = 2.57$. Solving the original equation by a quadratic, we get:

$$[H^+] = 2.6 \times 10^{-3} \quad \text{and} \quad pH = 2.57,$$

which shows that our initial assumption is correct in that X in the term $(0.0400 - X)$ was small enough to ignore.

### Common Ion Effect

If a large concentration of formate ions were added to the above solution (in the form of sodium formate, by the reaction HCOONa $\rightarrow$ HCOO$^-$ + Na$^+$), these additional formate ions would compete with the ones produced by the acid, and result in the reaction H$^+$ + HCOO$^-$ $\rightarrow$ HCOOH, thus resulting in an increase in the number of undisassociated formic acid molecules, and a decrease in the number of hydronium ions (represented as H$^+$). This is known as the "common ion effect."

Suppose we have one liter of the above 0.0400 *M* HCOOH solution. What will its pH be if we add 34.0 grams of HCOONa to it? (Assume no change in volume). The formula weight of HCOONa is 68.0 g/mol, and that gives us 0.500 moles of HCOONa. If the volume is one liter, then the concentration of HCOONa is 0.500 *M*. (Remember, the formula works only for *concentration*, not number of moles!) We can now use the previous formula and solve:

$$\frac{[H^+][HCOO^-]}{[HCOOH]} = K_a$$

As before, [HCOOH] = $0.0400 - X$, where X is the amount that has dissociated. [HCOO$^-$] = the amount of formate ions from both the salt and the acid. The sodium formate was determined to be .5000 molar, hence by stoichiometry so is the ion from this salt. The amount from the acid is X, as is the [H$^+$]. This gives us:

$$\frac{X(0.5000 + X)}{(0.0400 - X)} = 1.8 \times 10^{-4}$$

which can be solved as a quadratic. Again, however, if it is assumed that $X$ is very small with respect to the other numbers, it can be ignored in the subtraction and addition, giving us

$$\frac{0.500X}{.0400} = 1.8 \times 10^{-4}, \text{ or } X = [H^+] = 1.44 \times 10^{-5} M,$$

and the pH = 4.84. Had we solved the above equation as a quadratic, our answer would have been a pH of 4.87.

For slightly soluble compounds, a solubility constant, $K_{sp}$, is calculated in the same manner.

### *Example:*

The $K_{sp}$ at 25 °C for lead (II) carbonate is $1.5 \times 10^{-13}$. If 20.0 grams of $PbCO_3$ are mixed in 2.00 $L$ of water, 25 °C, how much of it will dissolve?

Our reaction is:

$$PbCO_3 \rightarrow Pb^{2+} + CO_3^{2-},$$

so we can write:

$$[Pb^{++}][CO_3^{2-}] = K_{sp}$$

We can tell from our stoichiometry that $[Pb^{++}] = [CO_3^=]$, which we will assign a value of $X$. Any material that is very insoluble, such as $PbCO_3$, is simply assigned a value of "1". Substituting in our above values yields:

$$(X)(X) = 1.5 \times 10^{-13}$$

$$X^2 = 1.5 \times 10^{-13}$$

$$X = 3.9 \times 10^{-7} M,$$

this is the concentration of the dissolved $PbCO_3$. Since it is in 2.00 liters, we have:

$$3.9 \times 10^{-7} \text{mol/L} \times 2.00 \text{ L} = 7.7 \times 10^{-7} \text{ mol}$$

total of $PbCO_3$. The formula weight of $PbCO_3$ is 267, we get

$$(7.7 \times 10^{-7} \text{ mol}) \times (267 \text{ g/mol}) = 2.1 \times 10^{-4}$$

grams of $PbCO_3$ in solution, or 210 micrograms have dissolved. (This is 0.0010% of the original 20.0 grams!)

# THERMODYNAMICS

## Standard States

The standard state corresponds to 25 °C and 1 atm. Heats of formation of substances in their standard states are indicated as $\Delta H°_f$.

## Some Commonly Used Terms in Thermodynamics

A system is that particular portion of the universe on which we wish to focus our attention.

Everything else is called the surroundings.

An **adiabatic process** occurs when the system is thermally isolated so that no heat enters or leaves.

An **isothermal process** occurs when the system is maintained at the same temperature throughout an experiment ($t_{final} = t_{initial}$).

An **isobaric process** occurs when the system is maintained at constant pressure (*i.e.*, $P_{final} = P_{initial}$).

The state of the system is some particular set of conditions of pressure, temperature, number of moles of each component, and their physical form (for example, gas, liquid, solid or crystalline form).

**State functions** depend only on the present state of the substance and not on the path by which the present state was attained. Enthalpy, energy, Gibbs free energy, and entropy are examples of state functions.

**Heat capacity** is the amount of heat energy required to raise the temperature of a given quantity of a substance one degree Celsius.

**Specific heat** is the amount of heat energy required to raise the temperature of 1g of a substance by 1.0 °C.

**Molar heat** capacity is the heat necessary to raise the temperature of 1 mole of a substance by 1.0 °C.

## The First Law of Thermodynamics

The first law of thermodynamics states that the change in internal energy is equal to the difference between the energy supplied to the system as heat and the energy removed from the system as work performed on the surroundings:

$$\Delta E = q - w$$

where $E$ represents the internal energy of the system (the total of all the energy possessed by the system). $\Delta E$ is the energy difference between the final and initial states of the system:

$$\Delta E = E_{final} - E_{initial}$$

The quantity $q$ represents the amount of heat that is added to the system as it passes from the initial to the final state, and $w$ denotes the work done by the system on the surroundings.

Heat added to a system and work done by a system are considered positive quantities (by convention).

For an ideal gas at constant temperature, $\Delta E = 0$ and $q - w = 0$ $(q = w)$.

Considering only work due to expansion of a system, against constant external pressure:

$$w = P_{external} \cdot \Delta V$$
$$\Delta V = V_{final} - V_{initial}$$

## Enthalpy

The heat content of a substance is called enthalpy, $H$. A heat change in a chemical reaction is termed a difference in enthalpy, or $\Delta H$. The term "change in enthalpy" refers to the heat change during a process carried out at a constant pressure:

$$\Delta H = q_p \; ; q_p \text{ means "heat at constant pressure."}$$

The change in enthalpy, $\Delta H$, is defined

$$\Delta H = \Sigma H_{products} - \Sigma H_{reactants}$$

When more than one mole of a compound is reacted or formed, the molar enthalpy of the compound is multiplied by the number of moles reacted (or formed).

Enthalpy is a state function. Changes in enthalpy for exothermic and endothermic reactions are shown in the figure below.

The $\Delta H$ of an endothermic reaction is positive, while that for an exothermic reaction is negative.

## Heats of Reaction

$\Delta E$ is equal to the heat absorbed or evolved by the system under conditions of constant volume:

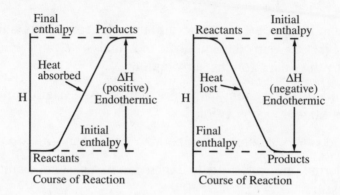

Course of Reaction        Course of Reaction

$$\Delta E = q_v; q_v \text{ means "heat at constant volume."}$$

Since

$$H = E + PV$$

at constant pressure $\Delta H = \Delta E + P\Delta V$. Note that the term $P\Delta V$ is just the pressure-volume work $((\Delta n)RT)$ for an ideal gas at constant temperature, where $\Delta n$ is the number of moles of gaseous products minus the number of moles of gaseous reactants. Therefore,

$$\Delta H = \Delta E + \Delta nRT$$

for a reaction which involves gases. If only solid and liquid phases are present, $\Delta V$ is very small, so that $\Delta H \approx \Delta E$.

## Hess's Law

Hess's law of heat summation states that when a reaction can be expressed as the algebraic sum of two or more reactions, the heat of the reaction, $\Delta H_r$, is the algebraic sum of the heats of the constituent reactions.

The enthalpy changes associated with the reactions that correspond to the formation of a substance from its free elements are called heats of formation, $\Delta H_f$.

$$\Delta H_r^0 = \Sigma \Delta H_f^0 \, (\text{products}) - \Sigma \Delta H_f^0 \, (\text{reactants})$$

## Heat of Vaporization and Heat of Fusion

The heat of vaporization of a substance is the number of calories required to convert 1 g of liquid to 1 g of vapor without a change in temperature.

The reverse process, changing 1 g of gas into a liquid without change in temperature, requires the removal of the same amount of heat energy (the heat of condensation).

The heat needed to vaporize 1 mole of a substance is called the molar heat of vaporization or the molar enthalpy of vaporization, $\Delta H_{vap}$, which is also represented as

$$\Delta H_{vaporization} = H_{vapor} - H_{liquid}$$

The magnitude of $\Delta H_{vap}$ provides a good measure of the strengths of the attractive forces operative in a liquid.

The number of calories needed to change 1 g of a solid substance (at the melting point) to 1 g of liquid (at the melting point) is called the heat of fusion.

The total amount of heat that must be removed in order to freeze 1 mole of a liquid is called its molar heat of crystallization. The molar heat of fusion, $\Delta H_{fus}$, is equal in magnitude but opposite in sign to the molar heat of crystallization and is defined as the amount of heat that must be supplied to melt 1 mole of a solid:

$$\Delta H_{fus} = H_{liquid} + H_{solid}$$

## Entropy

The degree of randomness of a system is represented by a thermodynamic quantity called the entropy, $S$. The greater the randomness, the greater the entropy.

A change in entropy or disorder associated with a given system is

$$\Delta S = S_2 - S_1$$

The entropy of the universe increases for any spontaneous process:

$$\Delta S_{universe} = (\Delta S_{system} + \Delta S_{surroundings})\ 0$$

When a process occurs reversibly at constant temperature, the change in entropy, $\Delta S$, is equal to the heat absorbed divided by the absolute temperature at which the change occurs:

$$\Delta S = \frac{q_{reversible}}{T}$$

## The Second Law of Thermodynamics

The second law of thermodynamics states that in any spontaneous process there is an increase in the entropy of the universe ($\Delta S_{total} > 0$).

$$\Delta S_{universe} \left( \Delta S_{total} \right) = \Delta S_{system} + \Delta S_{surroundings}$$

$$\Delta S_{surroundings} = \frac{-\Delta H_{system}}{T}$$

at constant $P$ and $T$

$$T\ \Delta S_{total} = -(\Delta H_{system} - T\ \Delta S_{system1})$$

The maximum amount of useful work that can be done by any process at constant temperature and pressure is called the change in Gibbs free energy, $\Delta G$;

$$\Delta G = \Delta H - T\Delta S$$

Another way in which the second law is stated is that in any spontaneous change, the amount of free energy available decreases.

Thus, if $\Delta G = 0$, then the system is at equilibrium.

## Standard Entropies and Free Energies

The entropy of a substance, compared to its entropy in a perfectly crystalline form at absolute zero, is called its absolute entropy, $S°$.

The third law of thermodynamics states that the entropy of any pure, perfect crystal at absolute zero is equal to zero.

The standard free energy of formation, $\Delta G^0{}_f$, of a substance is defined as the change in free energy for the reaction in which one mole of a compound is formed from its elements under standard conditions:

$$\Delta G_f^0 = \Delta H_f^0 - T\ \Delta S_f^0$$

$$\Delta S_f^0 = \Sigma S_f^0{}_{products} - \Sigma S_f^0{}_{reactants}$$

and $\quad \Delta G_r^0 = \Sigma \Delta G_f^0{}_{products} - \Sigma \Delta G_f^0{}_{reactants}$

The Gibbs Free energy change ($\Delta G°$) is related to the standard electrode potential, $E°$ by the following equation:

$$\Delta G° = -nFE°$$

where $n$ is the number of electrons involved in the half reaction and $F$ is the Faraday constant, which has a value of 23,061 calories/volt, or 96,487 coulombs.

## Example:

Calculate the Gibbs free energy change under standard conditions at 25 °C for the following reaction:

$$Br_2 + Pb \rightarrow PbBr_2$$

Consulting our table of half reaction we get:

$$2e^- + Br_2 \rightarrow 2Br^- = + 1.065 \text{ volts}$$

$$Pb° \rightarrow Pb^{++} + 2e^- = + 0.126 \text{ volts}$$

This gives a total of + 1.191 volts, and a total of 2 electrons changing atoms. Putting this data into the equation yields.

$$\Delta G° = -(2) \ (23,061) \ (1.191) = -54,930 \text{ calories.}$$

Notice that although a positive potential (+1.191 volts) designates a spontaneous reaction, a negative $\Delta G°$ (– 54,930 calories) designates the same phenomena.

$\Delta G°$ can also be related to the equilibrium constant, by the formula

$$\Delta G° = - RT \ln K$$

where $R$ is the ideal gas law constant (1.987 calories/mole Kelvin)*, $T$ is the temperature in Kelvin, and $K$ is the equilibrium constant ($K_a$, $K_{sp}$, etc.).

What is the $K$ of the above reaction?

$$\Delta G° = -54,930, T = 25 + 273 = 278K,$$

so $\quad - 54,930 = -(1.987) \ (278) \ln k, 99.4 = \ln K,$

$$e^{99.4} = e^{\ln k}, 2 \times 10^{43} = k$$

# DESCRIPTIVE CHEMISTRY

## Reactivity

**Group IA** elements are the most reactive of the metals. The outer "s" electron is loosely held and easily removed—and more easily removed for larger elements. Group IA elements react violently with water and are so reactive that they are never found naturally in an uncombined state. Hydroxides of IA elements are strong bases; increased size of the IA element will increase the base strength of the element's hydroxide.

---

* The numerical value for $R$ differs here because the units are different. $R$ can be expressed as 0.08205 $l$ atm/mole Kelvin, 1/.987 cal/mole Kelvin, etc., the actual value of $R$ is still the same.

**Group IIA** are also very reactive and do not tend to be found uncombined in nature. They react slowly with oxygen to form oxides and with water to form hydroxides.

**Transition metals** all react very slowly with oxygen or water, and some, do not react at all. The metals with lower reactivity can exist in uncombined in nature, and therefore were some of the first metals discovered by ancient civilizations.

The lightest of the **IIIA group** are non-metallic, while the remaining are all metals. Group IIIA elements are all mildly reactive. For example, aluminum resists combining with oxygen or reacting with water at normal temperatures, but it will react with hydrochloric acid.

The first element of the **group IVA** elements (carbon) is a non-metal. It is followed by two metalloids (silicon and germanium), and then by two metals (tin and lead). The first three elements are semi-conductors and fairly reactive.

**Group VA** consists of two non-metals, two metalloids, and a metal. The more reactive of these elements combine readily with oxygen and some of the more reactive metals.

**Group VIA** elements easily gain electrons, such as oxygen, with this ability decreasing with the larger elements.

**Group VIIA** elements gain electrons most easily, with the most highly reactive element being the smallest in this group (fluorine).

**Group VIIIA** are the inert gases and, because they have a full outer shell of electrons, do not combine easily with other elements. For example, the smaller inert gases exist as monoatomic gases. The largest in this group can combine with other elements, but only with highly electronegative elements (such as fluorine and chlorine) in coordinate covalent bonds.

## Naming Ionic Compounds

1. Monoatomic cations take the name of the element, *e.g.*, "sodium" for $Na^+$.

2. Cations with multiple possible oxidations states should have the oxidation state listed with a Roman numeral, *e.g.*, Tin (IV) oxide for $SnO_2$

3. Monoatomic anions take the name of the element, but end with "ide," *e.g.*, "fluoride" for $F^-$.

4.  Name the cation first, then the anion, *e.g.*, "sodium fluoride."

5.  Use Greek prefixes for multiple ions. mono-, di-, tri-, tetra-, penta-, hexa- hepta-, octa-, etc., *e.g.*, dinitrogen pentoxide for $N_2O_5$.

6.  Be sure to memorize the common cations and anions on the following charts.

## CATIONS

| NAME | FORMULA |
| --- | --- |
| Hydrogen | $H^+$ |
| Lithium | $Li^+$ |
| Sodium | $Na^+$ |
| Potassium | $K^+$ |
| Cesium | $Cs^+$ |
| Beryllium | $Be^{2+}$ |
| Magnesium | $Mg^{2+}$ |
| Calcium | $Ca^{2+}$ |
| Barium | $Ba^{2+}$ |
| Aluminum | $Al^{3+}$ |
| Iron II/III | $Fe^{2+}/Fe^{3+}$ |
| Copper I/II | $Cu^+/Cu^{2+}$ |
| Tin II/IV | $Sn^{2+}/Sn^{4+}$ |
| Lead II/IV | $Pb^{2+}/Pb^{4+}$ |
| Mercury I/II | $Hg^+/Hg^{2+}$ |
| Ammonium | $NH_4^+$ |

**ANIONS**

| NAME | FORMULA |
|---|---|
| Hydride | $H^-$ |
| Fluoride | $F^-$ |
| Chloride | $Cl^-$ |
| Oxide | $O^{2-}$ |
| Sulfide | $S^{2-}$ |
| Nitride | $N^{3-}$ |
| Phosphide | $P^{3-}$ |
| Carbonate | $CO_3^{2-}$ |
| Bicarbonate | $HCO_3^-$ |
| Hypochlorite | $ClO^-$ |
| Chlorite | $ClO_2^-$ |
| Chorate | $ClO_3^-$ |
| Perchlorate | $ClO_4^-$ |
| Iodite | $IO_2^-$ |
| Iodate | $IO_3^-$ |
| Acetate | $C_2H_3O_2^-$ |
| Permanganate | $MnO_4^-$ |
| Dichromate | $Cr_2O_7^-$ |
| Chromate | $CrO_4^-$ |
| Peroxide | $O_2^{2-}$ |
| Nitrite | $NO_2^-$ |
| Nitrate | $NO_3^-$ |
| Sulfite | $SO_3^{2-}$ |
| Sulfate | $SO_4^{2-}$ |
| Hydrogen sulfate | $HSO_4^-$ |
| Hydroxide | $OH^-$ |
| Cyanide | $CN^-$ |
| Phosphate | $PO_4^{3-}$ |
| Hydrogen phosphate | $HPO_4^{2-}$ |
| Dihydrogen phosphate | $H_2PO_4^-$ |

## Organic Chemistry

### *Alkanes*

Alkanes are hydrocarbon molecules with all single bonds between the carbons. Students should know the basic names of the members in the basic alkane series.

| ALKANE | FORMULA |
|--------|---------|
| Methane | $CH_4$ |
| Ethane | $C_2H_6$ |
| Propane | $C_3H_8$ |
| Butane | $C_4H_{10}$ |
| Pentane | $C_5H_{12}$ |
| Hexane | $C_6H_{14}$ |
| Heptane | $C_7H_{16}$ |
| Octane | $C_8H_{18}$ |
| Nonane | $C_9H_{20}$ |
| Decane | $C_{10}H_{22}$ |

### *Multiple Bonds: Alkenes and Alkynes*

Alkenes are hydrocarbons that contain a double bond between at least two carbons. Alkenes have the general formula, $C_nH_{2n}$. Alkynes are hydrocarbons that contain a triple bond between at least two carbons. Alkynes have the general formula, $C_nH_{2n-2}$.

The first covalent bond between two non-metals is a *sigma* bond ($\sigma$), where the electrons are paired along the axis between the two atoms. Any additional covalent bonds between non-metals are *pi* bonds ($\pi$), where the electrons are paired through overlap of *p*-orbitals above and below the inter-nuclear axis. For example, a double bond consists of one sigma and one *pi* bond. A triple bond consists of one *sigma* and two *pi* bonds. *Sigma* bonds are much stronger than *pi* bonds, and therefore have much higher bond energies and are more difficult to break.

## Organic Functional Groups

| Functional Group | General Formula | Example |
|---|---|---|
| Halohydrocarbon | $\begin{array}{c} H \\ \vert \\ R-C-Cl \\ \vert \\ H \end{array}$ | Carbon tetrachloride |
| Alcohol | $\begin{array}{c} H \\ \vert \\ R-C-OH \\ \vert \\ H \end{array}$ | Ethanol |
| Ether | $\begin{array}{c} H \quad\quad H \\ \vert \quad\quad \vert \\ R-C-O-C-R \\ \vert \quad\quad \vert \\ H \quad\quad H \end{array}$ | Diethyl ether |
| Aldehyde | $\begin{array}{c} H \\ \vert \\ R-C-H \\ \Vert \\ O \end{array}$ | Formaldehyde |
| Ketone | $\begin{array}{c} R-C-R \\ \Vert \\ O \end{array}$ | Methyl ethyl ketone |
| Carboxylic acid | $\begin{array}{c} R-C-OH \\ \Vert \\ O \end{array}$ | Acetic acid |
| Ester | $\begin{array}{c} H \\ \vert \\ R-C-O-C-R \\ \Vert \quad\quad \vert \\ O \quad\quad H \end{array}$ | Diphenyl ester |

## *Isomerism*

Isomers are molecules that have the same formula but different structure or arrangement of the atoms. Two isomers will have different physical and chemical properties, which will depend on how the atoms are arranged and the intermolecular forces that are created as a result.

**Structural isomers** exist when the two isomers have the same formula, but the atoms are arranged in a different sequences or arrangement. Below are the two structural isomers of butane, each with the same formula, but different structures.

n-butane:  $CH_3 - CH_2 - CH_2 - CH_3$

$$\begin{array}{c} CH_3 \\ | \end{array}$$
isobutane:  $CH_3 - CH - CH_3$

**Optical isomers** occur when two molecules have the same formula, and the same general structure, but the two structures are not superimposable on each other. This happens when the molecules are mirror images of one another, such as our right and left hands.

$$\begin{array}{ccc} Br & & Br \\ | & & | \\ R - C - Cl & & Cl - C - R \\ | & & | \\ H & & H \end{array}$$

## **Environmental Chemistry**

### *Acid Rain*

Acid rain is caused when oxides of nitrogen or sulfur combine with water to respectively form nitric and nitrous, or sulfuric and sulfurous, acids. Oxides of nitrogen are formed when the nitrogen gas in the atmosphere combines with the oxygen gas, which occurs when air is exposed to any high-temperature situation or combustion. Oxides of sulfur occur when fossil fuels—particularly coal—are combusted. Fossil fuels are created from decayed organisms, which originally contained proteins with sulfur-containing di-sulfide bonds. As the organisms decayed, the sulfur remained, and is converted to the oxide when the fossil fuel is burned.

With sulfur:

During combustion: $\quad$ S (in coal from ancient proteins) $+ O_2 \rightarrow SO_2$

Forms in atmosphere: $\quad$ $SO_2 + H_2O \rightarrow H_2SO_3$ (sulfurous acid)

Acidic proton dissociates: $\quad$ $H_2SO_3 \rightarrow H^+ + HSO_3^-$

With nitrogen (unbalanced reactions):

During combustion: $\quad$ $N_2$ (80% of atmosphere) $+ O_2 \rightarrow NO_2$

Forms in atmosphere: $\quad$ $NO_2 + H_2O \rightarrow HNO_3$ (nitric acid)

Acidic proton dissociates: $\quad$ $HNO_3 \rightarrow H^+ + NO_3^-$

### Hard Water

When some ions are dissolved in water, particularly $Ca^{2+}$, the resulting solution is called "hard water." Hard water decreases the sudsy action caused by soap; the calcium ion binds to the polar anionic side of the soap molecule and makes the soap molecule less available to bind to and remove grease.

Also, the dissolved ions in hard water create a crusty precipitate, called "scale," which clogs pipes and appliances. Water is "softened" using an ion-exchange process, where each calcium ion is replaced by two sodium ions. The resulting water does not decrease soap activity or deposit scale in pipes, but it does make the water taste saltier, and it increases sodium in the diet of people who drink the water. This is particularly disadvantageous for people with heart conditions or high blood pressure.

### Greenhouse Effect

Carbon dioxide and methane gas, as well as several other gases, absorb the low-frequency infrared heat energy that is radiated from the earth. Thus trapped, the heat that would otherwise escape into space is kept close to earth and heats the planet.

### Ozone Depletion

Normally, ozone gas in the earth's stratosphere absorbs damaging ultraviolet light that would otherwise penetrate the atmosphere and cause cellular damaging to living organisms. Certain industrial chemicals, most notably hydrocarbons that also contain chlorine and fluorine, cause the ozone ($O_3$) to be converted into atmospheric oxygen ($O_2$). This conversion allows more ultraviolet light to penetrate the atmosphere and is reflected in increased frequency of skin cancer among humans, and other types of cell damage.

## Laboratory

### *Equipment*

When introduced to laboratory equipment, students can easily be confused by equipment of different design but apparently similar function. The following comparisons represent the areas where students are most often confused.

1.  Funnels: a *Buchner funnel* is used to separate a solid from a solution using filter paper; whereas a *separatory funnel* is used to separate two liquids of different density and polarity (such as oil and water).

2.  Glassware to hold larger amounts of liquid, but not used to measure the volume of liquid. Students should know the names of these containers.

    a.  *Beakers* have straight sides and flat bottoms.

    b.  *Erlenmeyer flasks* have triangular sides that converge to a small neck at the top and a flat bottom.

    c.  *Florence flasks* have a narrow neck, rounded sides, and a round bottom.

3.  *Ceramic ware is*: an evaporating dish that is broad and flat to allow a solvent to evaporate and leave the solute behind; whereas a *crucible* is used to heat a material over the flame, which also involves a clay triangle, ring clamp, ring stand, and Bunsen burner. Tongs or a hot-mitt should be used to remove the crucible from the heat.

4.  Glassware to measure volume:

    a.  A *buret* is used to measure the volume of standard solution added to a sample during a chemical reaction.

    b.  A *volumetric pipette* is used to measure the specific amount of a solution. The narrow neck allows you to more accurately see when the desired volume is present.

    c.  A *measuring pipette* is used with a pipette bulb to draw up a variable amount of liquid to transfer it to another container.

    d.  Likewise, a *graduated cylinder* is used to measure a variable amount of liquid.

e. A *volumetric flask* is used to make a quantitative solution. When making the solution, measure a specific amount of concentrated or solid substance and put it in the flask. Then add a small amount of solvent and mix thoroughly by gently swirling the solution in the larger, round bottom of the flask. Finally, add enough solvent to go up to the measurement line in the neck of the flask.

## Safety

1. When diluting acids, "do it like you should, add the acid to the water." Adding water to concentrated acid will quickly cause the water to hydrolyze and the acid will splatter.

2. When lighting a Bunsen burner, use a match or sparking device; do not use a gas cigarette lighter.

3. If heating a material that may be flammable, set the beaker or test tube that contains the material in a water bath over the flame. This indirect heating assures that the temperature of the material will not be heated too quickly and never exceed the boiling temperature of water.

4. When heating material, heat slowly and be sure to point the container away from people. Sudden flashing may quickly push the material out of the container.

5. Assume that all chemicals you work with are toxic. Therefore, never touch your face during the laboratory and always wash you hands after leaving the laboratory. It is easier than imagined to have small amounts of substances on the hands. Report any spills to the teacher.

6. Wear proper protective gear: an apron and eye protection.

7. Know how to use emergency equipment, such as the eye-wash station, the shower, fire blanket, and fire extinguisher.

## Measurements and Accuracy

1. Understand the difference between precision and accuracy. Accuracy represents how close a measurement is to the real or accepted value. Measurements are precise when multiple measurements are close to each other. For example, a student might make a inaccurate standard solution for an acid-base titration. If the standard solution has a lower concentration

than thought, then more of it would be required to neutralize the sample, and the student will think that the sample has a higher concentration. The student attempts the neutralization several times and gets the same answer each time. The results would be precise, but not accurate.

2.  Be aware of significant figures in laboratory measurements. You are allowed one uncertain figure in your measurement. For example, in the following buret measurement described below, the volume is delineated by tenths of a milliliter (mL).

    a.  First, remember to read the bottom of the meniscus when measuring volume in glassware.

    b.  Since one uncertain digit is allowed, you should record 11.45 mL. It might be 11.44 mL, you are uncertain about the $\pm 0.01$ mL amount, but you are certain that the $\pm 0.1$ mL aspect of the measurement is between 11.4 and 11.5 mL.

    c.  Also with regard to significant figures, remember that if they are multiplied or divided together to get some final answer, the number of significant figures in the answer should match the least number of significant figures in the numbers that lead to the answer.

3.  When measuring the mass of a substance in a recently heated container, be sure to let the container cool before you put it on the balance. Air currents may decrease the accuracy of the measurement by artificially decreasing the measured mass.

4.  When making solutions, mix the solution slowly to be sure that all the solid dissolves. Your results might be affected if the solution is less concentrated than you think.

5.  When using a buret for titration, be sure to rinse the buret with the standard solution to be used in the titration. Rinsing with the sample to be titrated will neutralize some of the standard solution before the experiment begins. Rinsing with water will dilute the standard solution before the experiment begins.

6.  When you make solutions or use chemicals, you are assuming that they are pure—not a mixture with other chemicals. Therefore, be sure not to inadvertently add impurities. Be sure that a spatula is clean when you put it in a chemical. Do not touch the tip of a pipette to anything accept the solution that it holds.

## *Interpreting Results*

1.  First, never expect quantitative measurements to exactly match the expected value. Be sure to calculate the percent accuracy by dividing the difference between the measured and expected values, dividing by the expected value, and multiplying by 100. This figure should be a part of any laboratory report involving quantitative measurements.

2.  Analyze the precision of your measurements by making multiple measurements or comparing your value with your classmates. If measurements vary within the ± accuracy of your measuring devices, they are virtually the same value, even though the number as expressed on your calculator might be different. Use tables or graphs to better summarize multiple data points.

3.  As you examine the accuracy of your measurements, consider each step that you undertook to make the measurement. Consider how an inadvertent error in that step could have influenced the measurement, either by increasing or decreasing the value of the measurement relative to the expected value.

4.  When graphing a variable as you change another variable, the value that you measure should be on the *y-axis*; this is the *dependent variable*. It has changed as a result of you changing the *independent variable*, which should be on the *x-axis*. If such a graph shows an increasing slope, then the dependent variable is *directly proportional* to the independent variable. If such a graph shows a decreasing and rounded slope, then the dependent variable is *inversely proportional* to the independent variable.

# ▼

# PRACTICE
# TEST 1

This test is also on CD-ROM in our special interactive SAT Chemistry TEST*ware*®. It is highly recommended that you first take this exam on computer. You will then have the additional study features and benefits of timed conditions and instantaneous, accurate scoring. See page 5 for guidance on how to get the most out of our SAT Chemistry software.

# SAT Chemistry
# Practice Test 1

**(Answer sheets appear in the back of this book.)**

## PART A

**TIME:** 1 Hour
85 Questions

---

**DIRECTIONS**: Each set of questions below consists of five lettered choices followed by a list of numbered statements or questions. For each statement or question, select the answer choice that is most closely related to it. Each answer choice may be used once, more than once, or not at all.

---

*Note:* **For all questions involving solutions, assume that the solvent is water unless otherwise noted.**

**Questions 1–6** refer to the following groups.

(A)  Alkali metals

(B)  Alkaline earth metals

(C)  Metalloids

(D)  Halogens

(E)  Rare earths

1.    Used primarily in semiconductors

2.    Some occur as diatomic molecules

3.    Give oxides with the formula $X_2O$

4.    Produce acid salts with the formula $XSO_4$

5.    Have large electronegativity values

6.    Have small ionization energies

**Questions 7–10** refer to the following species.

   (A)  A Brønsted acid          (D)  A weak base

   (B)  A Brønsted base          (E)  A buffer

   (C)  A strong acid

7.  Is a solution made by the combination of a weak acid and the salt of its conjugate base

8.  Always dissociates nearly completely in aqueous solution

9.  Has a very high $K_a$

10. Always accepts a proton

**Questions 11–14** refer to the following species.

   (A)  A strong acid          (D)  A weak base

   (B)  A strong base          (E)  A salt

   (C)  A weak acid

11. $NH_3$

12. $Cl^-$

13. $NaHCO_3$

14. NaOH

**Questions 15–17** refer to the following values.

   (A)  0          (D)  –2

   (B)  –1          (E)  +2

   (C)  +1

15. The oxidation number of Na in NaCl

16. The oxidation number of Cl in $Cl_2$

17. The oxidation number of S in $Na_2S$

**Questions 18–20** refer to the following colors.

(A) Yellow                    (D) White

(B) Purple                    (E) Colorless

(C) Green

18. $S(s)$

19. $HCl(aq)$

20. $NaOH(aq)$

**Questions 21–23** refer to the following reaction and the given values.

$$4NH_3(g) + 5O_2(g) \rightarrow 4NO(g) + 6H_2O(g)$$

(A) 2.294                    (D) 25.3

(B) 36.49                    (E) 2.513

(C) 1.409

21. If you begin with 16.00 grams of ammonia, and an excess of oxygen, how many grams of water will be obtained?

22. If you begin with 66.00 grams of ammonia, and 54.00 grams of oxygen, how many grams of water will be obtained?

23. How many moles of $NH_3$ are needed to produce 2.513 moles of NO?

# PART B

DIRECTIONS: Each question below consists of two statements. Determine if Statement I is true or false <u>and</u> if Statement II is true or false and fill in the corresponding ovals on your answer sheet. Fill in oval CE if Statement II is a correct explanation of the true Statement I.

|  | (I) |  | (II) |
|---|---|---|---|

101. Acid rain is destructive to limestone

*because*

acid rain contains HCl.

102. The net ionic equation for the mixing of aqueous solutions of $CaCl_2$ and $Na_2SO_4$ is: $Na^+(aq) + Cl^-(aq) \rightarrow NaCl(s)$

*because*

NaCl precipitates out of the reaction.

103. Given that the $K_{sp}$ of AgBr and $BaCO_3$ are $5 \times 10^{-13}$ and $2 \times 10^{-9}$ respectively, AgBr is less soluble than $BaCO_3$

*because*

a larger *Ksp* indicates a larger conversion to products.

104. In any solution $[H^+] = 1 \times 10^{-7}$

*because*

$Kw = [OH^-][H^+]$ $= 1 \times 10^{-14}$

105. HF is considered a strong acid

*because*

strong acids ionize completely in an aqueous solution.

106. $NH_4^+$ is considered to be a strong acid

*because*

it is the conjugate acid of a strong base.

107. By the Lewis theory of acids and bases, $F^-$ is considered to be a base

*because*

it can accept protons.

108. A 1 *N* solution of
     $H_2SO_4$ is the same
     as a 1*M* solution
     of $H_2SO_4$

     *because*

     normality and
     molarity are both
     units of concentration
     and refer to the
     same thing.

109. A solution of NaOH
     and $Ba(OH)_2$ would
     be a good buffer

     *because*

     it contains $OH^-$
     as a common ion.

110. The oxidation
     number of Cl in $Cl_2$
     is +1

     *because*

     Cl is missing one
     electron to fill its
     shell.

111. Water has a high boiling
     point for its molecular
     weight

     *because*

     of polar covalent
     bonding.

112. Benzene is a poor electrolyte
     in water solution

     *because*

     it does not ionize.

113. The reaction of zinc with
     hydrochloric acid does not go
     to completion in an open
     container

     *because*

     hydrogen gas is
     not evolved.

114. Atoms of the same element
     combine covalently rather
     than by ionic attraction.

     *because*

     they have the same
     electronegativities.

115. Metals such as gold are
     malleable

     *because*

     the positive nuclei
     are surrounded by a "sea"
     of free electrons.

116. Acetic acid is a strong acid

     *because*

     it ionizes completely
     in water solution.

# PART C

**DIRECTIONS:** For each question in this section, select the best answer from among the given choices and fill in the corresponding oval on the answer sheet.

24. The element with atomic number 32 describes

    (A)  a metal            (D)  a halogen

    (B)  a nonmetal         (E)  a noble gas

    (C)  a metalloid

25. The Lewis dot structure of $N_2$ is best represented as

    (A)  $: \overset{.}{\underset{..}{N}} : \overset{..}{N} :$        (D)  $: N ::: N :$

    (B)  $: \overset{..}{\underset{..}{N}} :: N$        (E)  $\overset{.}{N} ::: \overset{.}{N}$

    (C)  $\cdot \overset{..}{\underset{..}{N}} :: \overset{..}{N} \cdot$

26. All of the following are chemical changes EXCEPT

    (A)  dissolving NaCl in water

    (B)  burning a piece of wood

    (C)  ozone absorbing ultraviolet light

    (D)  dissolving Na metal in water

    (E)  rusting of iron

27. Which of the following has the smallest mass?

    (A)  a hydrogen nucleus     (D)  a helium nucleus

    (B)  an alpha particle      (E)  a beta particle

    (C)  a neutron

28. 58.5 g of NaCl in

    (A) 1 liter of solution is 2 molar

    (B) 2 liters of solution is 0.75 molar

    (C) 1 liter of solution is 1 molal

    (D) 2 kilograms of solvent is 0.5 molal

    (E) 1 kilogram of solvent is 1 molar

29. The greatest reduction of kinetic energy of water molecules occurs when water is

    (A) cooled as a solid

    (B) cooled as a liquid

    (C) converted from a liquid to a gas

    (D) converted from a gas to a liquid

    (E) converted from a liquid to a solid

30. One formula unit of $Cr(NH_3)_5SO_4Br$ represents

    (A) 4 atoms          (D) 23 atoms

    (B) 8 atoms          (E) 27 atoms

    (C) 12 atoms

31. How many neutrons are there in the nucleus of an element of atomic weight 197?

    (A) 43          (D) 100

    (B) 79          (E) 118

    (C) 83

32. The extremely high melting point of diamond (carbon) may be explained by large numbers of

    (A) covalent bonds          (D) Van der Waals forces

    (B) ionic bonds          (E) polar bonds

    (C) hydrogen bonds

33. Which of the following best represents the geometry and atomic radii in a carbon dioxide molecule?

(A) o—O—o

(B) O—o—O

(C)

(D)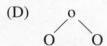

(E) o—O—O

Answer questions 34–37 using the phase diagram below.

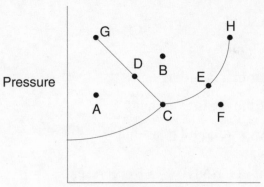

34. At which point can all three phases coexist at equilibrium?

(A) C        (D) G

(B) D        (E) H

(C) E

35. At which point can only the solid phase exist?

(A) A        (D) E

(B) B        (E) F

(C) C

36. Which is the critical point?

(A) B        (D) G

(B) E        (E) H

(C) F

37. At which point can only the solid and liquid phases coexist?

    (A) C                          (D) A

    (B) D                          (E) B

    (C) E

38. Which of the following is electrolytic?

    (A) mercury in water

    (B) a benzene solution of ethanol

    (C) sucrose dissolved in water

    (D) sodium chloride dissolved in water

    (E) vinegar in water

39. The oxidation number of sulfur in $NaHSO_4$ is

    (A) 0.                         (D) +4.

    (B) +2.                        (E) +6.

    (C) –2.

40. A small crystal of NaCl is added to a sodium chloride solution result-ing in the precipitation of more than 1 gram of sodium chloride. This solution had been

    (A) unsaturated                (D) dilute

    (B) saturated                  (E) concentrated

    (C) supersaturated

41. The salt produced by the reaction of perchloric acid with barium hydroxide is

    (A) $BaClO_3$                  (D) $Ba(ClO_4)_2$

    (B) $BaClO_4$                  (E) $BaCl_2$

    (C) $Ba(OH)_2$

42. A reaction that occurs only when heat is added is best described as

    (A) exothermic              (D) spontaneous

    (B) endothermic             (E) non-spontaneous

    (C) an equilibrium process

43. The transition metals are characterized by

    (A) highest energy electrons in $s$ subshells

    (B) highest energy electrons in $p$ subshells

    (C) highest energy electrons in $d$ subshells

    (D) highest energy electrons in $f$ subshells

    (E) stable electron configurations

44. Neutral atoms of F (fluorine) have the same number of electrons as

    (A) $B^{3-}$                (D) $Na^-$

    (B) $N^+$                   (E) $Mg^{3+}$

    (C) $Ne^-$

45. An equilibrium reaction may be forced to completion by

    (A) adding a catalyst

    (B) increasing the pressure

    (C) increasing the temperature

    (D) removing the products from the reaction mixture as they are formed

    (E) decreasing the reactant concentration

46. An acid $H_3X$ is classified as

    (A) monoprotic             (D) bidentate

    (B) diprotic               (E) polar covalent

    (C) triprotic

47. Which of the following salts will result in a basic solution when dissolved in water?

    (A) $Ba(NO_3)_2$        (D) $Pb_3(PO_4)_2$

    (B) $Na_2S$             (E) $NaCl$

    (C) $Al_2(SO_4)_3$

48. The Haber process is used for producing ammonia from nitrogen and hydrogen. This reaction could be forced to produce more ammonia by

    (A) increasing the reaction pressure

    (B) decreasing the reaction pressure

    (C) adding a catalyst

    (D) adding a salt

    (E) adding water

49. The ionization energy of an element is

    (A) a measure of its mass

    (B) the energy required to remove an electron from the element in its gaseous state

    (C) the energy released by the element in forming an ionic bond

    (D) the energy released by the element upon receiving an additional electron

    (E) the amount of ions in a molecule

50. The radioactive decay of plutonium −238 ( $^{238}_{94}Pu$) produces an alpha particle and a new atom. That new atom is

    (A) $^{234}_{92}Pu$        (D) $^{242}_{96}Pu$

    (B) $^{234}_{92}U$         (E) $^{242}_{96}Cm$

    (C) $^{234}_{92}Cm$

51. What is the approximate melting point of 0.2 liters of water containing 6.20 g of ethylene glycol ($C_2H_6O_2$)?

    (A) −1.86 °C             (D) 0.93 °C

    (B) −0.93 °C            (E) 1.86 °C

    (C) 0 °C

52. What is the empirical formula of a compound composed of 25.9% nitrogen and 74.1% oxygen?

    (A) NO                    (D) $N_2O_4$

    (B) $NO_2$                 (E) $N_2O_5$

    (C) $N_2O$

53. The molecular weight of a gas is 16. At STP, 4.48 liters of this gas weighs

    (A) 2.3 g                (D) 4.1 g

    (B) 2.7 g                (E) 4.9 g

    (C) 3.2 g

54. How many milliliters of 5 *M* NaOH are required to completely neutralize 2 liters of 3 *M* HCl?

    (A) 600 mL          (D) 1,500 mL

    (B) 900 mL          (E) 1,800 mL

    (C) 1,200 mL

55. How many moles of sulfate ion are in 200 mL of a 2 *M* sodium sulfate solution?

    (A) 0.2 mole         (D) 0.8 mole

    (B) 0.4 mole         (E) 1.0 mole

    (C) 0.6 mole

56. How many moles of electrons are required to reduce 103.6 g of lead from $Pb^{2+}$ to the metal?

    (A) 0.5 mole

    (B) 1 mole

    (C) 2 moles

    (D) 4 moles

    (E) 8 moles

57. How many grams of copper will be deposited from a solution of $CuSO_4$ by a current of 3 amperes in 2 hours?

    (A) 5 g

    (B) 7 g

    (C) 8 g

    (D) 11 g

    (E) 15 g

58. The standard electrode in electrochemistry is composed of

    (A) gold

    (B) platinum

    (C) copper

    (D) magnesium

    (E) hydrogen

59. $Zn \rightarrow Zn^{2+} + 2e^-$ ; $E^o_{ox} = +0.76$ V

    $Cr^{3+} + 3e^- \rightarrow Cr$ ; $E^o_{red} = -0.74$ V

    The anode in this cell is

    (A) Zn

    (B) Cr

    (C) $Zn^{2+}$

    (D) $Cr^{3+}$

    (E) $3e^-$

60. An $sp^2$ configuration is represented by which orientation?

    (A) tetrahedral

    (B) planar

    (C) linear

    (D) trigonal planar

    (E) square

61. A $sp^3d^2$ configuration is represented by which orientation?

    (A) tetrahedral          (D) trigonal bipyramidal

    (B) trigonal planar      (E) square planar

    (C) linear

62. The balanced molar relationship of the dissociation of water into hydrogen and oxygen is

    (A) 1:1:1               (D) 2:1:2

    (B) 2:1:1               (E) 2:2:1

    (C) 1:2:1

63. What volume of water is required to produce 5 liters of oxygen by the process below?

    $$H_2O(g) \rightarrow H_2(g) + O_2(g)$$

    (A) 3 liters            (D) 14 liters

    (B) 5 liters            (E) 16 liters

    (C) 10 liters

64. What is the molecular weight of $HClO_4$?

    (A) 52.5 g/mol          (D) 100.5 g/mol

    (B) 73.5 g/mol          (E) 116.5 g/mol

    (C) 96.5 g/mol

65. The structure of the third member of the alkyne series is

    (A) $H - C \equiv C - H$

    (B) $H - C \equiv C - CH_3$

    (C) $H - C \equiv C - CH_2 - CH_3$

    (D) $H - C \equiv C - C \equiv C - H$

    (E) $H - C \equiv C - CH = CH_2$

66. The systematic (IUPAC) name of this structure is

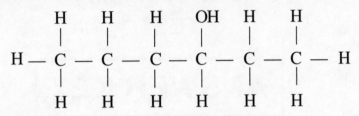

(A) hexanol

(D) 1-hexanol

(B) 3-hydroxyhexane

(E) isohexanol

(C) 3-hexanol

67. Which of the elements in Group IA of the periodic table has the greatest metallic character?

(A) Li

(D) Rb

(B) Na

(E) Fr

(C) K

68. The oxidation state of nitrogen in nitric acid ($HNO_3$) is

(A) +1

(D) +4

(B) +2

(E) +5

(C) +3

69. What volume does a sample of $1.50 \times 10^{23}$ atoms of helium at STP represent?

(A) 5.6 liters

(D) 22.4 liters

(B) 11.2 liters

(E) 1.5 liters

(C) 17.8 liters

# SAT Chemistry
# TEST 1

## ANSWER KEY

### PART A

| | | | | | | | |
|---|---|---|---|---|---|---|---|
| 1. | (C) | 7. | (E) | 13. | (E) | 19. | (E) |
| 2. | (D) | 8. | (C) | 14. | (B) | 20. | (E) |
| 3. | (B) | 9. | (C) | 15. | (C) | 21. | (D) |
| 4. | (B) | 10. | (B) | 16. | (A) | 22. | (B) |
| 5. | (D) | 11. | (D) | 17. | (D) | 23. | (E) |
| 6. | (A) | 12. | (D) | 18. | (A) | | |

### PART B

| | | | | | | | |
|---|---|---|---|---|---|---|---|
| 101. | T, F | 105. | F, T | 109. | F, T | 113. | F, F |
| 102. | F, F | 106. | F, F | 110. | F, T | 114. | T, T, CE |
| 103. | T, T, CE | 107. | T, T | 111. | T, F | 115. | T, T, CE |
| 104. | F, T | 108. | F, F | 112. | T, T, CE | 116. | F, F |

### PART C

| | | | | | | | |
|---|---|---|---|---|---|---|---|
| 24. | (C) | 36. | (E) | 48. | (A) | 60. | (D) |
| 25. | (D) | 37. | (B) | 49. | (B) | 61. | (E) |
| 26. | (A) | 38. | (D) | 50. | (B) | 62. | (E) |
| 27. | (E) | 39. | (E) | 51. | (B) | 63. | (C) |
| 28. | (D) | 40. | (C) | 52. | (E) | 64. | (D) |
| 29. | (D) | 41. | (D) | 53. | (C) | 65. | (C) |
| 30. | (E) | 42. | (B) | 54. | (C) | 66. | (C) |
| 31. | (E) | 43. | (C) | 55. | (B) | 67. | (E) |
| 32. | (A) | 44. | (E) | 56. | (B) | 68. | (E) |
| 33. | (A) | 45. | (D) | 57. | (B) | 69. | (A) |
| 34. | (A) | 46. | (C) | 58. | (E) | | |
| 35. | (A) | 47. | (B) | 59. | (A) | | |

# DETAILED EXPLANATIONS
# OF ANSWERS
## TEST 1

## PART A

1.  **(C)**
    The metalloids have characteristics of both the metals and the nonmetals. Metals are conductors while nonmetals are insulators.

2.  **(D)**
    The halogens (Group VII A) $Cl_2$, $Br_2$, and $I_2$ are examples of diatomic molecules. None of the other choices occur as diatomic molecules.

3.  **(A)**
    An oxide of formula $X_2O$ indicates that X has an oxidation state of $+1$ since oxygen has an oxidation state of $-2$. The alkali metals (Group IA) have an oxidation state of $+1$. The alkali earth metals (Group IIA) usually have an oxidation state of $+2$, thus giving an oxide with the formula XO. The metalloids have varying oxidation states as do the rare earths. The halogens usually have an oxidation state of $-1$.

4.  **(B)**
    The sulfate group has an oxidation number of $-2$. Thus, an oxidation number of $+2$ is required to produce an acid salt with the formula $XSO_4$. The alkaline earth metals usually have an oxidation number of $+2$.

5.  **(D)**
    The halogens have the largest electronegativity values since they require only one electron to completely fill their valence shell. The alkali metals have the smallest electronegativity values since they can lose one electron and have a complete valence shell. The alkali earth metals also have small electronegativities since they can lose two electrons to attain a noble gas configuration. The metalloids have intermediate electronegativity values.

6.  **(A)**

    The smallest ionization energies are realized when the removal of one electron yields a noble gas configuration. Thus, the alkali metals have the lowest ionization energies, then the alkali earth metals, metalloids, and halogens in order of increasing ionization energy.

7.  **(E)**

    A buffer is a solution made by the combination of a weak acid and a salt of its conjugate base. For example, acetic acid combined with sodium acetate would comprise a buffer. A buffer is intended to be insensitive to modest changes in pH.

8.  **(C)**

    Both strong acids and bases dissociate nearly completely in aqueous solution. For example, HCl is termed a strong acid because in aqueous solution it dissociates into $H^+$ and $Cl^-$ and the concentration of HCl itself is negligible.

9.  **(C)**

    As a strong acid dissociates essentially completely, its acid dissociation constant, $K_a$ will be extremely high. For HCl:

    $$K_a = \frac{[H^+][Cl^-]}{[HCl]}$$

Since $[H^+]$ and $[Cl^-]$ are very large compared with (HCl), $K_a$ will be very large as well.

10. **(B)**

    The Brønsted-Lowry notion of an acid-base reaction requires a proton to be transferred. In this concept an acid must donate a proton and a base must accept one.

11. **(D)**

    $NH_3$ is a weak base because in the reaction

    $$NH_3\,(aq) + H_2O \longleftrightarrow NH_4^+\,(aq) + OH^-\,(aq)$$

does not proceed very far to the right and the concentration of $OH^-$ is much, much less than that of $NH_3$.

12. **(D)**

Cl$^-$ is also considered to be a weak base. This is so because it is the conjugate base of a strong acid.

13. **(E)**

NaHCO$_3$ is a salt. It is a salt of the weak acid H$_2$CO$_3$.

14. **(B)**

NaOH is a strong base because it dissociates completely to give OH$^-$ ions.

15. **(C)**

The oxidation number of Na in NaCl is +1. In all monatomic ions, the oxidation number is that of the charge on that ion.

16. **(A)**

The oxidation number of Cl in Cl$_2$ is zero (0). In any elementary substance, the charge of an element is zero (0). The charge of O in O$_2$, H in H$_2$, are also 0, for example.

17. **(D)**

The oxidation number of S in Na$_2$S is −2. Because the charge on Na is +1 and there are two of them, in order to create a neutral compound, the oxidation number of S must be −2.

18. **(A)**

Solid sulfur is yellow. In addition, it smells like rotten eggs.

19. **(E)**

Aqueous hydrochloric acid is colorless.

20. **(E)**

Aqueous sodium hydroxide is colorless as well.

21. **(D)**

In the reaction given, since there is an excess of oxygen, it is the amount only of ammonia put in that will determine how much product there will be. For every 4 moles of ammonia put into the reaction, 6 moles of water will be obtained. The first step is to determine how many moles are in 16.00 grams of ammonia. Dividing 16.00 by the molecular weight of ammonia:

$$\frac{16.00 \text{ g}}{17.03 \text{ g/mole}} = 0.9395 \text{ moles NH}_3$$

Using cross multiplication, if for every 4 moles of NH$_3$ you get 6 moles of water:

$$\frac{4 \text{ moles ammonia}}{6 \text{ moles water}} = \frac{0.9395 \text{ moles ammonia}}{x \text{ moles water}}$$

$x = 1.409$ moles of water. To convert this to grams, we multiply by the molecular weight of water:

$$1.409 \text{ moles H}_2\text{O} \times 18.02 \text{ g/mol} = 25.39 \text{ g H}_2\text{O}.$$

This corresponds to choice (D).

22. **(B)**

Here you must determine which is the limiting reagent. First you must convert the masses of both the ammonia and the oxygen to their respective number of moles by dividing by the molecular weights.

$$\frac{66.00 \text{ g NH}_3}{17.04 \text{ g/mole}} = 3.873 \text{ moles NH}_3$$

$$\frac{54.00 \text{ g O}_2}{32.00 \text{ g/mole}} = 1.688 \text{ moles O}_2$$

Oxygen is therefore the limiting reagent.

For every 5 moles of oxygen put in, you get 6 moles of water out. Using cross multiplication:

$$\frac{5 \text{ moles oxygen}}{6 \text{ moles water}} = \frac{1.688 \text{ moles oxygen}}{x \text{ moles water}}$$

$x = 2.025$ moles water. Convert to grams by multiplying by the molecular weight of water:

$$2.025 \text{ moles} \times 18.02 = 36.49 \text{ grams O}_2$$

This corresponds to choice (B).

23. **(E)**

For every 4 moles of NH$_3$ that are put into the reaction, 4 moles of NO are produced. Therefore, if 2.513 moles of NH$_3$ are reacted, 2.513 moles will be produced. This is choice (E).

# PART B

### 101. T, F

Acid rain is generally considered to be destructive to limestone ($CaCO_3$) because acid rain contains sulfuric acid ($H_2SO_4$) or nitric acid ($HNO_3$). The reaction that occurs is

$$CaCO_3\,(s) + H_2SO_4\,(aq) \rightarrow CaSO_4\,(s) + CO_2\,(g) + H_2O$$

### 102. F, F

The correct net ionic equation is

$$Ca^{2+}\,(aq) + SO_4{}^{2-}\,(aq) \rightarrow CaSO_4\,(s).$$

NaCl is soluble in water and does not appear in the final net ionic equation.

### 103. T, T, CE

$K_{sp}$ equals the product of the equilibrium concentrations of the ions in a compound where each concentration is raised to the power of the ion coefficient.

### 104. F, T

In a *neutral* solution, $[H^+] = 1 \times 10^{-7}$. This is equivalent to saying that a solution has a pH of 7. This is not true in an acidic or basic solution. $K_w$ is, however, always equal to $1 \times 10^{-14}$.

### 105. F, T

Strong acids *do* ionize completely in an aqueous solution, but HF does not ionize completely and is therefore considered a weak acid.

### 106. F, F

$NH_4{}^+$ is a weak acid because it doesn't dissociate completely in water. $NH_4{}^+$ is the conjugate acid of $NH_3$, a weak base.

### 107. T, T

Both statements are true, but the latter is not a correct explanation of the former. By the Lewis definition, $F^-$ is a base because it can donate an electron pair.

### 108. F, F

Because normality depends on the number of transferable protons in a species and molarity doesn't, a $1N$ solution of $H_2SO_4$ is half as concentrated in terms of $H_2SO_4$ as a $1M$ solution of $H_2SO_4$.

109. **F, T**

These solutions together would not make a good buffer. A buffer is made by a weak acid and the salt of its conjugate base or *vice versa*. It is true that OH⁻ is a common ion, but this is irrelevant to use as a buffer here.

110. **F, T**

Like any other elementary substance, the Cl in $Cl_2$ has an oxidation number of 0.

111. **T, F**

Water has a high boiling point for its molecular weight due to hydrogen bonding. Polar covalent bonding also occurs in methane ($CH_4$) which has a boiling point of –162 °C.

112. **T, T, CE**

Benzene is a poor electrolyte because it does not ionize in water solution.

113. **F, F**

The reaction of zinc with hydrochloric acid goes to completion because the hydrogen gas which is evolved is allowed to escape. This is in effect removing one of the reaction products causing the equilibrium to shift towards completion of the reaction.

114. **T, T, CE**

Atoms of the same element form covalent bonds because their electronegativity values are the same. Bonds formed between elements whose electronegativities differ from 0.5 to 1.7 form polar covalent bonds. Differences greater than 1.7 in element electronegativities result in ionic bonds.

115. **T, T, CE**

Most metals characteristics such as malleability, flexibility, strength, and electrical conductivity are characteristic of the positive atomic nuclei surrounded by mobile electrons.

116. **F, F**

Acetic acid is a weak acid because it is only partially dissociated in a water solution.

# PART C

24. **(C)**
    Referring to the periodic table we see that element 32 is germanium. Germanium is a metalloid as are boron, silicon, arsenic, antimony, tellurium, polonium, and astatine. Chemically, metalloids exhibit both positive and negative oxidation states and combine with metals and nonmetals. They are characterized by electronegativity values between those of the metals and the nonmetals.

25. **(D)**
    The prime consideration in representing the bonding of a polyatomic element or compound is that each atom bonded should have a complete valence shell (eight electrons except hydrogen and helium which have two). Since nitrogen is in Group VA, it has five valence electrons illustrated as

    : N

Diatomic nitrogen must have the structure

    : N : : : N : (or : N ≡ N :)

to completely fill the valence shells of both atoms.

26. **(A)**
    Dissolving sodium chloride in water is an example of a physical change. A physical change alters the physical properties of a substance while maintaining its composition. If the water solution of NaCl were to be evaporated we would once again have solid sodium chloride. Chemical changes involve altering the composition and structure of a substance and are always associated with changes in energy. Wood and oxygen are changed to $CO_2$, $H_2O$ and nitrogen oxides while ozone is changed to diatomic oxygen and sodium and water are changed to sodium hydroxide and hydrogen gas.

27. **(E)**
    A beta particle is a fast electron of mass $9.11 \times 10^{-28}$ g while a proton and a neutron both have a mass of $1.67 \times 10^{-24}$ g. A hydrogen nucleus is a proton, and an alpha particle is a helium nucleus (two protons and two neutrons). Thus, the electron (beta particle) has the smallest mass of the choices given.

28. **(D)**
    One mole of NaCl weighs 58.5 g as obtained by: the atomic weight of Na plus the atomic weight of Cl from the periodic table. Thus, 58.5 g of NaCl in one liter of solution is 1 molar and 58.5 g of NaCl in one kilogram of solvent is 1 molal. By simple proportions, 58.5 g of NaCl in 2 kilograms of solvent is 0.5 molal.

29. **(D)**
    Molecules in the gaseous state have the greatest kinetic energy. The difference in energy between the liquid and gas phases is greater than the difference in energy between the solid and liquid phases. This may be readily seen by the energy changes occurring in water; the heat of fusion of water is 80 calories/gram, while the heat of vaporization is 540 calories/gram.

30. **(E)**
    $Cr(NH_3)_5SO_4Br$ represents 27 atoms. They are: $1 \times Cr$; $5 \times N$; $15 \times H$; $1 \times S$; $4 \times O$; and $1 \times Br$.

31. **(E)**
    The element of atomic weight 197 is gold (Au-atomic number 79). Since the atomic weight is equal to the number of protons and neutrons in the nucleus and the atomic number is equal to the number of protons in the nucleus, the number of neutrons in the nucleus is $197 - 79$ or 118.

32. **(A)**
    Diamond, composed solely of carbon cannot have ionic bonds or hydrogen bonds. Van der Waals attraction between the nucleus of one atom and the electrons of an adjacent atom are relatively weak compared to the covalent bonding network ($sp^3$ hybrid) between the carbon atoms in diamond. On the other hand, graphite (another allotropic form of carbon) is $sp^2$ hybrid and not strongly bonded as compared to diamond.

33. **(A)**
    Atomic radius decreases as one goes from left to right across a period, so the atomic radius of carbon is greater than that of oxygen. This eliminates choices (B) and (D). Now we must determine whether the $CO_2$ molecule is linear or bent. Linearity means the O–C–O bond angle is 180°. Recall that the nuclei of a molecule orient themselves so as to experience the smallest repulsions of the positive nuclei. Thus a triatomic molecule is expected to be linear as is $CO_2$. However, this is not always true. The lone electron pairs on oxygen in a water molecule bend the molecule so that the

hydrogen nuclei and the two electron pairs occupy the corners of a tetrahedron. Thus, the water molecule is bent. The same effect occurs in ammonia, $NH_3$, where a lone pair of electrons on nitrogen distorts the expected trigonal planar geometry. Shape of a $CO_2$ molecule is

$$: \overset{..}{O} = C = \overset{..}{O} :$$

$$180°$$

**34. (A)**

All three phases (solid, liquid and gas) may coexist at a single pressure/temperature combination known as the triple point. This point occurs at the intersection of the solid-liquid, solid-gas and liquid-gas equilibrium curves as illustrated by point C.

**35. (A)**

Examining a labeled phase diagram we see that the solid phase can only exist at point A.

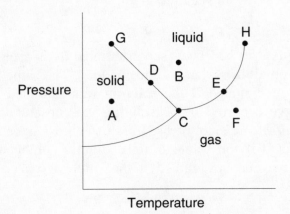

**36. (E)**

The critical point is the point above which a gas cannot change into a liquid. This means that a liquid cannot exist above this point, but at and below this point a liquid can exist. The temperature at the critical point is called the critical temperature and the pressure is called the critical pressure. The critical point in the phase diagram shown is the point H, since above it a gas cannot be liquefied.

37. **(B)**

Referring to the phase diagram previously given we see that the solid and liquid phases coexist on the line upon which point D is located.

38. **(D)**

An electrolyte is a substance which, when melted or dissolved in a suitable medium, conducts electricity. Therefore (D), a solution of sodium chloride dissolved in water, is electrolytic since the sodium and chloride ions are free to move. Neither (A) mercury in water, (B) a benzene solution of ethanol, nor (C) sucrose in water, are electrolytic.

39. **(E)**

The oxidation state of sulfur in sodium bisulfate may be determined by recalling that the oxidation states of sodium, hydrogen, and oxygen are usually +1, +1, and –2, respectively. Since the sum of the oxidation states for the atoms of a neutral compound are zero we have:

oxidation state of S + 1 + 1 + 4(–2) = 0; therefore

oxidation state of S = +6

So, the oxidation state of sulfur in $NaHSO_4$ is +6.

40. **(C)**

The solution in question had been supersaturated as is seen by the precipitation of more solute than what had been added. The same amount of solute would have precipitated if the solution was saturated and no precipitation would have occurred if the solution was unsaturated. The terms *dilute* and *concentrated* cannot be used in this context since a dilute solution may be saturated if the solute is only slightly soluble while a concentrated solution may be unsaturated if the solute is exceptionally soluble.

41. **(D)**

This is an example of a neutralization reaction where an acid and a base react to produce water and a salt. It must be known that barium has an oxidation number of +2 and that perchloric acid is $HClO_4$.

$$2HClO_4 + Ba(OH)_2 \rightarrow 2H_2O + Ba(ClO_4)_2$$

42. **(B)**

An endothermic reaction is one in which heat may be considered one of the "reactants." An exothermic reaction releases heat upon formation of the products. An equilibrium reaction may be either exothermic or endothermic. The same holds true for spontaneity; spontaneity can only be determined if one also knows the entropy change ($\Delta S$) for the reaction.

43. **(C)**

The transition metals have highest energy electrons in $d$ subshells ($3d$, $4d$, and $5d$). Lanthanides and actinides are characterized by highest energy electrons in the $4f$ and $5f$ subshells, respectively.

44. **(E)**

Neutral fluorine atoms have 9 electrons as determined by their atomic number. Magnesium atoms have 12 electrons so $Mg^{3+}$ has 9 electrons. Boron has 5 electrons so $B^{3-}$ has 8 electrons (the same as oxygen). Nitrogen has 7 electrons so $N^+$ has 6 electrons (the same as carbon). Neon has 10 electrons so $Ne^-$ has 11 electrons (the same as sodium). Sodium has 11 electrons so $Na^-$ has 12 electrons (the same as magnesium).

45. **(D)**

Le Chatelier's Principle may be used to predict equilibrium reactions. If a stress is placed on a system in equilibrium, the equilibrium shifts so as to counteract that stress. Hence, increasing the reactant concentration favors formation of the products while decreasing the reactant concentration favors formation of the reactants. The same holds true for altering the product concentrations. Increasing the temperature favors the reaction that absorbs heat while decreasing the temperature favors the reaction that releases heat. Increasing the pressure favors the reaction that decreases the volume of a closed system while decreasing the pressure favors the reaction resulting in an increased volume (moles of gaseous product produced are the only things counted since liquids and solids occupy a relatively small volume in comparison). However, temperature and pressure dependencies cannot be inferred from this question. The addition of a catalyst alters the reaction rate but not the position of equilibrium. The only way completion can be obtained is that we remove the products as they are formed. Now the state of the reaction becomes nonequilibrium, but it tries to come into an equilibrium state once again. This leads to formation of more products which in turn leads to completion of the given reaction.

46. **(C)**

An acid $H_3X$ is classified as triprotic since it may "give up" three protons to a base. An example of a triprotic acid is phosphoric acid, $H_3PO_4$. Examples of monoprotic and diprotic acids are hydrochloric, HCl and sulfuric, $H_2SO_4$, respectively. The term bidentate, rather than referring to acids, is associated with ligands. Bidentate ligands have two atoms that may coordinate to a metal ion.

47. **(B)**

The salts of strong bases and weak acids hydrolyze to form a basic solution while the salts of weak bases and strong acids hydrolyze to form an acidic solution.

$$Ba(NO_3)_2 + 2H_2O \rightarrow 2HNO_3 + Ba(OH)_2$$

A neutral solution is produced since both nitric acid and barium hydroxide are completely dissociated, and each is present in the same concentration (barium hydroxide has 2 hydroxy groups)

$$Na_2S + 2H_2O \rightarrow H_2S + 2NaOH$$

A basic solution is produced since hydrosulfuric acid is a weak acid and sodium hydroxide is a strong base.

$$Al_2(SO_4)_3 + 6H_2O \rightarrow 3H_2SO_4 + 2Al(OH)_3$$

An acidic solution is produced since aluminum hydroxide is insoluble and sulfuric acid is a strong acid.

$$Pb_3(PO_4)_2 + 6H_2O \rightarrow 2H_3PO_4 + 3Pb(OH)_2$$

An acidic solution is produced since phosphoric acid is a weak acid and lead (II) hydroxide is insoluble.

$$NaCl + H_2O \rightarrow HCl + NaOH$$

A neutral solution is produced since hydrochloric acid is a strong acid and sodium hydroxide is a strong base.

48. **(A)**

The reaction of the Haber process is:

$$N_2\,(g) + 3H_2\,(g) \longleftrightarrow 2NH_3\,(g) + \text{heat}$$

We see that there are 4 moles of gas on the left side of the reaction and 2 moles of gas on the right. According to Le Chatelier's Principle, increasing the pressure would force the reaction to the right to produce more ammonia. (Note: Change in pressure affects only those equilibrium in which a gas or gases are reactants or products.)

110

49. **(B)**

The ionization energy is defined as the energy required to remove the most loosely bound electron from an element in the gaseous state. The energy released by an element in forming an ionic solid with another element is the lattice energy of that ionic compound. The electronegativity of an element gives the relative strength with which the atoms of that element attract valence electrons.

50. **(B)**

Plutonium-238 has a mass of 238 and an atomic number of 94. The atomic mass tells us the number of protons and neutrons in the nucleus while the atomic number tells us the number of protons. An alpha particle ($\alpha$) is a helium nucleus $^4_2\text{He}$ composed of 2 neutrons and 2 protons (atomic mass of 4). Hence, upon emitting an alpha particle, the atomic number decreases by 2 and the atomic mass decreases by 4. This gives us $^{234}_{92}\text{X}$. Examining the periodic table we find that element 92 is uranium. Thus, our new atom is $^{234}_{92}\text{U}$. $^{234}_{92}\text{Pu}$ and $^{234}_{92}\text{Cm}$ are impossible since the atomic number of plutonium is 94 and that of curium is 96. $^{242}_{96}\text{Pu}$ and $^{242}_{96}\text{Cm}$ are impossible since these nuclei could only be produced by fusion of $^{238}_{94}\text{Pu}$ with an alpha particle. In addition, $^{242}_{96}\text{Pu}$ is incorrectly named.

The reaction (decay) is $^{238}_{94}\text{Pu} \rightarrow {}^{234}_{92}\text{U} \rightarrow {}^4_2\text{He}$

51. **(B)**

First we determine the number of moles present in solution taking the molecular weight of ethylene glycol to be 62 g. Thus,

$$6.20 \text{ g} \times = 0.1 \text{ mole of ethylene glycol}$$

We must also know the molality—the ratio of moles of solute to kilograms of solvent. The number of kilograms of solvent is

$$0.2 \text{ L} \times \frac{1 \text{ kg}}{1 \text{ L}} = 0.2 \text{ kg}$$

since the density of water is 1 g/mL. The molality of the solution is

$$\frac{0.1 \text{ mole}}{0.2 \text{ kg}} = 0.5 \text{ molal.}$$

For $H_2O$, the molal freezing point depression constant is 1.86 °C/molal. Thus, the freezing point depression is

$$0.5 \text{ molal} \times \frac{1.86\ ^\circ C}{\text{molal}} = 0.93\ ^\circ C$$

Thus, the melting point would be

$$0\ ^\circ C - 0.93\ ^\circ C = -0.93\ ^\circ C$$

52. **(E)**
A 100 g sample of this gas contains 25.9 g of nitrogen and 74.1 g of oxygen. Dividing each of these weights by their respective atomic weights gives us the molar ratio of N to O for the gas. This gives

$$N_{\frac{25.9}{14}} O_{\frac{74.1}{16}} = N_{1.85} O_{4.63}$$

Dividing both subscripts by the smallest subscript gives

$$N_{\frac{1.85}{1.85}} O_{\frac{4.63}{1.85}} = N_1 O_{2.5}$$

Doubling both subscripts so as to have whole numbers gives us $N_2 O_5$.

53. **(C)**
A molecular weight of 16 g tells us that a volume of 22.4 liters (molar volume) of that gas weighs 16 g. To determine the weight of a 4.48 L sample we multiply

$$4.48 \text{ L} \times \frac{16 \text{ g}}{22.4 \text{ L}} = 3.2 \text{ g}$$

54. **(C)**
The relationship $M_1 V_1 = M_2 V_2$ in neutralization problems involving a strong acid and strong base. We have

$$(3\ M \text{ HCl})(2{,}000 \text{ mL}) = (5\ M \text{ NaOH})(V_2 \text{ mL})$$

$$V_2 = \frac{(3M)(2{,}000 \text{ mL})}{(5M)} = 1{,}200 \text{ mL}$$

55. **(B)**
A 1 $M$ sodium sulfate ($Na_2SO_4$) solution contains one mole of sulfate ion per liter of solution. Thus 0.2 L of a 1 $M$ solution contains 0.2 mole of sulfate ion. 0.2 L of a 2 $M$ solution would then contain 0.4 mole of sulfate ion.

56. **(B)**

The atomic weight of lead is 207.2 g/mole from the periodic table. The number of moles present in 103.6 g of lead is given by

$$103.6 \text{ g} \times \frac{1 \text{ mole}}{207.2 \text{ g}} = 0.5 \text{ mole}$$

Since lead is in the +2 oxidation state, two moles of electrons are required for every mole of lead to reduce it to the metals. However only one mole of electrons is required to reduce 0.5 mole of $Pb^{2+}$ to $Pb°$.

57. **(B)**

Copper is being reduced from $Cu^{2+}$ to the metal according to

$$Cu^{2+} + 2e^- \rightarrow Cu$$

The amount of electricity that allows one mole of electrons to undergo reaction is the faraday ($F$) which is equal to 96,500 coulombs. Thus, two faradays of charge are required to reduce one mole of $Cu^{2+}$ to the metal. Now we must calculate the number of coulombs provided by the applied current

$$3.0 \text{ amps} \times 2 \text{ hours} \times \frac{3,600 \text{ sec}}{1 \text{ hour}} \times \frac{1 \text{ coulomb}}{1 \text{ amp sec}} = 21,600 \text{ coulombs}$$

Calculating the number of faradays donated to the copper we obtain

$$21,600 \text{ coulombs} \times \frac{1\ F}{96,500 \text{ coulombs}} = 0.22\ F$$

Now we may compute the amount of copper deposited by this amount of charge since we know that 2F of charge reduces one mole of $Cu^{2+}$ to $Cu°$. Thus, we have

$$0.22\ F \times \frac{1 \text{ mole Cu}}{2\ F} \times \frac{63.5 \text{ g Cu}}{1 \text{ mole Cu}} = 7.1 \text{ g}$$

7.0 g of copper deposited.

58. **(E)**

The hydrogen electrode has been chosen as the standard electrode with an assigned value of $E° = 0.00\ V$.

59. **(A)**
     The anode of any electrochemical cell is defined to be the site of oxidation. Thus, since Zn is being oxidized to $Zn^{2+}$ in this cell it is determined to be the anode. The cathode, the site of reduction, is Cr in this cell. The solutions of the metal ions are not the anode or the cathode but rather the electrolytic medium.

60. **(D)**
     An $sp^2$ configuration is represented by the trigonal planar orientation, which looks like

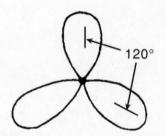

61. **(E)**
     An $sp^3d^2$ configuration is represented by the square planar orientation, which looks like the following. Note: two hybridizal pairs of electrons are unbounded.

62. **(E)**
     Examining the balanced reaction equation of $2H_2O \rightarrow 2H_2 + O_2$ yields the ratio 2:2:1.

63. **(C)**
     Balancing the reaction equation gives

$$2H_2O \rightarrow 2H_2 + O_2$$

As may be seen from the equation, two units of water react to produce one unit of oxygen. Thus 10 L of water are required to produce 5 L of oxygen.

64. **(D)**

The molecular weight of a compound is the sum of its constituents' atomic weights. Elements or groups followed by a subscript have their atomic weight multiplied by that subscript. Thus, the molecular weight of perchloric acid ($HClO_4$) is

> atomic weight of H + atomic weight of Cl
> $+ 4 \times$ atomic weight of O

or $1 \text{ g/mol} + 35.5 \text{ g/mol} + 4(16 \text{ g/mol}) = 100.5 \text{ g/mol}$

65. **(C)**

The first member of the alkyne series is acetylene (or ethyne), whose structure is

$$HC \equiv CH$$

The second is propyne: $\quad HC \equiv C - CH_3$

The third is butyne: $\quad HC \equiv C - CH_2 - CH_3$

Note that there are no analogous compounds in the alkene or alkyne series for the first member of the alkane series (methane – $CH_4$).

66. **(C)**

Alcohols are named by replacing the *-e* of the corresponding hydrocarbon name by the suffix *-ol*. The position of the hydroxy substituent is numbered from the shorter end of the chain. Thus, the structure is named 3-hexanol. It is a hexanol because the parent hydrocarbon has six carbons and the prefix *3-* (not *1-*) is used to indicate the location of the hydroxy group on the third carbon.

67. **(E)**

The metals are found on the left side of the periodic table, with metallic character increasing as one goes down a group. All the choices given are in Group IA, so the one farthest down in the group has the greatest metallic character. This is francium (Fr).

68. **(E)**

The oxidation states of the element comprising a neutral compound must have a sum of zero. Thus, nitrogen in $HNO_3$ has an oxidation state of +5, since hydrogen and oxygen have oxidation states of +1 and –2, respectively.

*i.e.,* $\quad (1) + (n) + (-6) = 0$; therefore

$$n = 5$$

69. **(A)**

A mole is defined to be $6.02 \times 10^{23}$ atoms, molecules, ions, particles, etc. Thus, $1.5 \times 10^{23}$ atoms represents 0.25 mole. Recalling that the molar volume of any ideal gas at STP is 22.4 liters, we may calculate the volume of $1.5 \times 10^{23}$ atoms to be

$$(0.25 \text{ L})(22.4 \text{ L/mol}) = 5.6 \text{ L}$$

# PRACTICE
# TEST 2

This test is also on CD-ROM in our special interactive SAT Chemistry TEST*ware*®. It is highly recommended that you first take this exam on computer. You will then have the additional study features and benefits of timed conditions and instantaneous, accurate scoring. See page 5 for guidance on how to get the most out of our SAT Chemistry software.

# SAT Chemistry
# Practice Test 2

**(Answer sheets appear in the back of this book.)**

# PART A

**TIME:**    1 Hour
                   85 Questions

**DIRECTIONS**: Each set of questions below consists of five lettered choices followed by a list of numbered statements or questions. For each statement or question, select the answer choice that is most closely related to it. Each answer choice may be used once, more than once, or not at all.

*Note:* **For all questions involving solutions, assume that the solvent is water unless otherwise noted.**

**Questions 1–9**

Use the partial periodic chart below and the letters in parentheses to answer the following questions.

IA    IIA    IIIA    IVA    VA    VIA    VIIA    VIII

$_1^1 H$                                                                                   $_4^2 He$

(A)    (B)    (C)                                            (D)    (E)

1.  The element which forms a highly basic solution in water

2.  The element displaying both metallic and non-metallic qualities

3.  The element with a possible oxidation number of −1

4.  The element with the smallest electron affinity

5.  The element with the smallest atomic radius

6.   An inert gas

7.   A member of the alkaline earth metals

8.   The one that reacts in a 2-to-1 ratio with (B)

9.   The element with a complete 2s orbital and empty 2p orbital

**Questions 10–13** refer to the following periodic table trends.

(A)  Property which decreases as one moves from left to right along the periodic table and increases as one moves from top to bottom.

(B)  Property which increases as one moves from left to right along the periodic table and decreases as one moves from top to bottom.

(C)  Property which decreases as one moves from left to right along the periodic table and decreases as one moves from top to bottom.

(D)  Property which increases as one moves from left to right along the periodic table and increases as one moves from top to bottom.

(E)  Property which is not related to the position along the periodic table.

10.  Atomic radius

11.  Electronegativity

12.  Atomic mass

13.  Ionization energy

**Questions 14–17** refer to the following geometries.

(A)  Linear geometry

(B)  Bent geometry

(C)  Tetrahedral geometry

(D)  Pyramidal geometry

(E)  Equilateral triangle geometry

14. $NH_3$

15. $H_2O$

16. $BeF_2$

17. $CH_4$

**Questions 18–21** refer to the following choices.

    (A) temperature(s)

    (B) universal gas constant

    (C) volume(s)

    (D) pressure(s)

    (E) molecular weight(s)

18. At a constant number of moles and pressure, the volume of an ideal gas is directly proportional to its

19. The kinetic energy of a sample of an ideal gas is a property only of

20. The rate of effusion of two gasses is inversely proportional to the square root of their

21. At constant temperature the volume of a given amount of an ideal gas is inversely proportional to its

**Questions 22–24** refer to the following values.

    (A) 0          (D) –2

    (B) –1        (E) +2

    (C) +1

22. The oxidation number of Na in NaCl

23. The oxidation number of Cl in $Cl_2$

24. The oxidation number of S in $Na_2S$

# PART B

(I)                                                    (II)

101. The vaporization of          *because*     heat must be supplied
water is considered to                         to convert it from
be spontaneous                                 liquid to gas.
(at constant temperature
and pressure)

102. When two moles of            *because*     the system has
gas are converted to                           become more
one mole, entropy                              disordered.
decreases

103. If $\Delta H$ of a reaction    *because*     $\Delta G = \Delta H - T\Delta S$
(at a given pressure)
is positive and $\Delta S$ is
positive, then $\Delta G$ must
be positive

104. $K_c$ for the reaction:       *because*     the system is in
$2HBr(g) \rightleftharpoons Br_2(g) + H_2(g)$     equilibrium and the
is the same as that                            concentrations are the
for the reaction                               same on both sides of
$H_2(g) + Br_2(g) \rightleftharpoons 2HBr(g)$    the reaction.

105. In the system                            there is no net change
$N_2(g) + O_2(g)\ 2NO(g)$     *because*         in the number of moles
decreasing the pressure                        of gas from one side of
will not cause a shift                         the reaction to the other.
in the position of the
equilibrium

106. The time it takes for half of a 2 *M* sample of cyclobutane to decompose is the same for half of a 4 *N* sample to decompose (Assume first-order kinetics)   *because*   the time required for a given fraction of a reactant to decompose in a first order reaction is independent of concentration.

107. A catalyst increases the rate of a reaction   *because*   it raises the energy of the products so it is closer to that of the reactants.

108. Increasing the temperature increases the reaction rate   *because*   at high temperatures, molecules (or atoms) tend to be further apart.

109. $SO_3$ is called an acid anhydride   *because*   it forms sulfuric acid when added to water.

110. When HCl and NaOH are mixed in equal amounts, in theory one could drink from the resulting solution   *because*   the salt neutralizes both the acid and the base.

111. The reaction of lead (II) nitrate with sodium sulfate does not go to completion   *because*   lead sulfate precipitates out of solution.

112. A compound formed endothermically is stable   *because*   heat is released during the formation.

113. The atomic radius of a metal atom is larger than that of its ion   *because*   the valence electrons of a metal are tightly held.

114. 10 g of water are heated from 80 °C to 95 °C by the addition of 1,500 calories   *because*   the specific heat of water is 1 k cal/kg C°.

115. Decreasing the volume of a    *because*    pressure and volume are
     closed system decreases                 inversely related.
     the pressure

116. The activation energy of a    *because*    it is not used up by the
     reaction is decreased by a                reaction process.
     catalyst

# PART C

> **DIRECTIONS:** For each question in this section, select the best answer from among the given choices and fill in the corresponding oval on the answer sheet.

25. Which of the following compounds has an approximate formula weight of 120?

    (A) $Ca(OH)_2$

    (B) $KNO_3$

    (C) $MgSO_4$

    (D) $AlCl_3$

    (E) $BeCl_2$

26. Which of the following occurs naturally as a diatomic element?

    (A) $I_2$

    (B) $O_3$

    (C) $NO$

    (D) $S$

    (E) $He$

27. Which of the following serves as a catalyst in the reaction

    $$CH_2 = CH_2 + H_2 + Pt \rightarrow CH_3CH_3 + Pt$$

    (A) $C$

    (B) $CH_2 = CH_2$

    (C) $H_2$

    (D) $Pt$

    (E) $CH_3CH_3$

28. The expected electron configuration of propanal is:

    (A)
    $$
    \begin{array}{ccc}
    H & H & H \\
    & & \\
    H : \ddot{C} : \ddot{C} : \ddot{C} : \ddot{O} : \\
    \ddot{} & \ddot{} & \ddot{} \\
    H & H & \\
    \end{array}
    $$

    (B)
    $$
    \begin{array}{ccc}
    H & H & H \\
    & & \\
    H : \ddot{C} :: \ddot{C} : \ddot{C} : \ddot{O} : \\
    & \ddot{} & \ddot{} \\
    & & H \\
    \end{array}
    $$

(C)    H        H        (D)                          H

H : C̈ :: C :: C̈ :                    H : C : : : C : C̈ :: Ö :

(E)    H  H  H

H : C̈ : C̈ : C̈ :: O

    H  H

29. The contribution of the electron to the atomic weight is

(A) zero

(B) 1/1,837 that of a proton or a neutron

(C) equal to that of a proton

(D) equal to that of a neutron

(E) less than that of a proton

30. Which region of the periodic table represents the element with the largest atomic radius?

(A) upper left          (D) lower right

(B) upper right         (E) middle

(C) lower left

31. Which of the following formula units consists of 17 atoms?

(A) $Al_2(SO_4)_3$          (D) $Mg(IO_3)_2$

(B) $Al(NO_3)_3$           (E) $H_2O$

(C) $Ca(HCO_3)_2$

32. The attractive force between the protons of one molecule and the electrons of another molecule are strongest

(A) in the solid phase          (D) during sublimation

(B) in the liquid phase         (E) during fusion

(C) in the gas phase

33. Sodium chloride (NaCl) would be most soluble in

    (A) ether

    (B) benzene

    (C) water

    (D) carbon tetrachloride

    (E) gasoline

34. Hydrolysis of sodium acetate yields

    (A) a strong acid and a strong base

    (B) a weak acid and a weak base

    (C) a strong acid and a weak base

    (D) a weak acid and a strong base

    (E) water

35. The oxidation state of manganese in $KMnO_4$ is

    (A) +1

    (B) +2

    (C) +3

    (D) +4

    (E) +7

36. An increase in pressure will change the equilibrium constant by

    (A) shifting to the side where a smaller volume results

    (B) shifting to the side where a larger volume results

    (C) favoring the exothermic reaction

    (D) favoring the endothermic reaction

    (E) having no effect

37. The salt, sodium chlorite, is produced in the reaction of sodium hydroxide with

    (A) HCl

    (B) $HClO_2$

    (C) $HClO_3$

    (D) $HClO_4$

    (E) NaCl

38. A liquid containing some microscopic particles just like particles from tobacco smoke can be detected not by the naked eye, but by the fact that they reflect light. These particles could probably be described as

(A) a saturated solution
(B) an unsaturated solution
(C) a supersaturated solution
(D) colloid
(E) a suspension

39. A reaction involving oxidation and reduction in which electrons are transferred by means of an external power source is best described as

(A) exothermic
(B) endothermic
(C) photochemical in nature
(D) electrolytical
(E) galvanic

40. Two atoms, X and Y, have the same number of protons and electrons, but different numbers of neutrons. This illustrates

(A) the Law of Definite Composition
(B) the Law of Multiple Proportions
(C) the existence of isotopes
(D) the probability of combination
(E) conservation of energy

41. The most active metal of the alkali metals is

(A) Li
(B) Mg
(C) K
(D) Sr
(E) Cs

42. How many moles of electrons must be removed from 0.5 mole of $Fe^{2+}$ to produce $Fe^{3+}$?

(A) 0.5
(B) 1.0
(C) 1.5
(D) 2.0
(E) 2.5

43. A gas has a volume of 10 liters at 50 °C and 200 mm Hg pressure. What correction factor is needed to give a volume at STP?

(A) $\dfrac{0}{50} \times \dfrac{200}{760}$

(D) $\dfrac{273}{323} \times \dfrac{760}{200}$

(B) $\dfrac{0}{50} \times \dfrac{760}{200}$

(E) $\dfrac{323}{273} \times \dfrac{760}{200}$

(C) $\dfrac{273}{323} \times \dfrac{200}{760}$

44. What is the pH of a 0.01 $M$ NaOH solution?

(A) 2

(D) 10

(B) 4

(E) 12

(C) 7

45. Twenty liters of NO gas react with excess oxygen. How many liters of $NO_2$ gas are produced if the NO gas reacts completely?

(A) 5 liters

(D) 40 liters

(B) 10 liters

(E) 50 liters

(C) 20 liters

46. How much reactant remains if 92 g of $HNO_3$ is reacted with 24 g of LiOH assuming the reaction to be complete?

(A) 46 g of $HNO_3$

(D) 2 g of LiOH

(B) 29 g of $HNO_3$

(E) 12 g of LiOH

(C) 12 g of $HNO_3$

47. What is the molar concentration of $I^-$ in 1 liter of a saturated water solution of $PbI_2$ if the $K_{sp}$ of lead iodide is $1.4 \times 10^{-8}$?

(A) $3.0 \times 10^{-3}$

(D) $2.4 \times 10^{-3}$

(B) $1.2 \times 10^{-4}$

(E) $1.4 \times 10^{-8}$

(C) $5.9 \times 10^{-5}$

48. What is the density of a diatomic gas whose gram-molecular weight is 80 g/mol?

    (A) 1.9 g/L            (D) 4.3 g/L

    (B) 2.8 g/L            (E) 5.0 g/L

    (C) 3.6 g/L

49. How many liters of $H_2$ can be produced by the decomposition of 3 moles of $NH_3$?

    (A) 4.5 liters         (D) 96 liters

    (B) 27 liters          (E) 101 liters

    (C) 67.2 liters

The following drawing can be used to answer questions 50–54.

$H_2O$ + dilute $H_2SO_4$

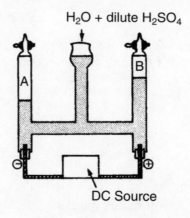

DC Source

50. What type of reaction is occurring with the following set-up?

    (A) single replacement     (D) acid-base neutralization

    (B) double replacement     (E) precipitation

    (C) electrolysis

51. What will be found at point A in the drawing above?

    (A) $O_2$              (D) $H_2SO_4$ vapor

    (B) $H_2$             (E) free electrons

    (C) $H_2O$ vapor

52. What will be found at point B?

    (A) $O_2$                    (D) $H_2SO_4$ vapor

    (B) $H_2$                    (E) free electrons

    (C) $H_2O$ vapor

53. Which of the following is the anode reaction?

    (A) $2H_2O \longrightarrow H_3O^+ + OH^-$

    (B) $H_2O \longrightarrow \frac{1}{2}O_2 + H_2$

    (C) $H_2O \longrightarrow H^+ + OH^-$

    (D) $H_2O \longrightarrow \frac{1}{2}O_2 + 2H^+ + 2e^-$

    (E) $2H_2 + 2e^- \longrightarrow H_2 + 2OH^-$

54. Which of the following is the cathode reaction?

    (A) $2H_2O \longrightarrow H_3O^+ + OH^-$

    (B) $H_2O \longrightarrow \frac{1}{2}O_2 + H_2$

    (C) $H_2O \longrightarrow H^+ + OH^-$

    (D) $H_2O \longrightarrow \frac{1}{2}O_2 + 2H^+ + 2e^-$

    (E) $2H_2O + 2e^- \longrightarrow H_2 + 2OH^-$

Use the following drawing to answer questions 55–57.

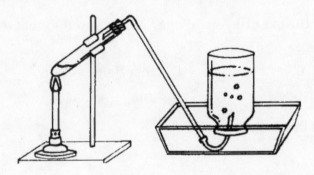

55. The setup shown above is used to prepare a gas

    (A) that is water soluble        (D) lighter than air

    (B) that is water insoluble       (E) for electrochemistry

    (C) heavier than air

56. What is the product gas if $KClO_3$ and $MnO_2$ are used as reactants?

   (A) $O_2$                      (D) $H_2$

   (B) $Cl_2$                     (E) no gas is produced

   (C) $N_2$

57. Which of the following could not be prepared by this method assuming that suitable reactants were available?

   (A) $O_2$                      (D) $NH_3$

   (B) $CO_2$                     (E) KCl

   (C) $N_2$

58. Which of the following is a conclusion as opposed to an observation?

   (A) A mixture of water and ethyl ether is immiscible; the ether separates into a layer above the water.

   (B) A glowing splint is placed in an oxygen environment; the splint catches fire.

   (C) A mixture of $Na_2Cr_2O_7$ and $Pb(NO_3)_2$ in solution results in precipitation of $Pb(Cr_2O_7)_2$; lead dichromate is insoluble.

   (D) A sample of water is heated; boiling occurs at 100 °C.

   (E) A piece of litmus paper is placed in a 0.1 $M$ HCl solution; the litmus paper changes color.

59. The rate of effusion of hydrogen gas as compared to that of oxygen gas is

   (A) one-half as fast            (D) four times as fast

   (B) identical                   (E) eight times as fast

   (C) twice as fast

Questions 60–62 refer to the chart below.

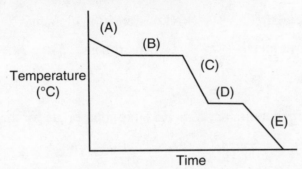

60. Where is the state of the substance a mixture of vapor and liquid?

61. Where is the heat required to change the state of the compound the least (assume constant heating)?

62. Where is the specific heat of the compound the greatest (assume constant heating)?

63. The name of the compound $HClO_2$ is

    (A) hydrochloric acid        (D) chloric acid

    (B) hypochlorous acid        (E) perchloric acid

    (C) chlorous acid

64. A 0.5 molal solution could be prepared by dissolving 20 g of NaOH in

    (A) 0.5 L of water          (D) 1 kg of water

    (B) 0.5 kg of water         (E) 2 L of water

    (C) 1 L of water

65. Which statement is true for a liquid/gas mixture in equilibrium?

    (A) The equilibrium constant is dependent on temperature.

    (B) The amount of the gas present at equilibrium is independent of pressure.

    (C) All interchange between the liquid and gas phases has ceased.

    (D) A catalyst will shift equilibrium.

    (E) The mixture will sublime.

66. We find that the ionization energy is greatest for the

    (A) alkali metals          (D) transition elements

    (B) alkali earth metals    (E) inert gases

    (C) halogens

67. The equilibrium expression, $K_e = [CO_2]$ is appropriate for the reaction

    (A) $C\ (s) + O_2\ (g) \rightleftharpoons CO_2\ (g)$

    (B) $CO\ (g) + \frac{1}{2}O_2\ (g) \rightleftharpoons CO_2\ (g)$

    (C) $CaCO_3\ (s) \rightleftharpoons CaO\ (s) + CO_2\ (g)$

    (D) $CO_2\ (g) \rightleftharpoons C\ (s) + O_2\ (g)$

    (E) $CaO\ (s) + CO_2\ (g) \rightleftharpoons CaCO_3\ (s)$

68. Calculate the concentration of HI present in an equilibrium mixture produced by the reaction

    $$H_2\ (g) + I_2\ (g) \rightleftharpoons 2HI\ (g) \text{ if } K_e = 3.3 \times 10^{-1}$$

    and the concentrations of $H_2$ and $I_2$ are $0.1\ M$ and $0.3\ M$, respectively at equilibrium.

    (A) $0.01\ M$          (D) $0.1\ M$

    (B) $0.03\ M$          (E) $1\ M$

    (C) $0.05\ M$

69. The following reaction coordinates cannot be associated with

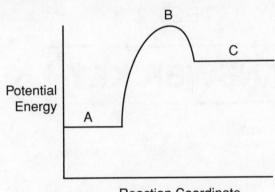

(A)  an endothermic reaction from A to C

(B)  an exothermic reaction from A to C

(C)  the activation energy for the reaction

(D)  the energy for the intermediate

(E)  the energy absorbed in the reaction from A to C

# SAT Chemistry
# TEST 2

## ANSWER KEY

## PART A

| | | | | | | | |
|---|---|---|---|---|---|---|---|
| 1. | (A) | 7. | (B) | 13. | (B) | 19. | (A) |
| 2. | (C) | 8. | (D) | 14. | (D) | 20. | (E) |
| 3. | (D) | 9. | (B) | 15. | (B) | 21. | (D) |
| 4. | (D) | 10. | (A) | 16. | (A) | 22. | (C) |
| 5. | (E) | 11. | (B) | 17. | (C) | 23. | (A) |
| 6. | (E) | 12. | (D) | 18. | (A) | 24. | (D) |

## PART B

| | | | | | | | |
|---|---|---|---|---|---|---|---|
| 101. | F, T | 105. | T, T, CE | 109. | T, T, CE | 113. | T, F |
| 102. | T, F | 106. | T, T, CE | 110. | T, F | 114. | F, T |
| 103. | F, T | 107. | T, F | 111. | F, T | 115. | F, T |
| 104. | F, F | 108. | T, T | 112. | F, F | 116. | T, T |

## PART C

| | | | | | | | |
|---|---|---|---|---|---|---|---|
| 25. | (C) | 37. | (B) | 49. | (E) | 61. | (D) |
| 26. | (A) | 38. | (D) | 50. | (C) | 62. | (A) |
| 27. | (D) | 39. | (D) | 51. | (B) | 63. | (C) |
| 28. | (E) | 40. | (C) | 52. | (A) | 64. | (D) |
| 29. | (B) | 41. | (E) | 53. | (D) | 65. | (A) |
| 30. | (C) | 42. | (A) | 54. | (E) | 66. | (E) |
| 31. | (A) | 43. | (C) | 55. | (B) | 67. | (C) |
| 32. | (A) | 44. | (E) | 56. | (A) | 68. | (D) |
| 33. | (C) | 45. | (C) | 57. | (D) | 69. | (B) |
| 34. | (D) | 46. | (B) | 58. | (C) | | |
| 35. | (E) | 47. | (A) | 59. | (D) | | |
| 36. | (E) | 48. | (C) | 60. | (B) | | |

# DETAILED EXPLANATIONS
# OF ANSWERS
## TEST 2
## PART A

1.  **(A)**
    The alkali metals react with water to produce strong bases. For example,

    $$Na + H_2O \rightarrow NaOH + {}^1/_2H_2 \, (g)$$

    The alkali earth metals (B) also react to form bases but those produced are not as strong.

2.  **(C)**
    Elements having both metallic and nonmetallic characteristics are termed metalloids and are found bordering the heavy line on the right side of the periodic table.

3.  **(D)**
    The possible oxidation numbers of a compound are usually given by the group number or by the group number minus 8. Thus, Group VIIA characteristically has an oxidation number of –1.

4.  **(D)**
    Electron affinity is the energy given off when an electron is removed from an atom in the gas phase. Since electron affinity is an exothermic value, a stronger attraction of an electron to an element is represented by a more negative value. Therefore, electron affinity generally decreases as one goes from left to right across a row in the periodic table (excluding VIIIA, which already have filled shells), and also decreases as one goes from bottom to top within a family.

5.  **(E)**
    The atomic radii of the elements decreases as one proceeds from left to right across a period and increases as one goes from top to bottom along a group. Thus, the element with the smallest atomic radius occupies the upper right-hand corner of the periodic table.

6.  **(E)**

The inert gases, Group VIII, are characterized by a completely filled outer electron shell.

7.  **(B)**

The alkaline earth metals, characterized by a complete s subshell are found in Group IIA.

8.  **(D)**

Element B is found in Group IIIA, signifying that it has an oxidation number of +2. If two atoms of the same element are to produce a neutral compound with B, they must each have an oxidation number of –1. This is characteristic of the halogens, Group VIIA.

9.  **(B)**

The given electronic configuration places two electrons in the second energy level. This indicates an alkaline earth metal, Group IIA (more specifically magnesium).

10. **(A)**

Typically, atomic radius is a property which decreases as one moves from left to right along the periodic table and increases as one moves from top to bottom. This can be rationalized in terms of electronic configuration. Moving down the table, each successive atom has the same configuration in the outer shell, but the outer shell is progressively more shielded from the positive charge of the nucleus by the inner electrons through the addition of another energy level, which also increases the size of the atomic radius. Therefore, the outer electrons are held less tightly and the atomic radius becomes larger as one moves down a group or column on the periodic table. The decrease going across the table can be explained similarly. As one moves across the table, the effective nuclear charge increases. Electrons are added in the same energy level and thus act as poor shields for each other since they are all the same distance from the nucleus. As the effective nuclear charge increases, outer electrons are pulled in more tightly and atomic radius decreases.

11. **(B)**

Electronegativity on the other hand, increases left to right and decreases top to bottom. Electronegativity is defined as the tendency of an atom to attract electrons. This is consistent with the trend in atomic radius—the smaller the atomic radius, the smaller the atom, the more strongly electrons are attracted to it.

## 12. **(D)**

Atomic mass increases from left to right and increases top to bottom. This can be seen on the periodic table. As the total number of protons, neutrons, and electrons increases, atomic mass does as well.

## 13. **(B)**

Ionization energy, is a complement of electronegativity. The more electronegative the element, the stronger it holds its electrons and the harder it is to pull one off and ionize the atom. Therefore, the trend is the same as for electronegativity.

## 14. **(D)**

Lone electron pairs on an atom take up space just as attached atoms do. In fact, lone pairs tend to take up even more room and are repelled by the electron clouds around atoms. $NH_3$ has pyramidal geometry because the three hydrogens occupy the three corners of an equilateral triangle acting as the base, and the one lone electron pair on the nitrogen occupies the apex of the pyramid. This allows the lone pair the maximum distance away from the hydrogens.

## 15. **(B)**

$H_2O$ has bent geometry because the two hydrogens on the oxygen and oxygen's two lone electron pairs occupy the four corners of a tetrahedron, leaving $H_2O$ appearing bent.

## 16. **(A)**

$BeF_2$ has linear geometry. There are no lone pairs on the Be atom to "push" the F out of the way.

## 17. **(C)**

$CH_4$ has tetrahedral geometry. Since there are no lone electron pairs on the carbon, the four hydrogens may take equal space and thus form the corners of a tetrahedron.

## 18. **(A)**

This is Charles' and Gay-Lussac's Law.

## 19. **(A)**

This is one of the postulates of the kinetic theory of gases. The energy resulting from the motion of a molecule depends only on the temperature. It does not depend on the pressure, volume, or any quality of the molecule.

20. **(E)**

This refers to Graham's Law of gaseous effusion. Effusion is the rate at which a gas will pass through a small orifice into a vacuum. Graham's Law states that given two gasses, the effusion rates are proportional to the square root of their molecular weights, *i.e.*,

$$\text{rate of effusion of gas } 1 = (MW_{gas\ 1} / MW_{gas\ 2})^{1/2}$$

21. **(D)**

This is Boyle's Law.

22. **(C)**

The oxidation number of Na in NaCl is +1. In all monatomic ions, the oxidation number is the charge on that ion.

23. **(A)**

The oxidation number of Cl in $Cl_2$ is zero (0). In any elementary substance, the charge of an element is zero (0). For example, the charge of O in $O_2$, H in $H_2$, is also zero (0).

24. **(D)**

The oxidation number of S in $Na_2S$ is –2. Because the charge on Na is +1 and there are two of them, in order to create a neutral compound, the oxidation number of S must be –2.

# PART B

101. **F, T**

Vaporization of water is an equilibrium process. Spontaneity of a process depends on $\Delta G$, which is a function of $\Delta H$ and $\Delta S$. An endothermic process (requiring heat) may or may not be spontaneous, depending on the entropy ($\Delta S$).

102. **T, F**

When the number of moles in a system is decreased, entropy decreases because the system has become more organized, or less disordered

$$(\Delta S < 0).$$

## 103. **F, T**

While $\Delta G = \Delta H - T\Delta S$ is the correct Gibbs-Helmholtz equation, if $\Delta H$ and $\Delta S$ are positive, $\Delta G$ may be positive or negative depending on the temperature.

## 104. **F, F**

If $K_c$ is the equilibrium constant for a forward reaction, then it is the equilibrium constant for the reverse reaction. While, as it is written, the system is in equilibrium, this does not necessarily mean that the concentrations are the same on both sides.

## 105. **T, T, CE**

Le Chatelier's Principle says that placing a stress on a system will cause the system to react to relieve the stress. Here, because both sides have the same number of moles, a shift will not relieve the stress of added pressure, so the system's equilibrium will remain where it is.

## 106. **T, T, CE**

Both statements are true and the second is a correct explanation of the former. The equation for half life is

$$t_{1/2} = \frac{0.693}{K}$$

so $t^1/_2$ is independent of concentration and depends only upon the rate constant.

## 107. **T, F**

A catalyst increases the rate of a reaction by lowering the activation energy.

## 108. **T, T**

Increasing temperature increases the reaction rate because more molecules have greater kinetic energies, making them more likely to collide, even though they tend to be further apart.

## 109. **T, T, CE**

The reaction of an acid anhydride with water produces the corresponding acid. For the case presented in the question:

$$SO_3 (g) + H_2O \rightarrow H_2SO_4$$

110. **T, F**

The reaction of hydrochloric acid with sodium hydroxide is an example of an acid-base neutralization in which water and the corresponding salt are produced. The reason given gives the opposite of this conclusion.

$$HCl + NaOH \rightarrow H_2O + NaCl$$

111. **F, T**

The reaction of $Pb(NO_3)_2$ with $Na_2SO_4$ goes to completion because $PbSO_4$ precipitates out of the solution.

112. **F, F**

A compound produced by an endothermic reaction is generally unstable since heat was added to the reactant mixture in its production.

113. **T, F**

The ionic radius of a metal atom is smaller than the atomic radius since the nuclear attraction for the remaining electrons increases (thereby decreasing the radius) once the valence electrons are removed. Note that removal of a metal's valence electron(s) requires minimum energy.

114. **F, T**

150 calories of heat are required to raise the temperature of 10 g of water from 80 °C to 95 °C since the specific heat of water is 1 cal/g C°.

$$q = mc \, \Delta t = (10)\,(1)\,(95 - 80) = 150 \text{ calories}$$

115. **F, T**

Decreasing the volume of a system increases the pressure since pressure and volume are inversely related at constant temperature (Boyle's law).

$$P_1 V_1 = P_2 V_2 \text{ or } \frac{P_1}{P_2} = \frac{V_2}{V_1}$$

116. **T, T**

Catalysts increase the rate of a reaction by lowering the activation energy.

# PART C

25. **(C)**

Consulting the periodic table, we find that the atomic weights of magnesium, sulfur, and oxygen are approximately 24.3, 32, and 16, respectively. Therefore, the formula weight of magnesium sulfate is given by:

$$24.3 + 32 + 4(16) = 120.3 \approx 120$$

In a likewise manner, the formula weights of $Ca(OH)_2$, $KNO_3$, $AlCl_3$, and $BeCl_2$ are 74, 101, 133.5, and 80, respectively.

26. **(A)**

Iodine occurs naturally as a diatomic element. Ozone, $O_3$, an allotrope of diatomic oxygen, is a triatomic element. Nitric oxide, NO, is not an element but rather a compound. Sulfur and helium exist as monoatomic elements.

27. **(D)**

One characteristic of a catalyst is that it remains unchanged by the reaction process. It may now be seen that the platinum, Pt, is the catalyst for this reaction.

28. **(E)**

From the name propanal, we find that we must describe an aldehyde (from the *-al* suffix) composed of a 3-carbon skeleton (from the prop-prefix) with no multiple bonds (from the *-ane* root). Remembering that an aldehyde is characterized by the functional group

$$
\begin{array}{c}
O \\
\parallel \\
-C-H
\end{array}
$$

we obtain

$$
\begin{array}{c}
O \\
\parallel \\
CH_3 - CH_2 - C - H
\end{array}
$$

as a result. This is equivalent to the electron configuration in (E) since each bond (1) represents two electrons.

29. **(B)**

The mass of an electron is 1/1,837 that of a proton or that of a neutron.

30. **(C)**

The atomic radii of the elements decreases as one proceeds from left to right across a row of the periodic table and increases as one proceeds from top to bottom along a column. Thus, the element with the largest atomic radius would be found in the lower left corner of the periodic table.

31. **(A)**

Summing the subscripts gives:

$Al_2(SO_4)_3 : 2 + 3 + 12 = 17$ atoms

$Al(NO_3)_3 : 1 + 3 + 9 = 13$ atoms

$Ca(HCO_3)_2 : 1 + 2 + 2 + 6 = 11$ atoms

$Mg(IO_3)_2 : 1 + 2 + 6 = 9$ atoms

32. **(A)**

The attractive force between the protons of one atom and the electrons of another is inversely proportional to the square of the distance between the atoms, *i.e.*, $(F \propto \frac{1}{d^2})$ where $F$ = force and $d$ = distance between two atoms. This shows that the attraction is strongest at small distances (as in solids) and weakest at large distances (as in gases).

33. **(C)**

Polar solutes such as sodium chloride are more soluble in polar solvents than in non-polar solvents and non-polar solutes are more soluble in non-polar solvents ("like dissolves like"). Water is the only polar solvent given.

34. **(D)**

The hydrolysis reaction for sodium acetate proceeds as follows:

$$\underset{\text{CH}_3\text{CONa}}{\overset{\overset{\textstyle O}{\|}}{}} + H_2O \rightarrow \underset{\text{CH}_3\text{COH}}{\overset{\overset{\textstyle O}{\|}}{}} + NaOH$$

The products of the reaction are a weak acid (acetic acid) and a strong base (sodium hydroxide).

35. **(E)**

The oxidation states of the atoms of a neutral compound must add up to equal zero. For $KMnO_4$, the oxidation state of K must be +l since it is in Group IA and the oxidation state of O must be –2 since it is in Group VIA. Thus we have:

$$1 + Mn + 4(-2) = 0 \text{ and } Mn = +7$$

36. **(E)**

The equilibrium constant is independant of pressure and volume but dependent on temperature.

37. **(B)**

The reaction of chlorous acid, $HClO_2$ with sodium hydroxide produces sodium chlorite since *-ous* acids form *-ite* salts. Hydrochloric acid and sodium hydroxide give sodium chloride since *hydro-* root *-ic* acids form *-ide* salts. Chloric acid, $HClO_3$, and perchloric acid, $HClO_4$ and sodium hydroxide give sodium chlorate and sodium perchlorate, respectively, since *-ic* acids form *-ate* salts.

38. **(D)**

These are examples of colloids. Usually colloids are not visible to the naked eye (diameter in the range of 1 to 500 nm). Colloids however are large enough to reflect light from their surfaces (Tyndall effect). The scattered light can be viewed at right angles to the beam. True solutions do not display this effect due to the smaller solute particles.

39. **(D)**

Electrolysis involves chemically induced changes by the passage of an external current through a substance. This method can be used to convert $H_2O$ to $H_2$ and $O_2$, or to produce Na metal from molten salt. In contrast to an electrolytic cell, a galvanic or voltaic cell spontaneously generates a current by virtue of the electron transfer reactions within the cell. In essence, an electrolytical cell requires electricity, while a voltaic cell produces it.

40. **(C)**

Isotopes are atoms of the same element differing in the number of neutrons.

41. **(E)**

Activity increases as one moves down a group of the periodic table since the outermost electrons are further away from the nucleus and not held as tightly as those of the smaller atoms. Also, metallic character is greatest at the far left of the periodic table.

42. **(A)**

Iron loses 1 mole of electrons when one mole of $Fe^{2+}$ reacts to produce $Fe^{3+}$. The removal of 0.5 mole of electrons is required to oxidize iron from the +2 to the +3 state.

43. **(C)**

This problem is solved by applying the combined as law:

$$\frac{P_1 V_1}{T_1} = \frac{P_2 V_2}{T_2}$$

Rearranging gives:

$$V_2 = V_1 \times \frac{T_2}{T_1} \times \frac{P_1}{P_2} \text{; converting Celsius degrees to Kelvins}$$

K = (°C + 273) and using the same pressure units (mm Hg): STP means 0 °C and 1 atm or 760 mm Hg.

Substituting given values:

$$V_2 = 10 \times \frac{273}{323} \times \frac{200}{760}$$

This gives the correction factor:

$$\frac{273}{323} \times \frac{200}{760}$$

44. **(E)**

The pH of a solution is defined as

$$pH = -\log[H^+]$$

We are not given the $[H^+]$ however. There are two ways of solving this problem. The first relies on the fact that:

$$K_w = [H^+][OH^-] = 1 \times 10^{-14}$$

Rearranging gives

$$[H^+] = \frac{K_w}{[OH^-]} = \frac{1 \times 10^{-14}}{1 \times 10^{-2}} = 1 \times 10^{-12}$$

and    $pH = -\log 1 \times 10^{-12} = 12$

Alternatively, we define pOH as

$pOH = -\log[OH^-]$

which gives

$pOH = -\log 1 \times 10^{-2} = 2.$

Recalling that $pH + pOH = 14$ we have upon rearrangement:

$pH = 14 - pOH = 12$

45. **(C)**

The reaction in question is

$NO + \frac{1}{2}O_2 \rightarrow NO_2$

or using the given coefficients

$20\ NO + 10\ O_2 \rightarrow 20\ NO_2$

Note that the unit of the coefficients used is liters, not moles. This does not affect the calculation since moles and liters are directly related in the case of gases (1 mole of a gas occupies 22.4 liters of STP (standard temperature and pressure)).

46. **(B)**

The molecular weight of $HNO_3$ is 63 grams/mole and that of LiOH is 24 grams/mole. $HNO_3$ and LiOH react in a 1:1 ratio by mole as seen by

$HNO_3 + LiOH \rightarrow H_2O + LiNO_3$

There is an excess of $HNO_3$, since only one mole of it can react with the one mole of LiOH available. Thus, there is an excess of $92 - 63$ or 29 grams of nitric acid.

47. **(A)**

The solubility product of lead (II) iodide is given by

$K_{sp} = [Pb^{2+}]\ [I^-]^2$

where $[Pb^{2+}]$ and $[I^-]$ are the concentrations of lead ion and iodide in solution, respectively. We know that $K_{sp} = 1.4 \times 10^{-8}$ and that the concentration of iodide in solution is twice that of the lead ion from the dissociation:

$PbI_2 \rightarrow Pb^{2+} + 2I^-$

Setting $[Pb^{2+}] = x$, we know that $[I^-] = 2x$. Thus,

$$K_{sp} = [Pb^{2+}] [I^-]^2 = (x) (2x)^2 = 1.4 \times 10^{-8}.$$

Solving for $x$ gives

$$4x^3 = 1.4 \times 10^{-8}$$

and $\qquad x = 1.5 \times 10^{-3}$

Recalling that $[I^-] = 2x$ we have

$$[I^-] = 2(1.5 \times 10^{-3}) = 3 \times 10^{-3}$$

48. **(C)**

Recalling that density equals

$$\text{Density} = \frac{m}{v}$$

gives $\quad \text{Density} = \dfrac{80 \text{ g/mol}}{22.4 \text{ L/mol}} = 3.6 \text{ g/L}$

49. **(E)**

The equation for the reaction is:

$$2NH_3 \rightarrow N_2 + 3H_2$$

Multiplying each coefficient by $^3/_2$ gives

$$3NH_3 \rightarrow \frac{3}{2}N_2 + \frac{9}{2}H_2.$$

Thus, 3 moles of $NH_3$ decompose to produce 4.5 moles of $H_2$. Converting to liters (since 1 mole = 22.4 L):

$$4.5 \text{ moles H}_2 \times \frac{22.4 \text{ L of H}_2}{1 \text{ mole of H}_2} \approx 101 \text{ L of H}_2$$

50. **(C)**

The electrical source indicates that an electrolysis is occurring. Both oxidation and reduction are taking place in the reaction.

51. **(B)**

The reaction in question is

$$2H_2O \rightarrow 2H_2 + O_2$$

where oxygen is being oxidized at the anode,

$$O^{2-} \rightarrow {}^1/_2O_2 + 2e^-,$$

and hydrogen is being reduced at the cathode,

$$2H^+ + 2e^- \rightarrow H_2.$$

The side of the apparatus labelled A is the cathode (reduction site) since it is connected to the negative terminal of the source. Therefore $H_2$ will be found at A.

52. **(A)**

Point B, the anode (oxidation site), will be the site where $O_2$ is found since it is the oxidation product.

53. **(D)**

The oxidation reaction is

$$H_2O \rightarrow {}^1/_2O_2 + 2H^+ + 2e^-$$

Reaction E is a reduction while the other reactions as depicted are not electrochemical in nature.

54. **(E)**

The reduction reaction is

$$2H_2O + 2e^- \rightarrow H_2 + 2OH^-$$

55. **(B)**

This particular setup is used to prepare a gas which is nonsoluble in water from solid reactants.

56. **(A)**

The reaction is

$$2KClO_3\,(s) + MnO_2\,(s) \rightarrow 2KCl + 3O_2 + MnO_2$$

57. **(D)**

A water soluble gas such as ammonia could not be prepared in this manner.

58. **(C)**

An observation is something you detect with your senses or a piece of equipment. A conclusion is the interpretation of one or many observations.

59. **(D)**

Graham's law states that the relative rate of effusion of a gas is inversely proportional to the square root of its molecular weight. Expressed as a ratio we have

$$\frac{\text{diffusion rate of H}_2}{\text{diffusion rate of O}_2} = \sqrt{\frac{\text{molecular weight of O}_2}{\text{molecular weight of H}_2}}$$

$$= \sqrt{\frac{32}{2}} = \sqrt{16} = 4$$

Thus, the rate of $H_2$ diffusion is 4 times as fast as the rate of $O_2$ diffusion.

60. **(B)**

The states present on this cooling curve are as follows:

(A) vapor phase being cooled to the boiling point

(B) mixture of vapor and liquid at a constant temperature (the boiling point)

(C) all the vapor has been converted to the liquid which is being cooled to the freezing point

(D) mixture of liquid and solid at a constant temperature (the freezing point)

(E) all the liquid has been converted to the solid which continues to cool.

61. **(D)**

The phase changes occur at a constant temperature thus they are depicted as horizontal lines on the cooling curve. Assuming constant heating, the phase change requiring the least energy will be the one that requires the shortest time interval to occur. This is depicted to be region D.

62. **(A)**

A large value for the specific heat of a substance indicates a small change in temperature results for every unit of heat introduced or removed to or from the system. Assuming constant heating, a longer period of time will be required to change the temperature a given amount if there is a large specific heat. This appears as the smallest non-zero slope on the cooling curve. In our example, region A gives the phase with the largest specific heat.

63. **(C)**

The structure $HClO_2$ is chlorous acid. Binary acids, such as HCl, are given the prefix *hydro-* in front of the stem of the nonmetallic element and the ending *-ic*. Ternary acids (composed of three elements—usually hydrogen, a nonmetal, and oxygen) usually have a variable oxygen content so the most common member of the series has the ending *-ic*. The acid with one less oxygen than the *-ic* acid has the ending *-ous*. The acid with one less oxygen than the *-ous* acid has the prefix *hypo-* and the ending *-ous*. The acid containing one more oxygen than the *-ic* acid has the prefix *per-* and the ending *-ic*. For example

| | |
|---|---|
| HCl | hydrochloric acid |
| HClO | hypochlorous acid |
| $HClO_2$ | chlorous acid |
| $HClO_3$ | chloric acid |
| $HClO_4$ | perchloric acid |

64. **(D)**

The molality of a solution ($m$) is defined as the number of moles of solute dissolved in one kilogram of solvent. The number of moles of NaOH to be used is determined to be:

$$20 \text{ g of NaOH} \times \frac{1 \text{ mole of NaOH}}{40 \text{ g of NaOH}} = 0.5 \text{ mole of NaOH}$$

Thus:

$$0.5 \ m = \frac{0.5 \text{ mole of NaOH}}{x \text{ kilograms of water}}$$

Rearranging:

$$x = \frac{0.5}{0.5} = 1 \text{ kg of water}$$

65. **(A)**

The equilibrium constant is dependent only on temperature but the amount of each substance present at equilibrium is dependent on pressure, volume, and temperature. There is still an interchange between the phases, but the same number of molecules leave and enter both phases so the equilibrium concentrations and equilibrium constant are the same for a given pressure, volume, and temperature.

66. **(E)**

The ionization energy is the energy required to remove an electron from the valence shell of an atom. The greatest ionization energy is found in the inert gases since they have a stable (complete) outer electron configuration, while the least electronegative element would have the lowest ionization energy.

67. **(C)**

The equilibrium constant is defined as the product of the concentrations of the gaseous products raised to the power of their coefficients divided by the product of the gaseous reactant concentrations raised to the power of their coefficients. Only gaseous reactants and products are included in $K_e$ since the concentrations of liquids and solids participating in the reaction are assumed to be large ( as compared to those of the gases) and relatively constant. The expressions of the equilibrium constants for the reactions given are:

(A)  $K_e = \dfrac{[CO_2]}{[O_2]}$

(B)  $K_e = \dfrac{[CO_2]}{[CO][O_2]^{1/2}}$

(C)  $K_e = [CO_2]$

(D)  $K_e = \dfrac{[O_2]}{[CO_2]}$

(E)  $K_e = \dfrac{1}{[CO_2]}$

68. **(D)**

The equilibrium constant expression for the reaction is:

$$K_e = \frac{[HI]^2}{[H]^2 \, [I]^2}$$

Substituting given values, we obtain:

$$3.3 \times 10^{-1} = \frac{[HI]^2}{(0.1)(0.3)}$$

Rearranging:

$$[HI]^2 = (3.3 \times 10^{-1})(0.1)(0.3) = 9.9 \times 10^{-3}$$

and    $[HI] = 0.1 \, M$

69. **(B)**

Heat was absorbed by the system during the reaction as indicated by the products having a greater potential energy than the reactants. A reaction in which heat is absorbed in order to produce the products is said to be endothermic.

# PRACTICE
# TEST 3

# SAT Chemistry
# Practice Test 3

**(Answer sheets appear in the back of this book.)**

## PART A

**TIME:** 1 Hour
85 Questions

**DIRECTIONS**: Each set of questions below consists of five lettered choices followed by a list of numbered statements or questions. For each statement or question, select the answer choice that is most closely related to it. Each answer choice may be used once, more than once, or not at all.

*Note:* **For all questions involving solutions, assume that the solvent is water unless otherwise noted.**

**Questions 1–3** refer to the following species.

(A) Li

(D) Mn

(B) Br

(E) Ge

(C) Cl⁻

1. Is considered to be a metalloid

2. Has only one electron in its $2s$ orbital

3. Has the same electron configuration as a noble gas

**Questions 4–7** refer to the variables or constants.

(A) $PV = k$ at constant $n$ and $T$

(B) $P_r = P_A + P_B + P_C$

(C) $PV = nRT$

(D)  $V = kT$ at constant $n$ and $P$

(E)  $V = kn$ at constant $P$ and $T$

4.  The combined gas law

5.  Boyle's Law

6.  Charles' and Gay-Lussac's Law

7.  Avogadro's Law

**Questions 8–13** refer to the following classifications.

(A)  Acid                     (D)  Basic salt

(B)  Base                     (E)  Amphoteric

(C)  Acid salt

8.  Amino acids

9.  Ammonia

10.  Ammonium sulfate

11.  Aluminum chloride

12.  Arsenic

13.  Group IA element + water

**Questions 14–20**

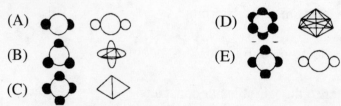

Note that these molecules are not drawn to scale and that the black spheres represent either atoms bonded to the central atom or lone electron pairs on the central atom.

14. $CS_2$

15. $H_2O$

16. $H_3O^+$

17. $BF_3$

18. $SF_6$

19. $CO_2$

20. $NH_3$

**Questions 21–23** refer to the following answers.

    (A) 1-butene            (D) 2-methylpropane

    (B) 2,3-dimethylbutane     (E) *trans*-2-butene

    (C) *cis*-2-butene

21.
```
        H     H
        |     |
  H  -  C  -  C  -   C  =  C  -  H
        |     |      |     |
        H     H      H     H
```

22.
```
        H            H     H
        |            |     |
  H  -  C  -  C  =   C  -  C  -  H
        |     |            |
        H     H            H
```

23.
```
                  H
                  |
          H  H-C -H H      H
          |    |    |      |
  H  -  C  -   C  -  C  -C  -  H
          |    |    |      |
          H      H  H-C -H H
                    |
                    H
```

# PART B

> **DIRECTIONS:** Each question below consists of two statements. Determine if Statement I is true or false <u>and</u> if Statement II is true or false and fill in the corresponding ovals on your answer sheet. Fill in oval CE if Statement II is a correct explanation of the true Statement I.

| (I) | | (II) |
|---|---|---|
| 101. In the reaction of Mg *(s)* with acid to form $Mg^{2+}$ *(aq)* and $H_2$ *(g)*, Mg is oxidized | *because* | Mg looses electrons. |
| 102. Positive ions move toward a cathode | *because* | that is where oxidation occurs. |
| 103. The standard reduction potential for $Ag^+$ t $e^- \rightarrow Ag$ is half that as for $2Ag^+ + 2e^- \rightarrow 2Ag$ | *because* | standard potential is dependent on the number of electrons transferred. |
| 104. $CO_2$ is drawn as a series of resonance structures | *because* | its bonds are a hybrid of single and double bond character. |
| 105. Hydrofluoric acid etches glass | *because* | it is a strong acid. |
| 106. The metalloids share similar characteristics | *because* | their valence shells have the same configuration. |
| 107. Cobalt nitrate is frequently used in qualitative tests | *because* | it gives precipitates with very characteristic colors. |
| 108. NaCl is an electrolyte | *because* | it forms ions in solution. |

109. Adding a catalyst to a reaction mixture alters the reaction rate

    *because*

    Le Chatelier's principle is followed for equilibrium reactions.

110. A reaction having a negative value of $\Delta H$ is said to be exothermic

    *because*

    the reaction spontaneously goes to completion.

111. Equilibrium of a reaction mixture at a given temperature, pressure, and volume is characterized by constant product and reactant concentrations

    *because*

    both the forward and the reverse reactions have stopped.

112. The equilibrium constant is independent of temperature

    *because*

    the concentrations of the products are dependent on volume and pressure.

113. A catalyst increases the rate of a reaction

    *because*

    it lowers the free energy charge of the reaction.

114. Ge is an excellent conductor of electricity

    *because*

    it contains $d$ electrons.

115. NO is paramagnetic

    *because*

    it has 3 unpaired electrons.

116. Table salt, NaCl *(s)* may not be considered to be a pure substance

    *because*

    it is composed of two different elements.

# PART C

**DIRECTIONS:** For each question in this section, select the best answer from among the given choices and fill in the corresponding oval on the answer sheet.

24. Which of the following illustrates a chemical change?

    (A)  the melting of ice at 0 °C

    (B)  the burning of wood in a fireplace

    (C)  the evolution of heat while rubbing two sticks together

    (D)  the decrease in fluid viscosity at high temperatures

    (E)  water freezing at 0 °C

25. The primary products of hydrocarbon combustion are

    (A)  water and carbon

    (B)  water and carbon monoxide

    (C)  water and carbon dioxide

    (D)  hydrogen and carbon monoxide

    (E)  hydrogen and carbon

26. The prefix *deci-* means

    (A)  $10^{-3}$          (D)  $10^3$

    (B)  $10^{-1}$          (E)  $10^5$

    (C)  $10^1$

27. How many moles of $CO_2$ are represented by $1.8 \times 10^{24}$ atoms?

    (A)  1          (D)  4

    (B)  2          (E)  5

    (C)  3

28. The Law of Conservation of Matter states that matter is conserved in terms of

    (A) pressure          (D) mass

    (B) volume            (E) density

    (C) temperature

29. The temperature above which a liquid cannot exist is indicated by

    (A) the triple point       (D) the boiling point

    (B) the critical point     (E) the sublimation point

    (C) the eutectic point

30. An alkaline earth metal may be described by the atomic number

    (A) 11                (D) 32

    (B) 12                (E) 52

    (C) 24

31. The production of alkanes from alkenes is accomplished by

    (A) burning in the presence of water

    (B) distillation

    (C) methylation

    (D) catalytic hydrogenation

    (E) hydrolysis

32. Water is immiscible with most organic compounds due to differences in

    (A) molecular weight       (D) polarity

    (B) atomic composition     (E) temperature

    (C) density

33. A tetrahedral geometry with one corner occupied by a lone electron pair best represents

   (A) $H_2O$

   (B) $H_3O^+$

   (C) $BF_3$

   (D) $AlCl_3$

   (E) $NH_4^+$

34. When the electrons of a bond are shared unequally by two atoms, the bond is said to be

   (A) covalent

   (B) polar covalent

   (C) coordinate covalent

   (D) ionic

   (E) metallic

35. $sp^2$ hybridization will be found for carbon in

   (A) $CH_4$

   (B) $C_2H_4$

   (C) $C_2H_2$

   (D) $CH_3OH$

   (E) $CH_3OCH_3$

36. Which of the following is responsible for the abnormally high boiling point of water?

   (A) covalent bonding

   (B) hydrogen bonding

   (C) high polarity

   (D) large dielectric constant

   (E) low molecular weight

37. Which of the following contains a coordinate covalent bond?

   (A) HCl

   (B) $H_2O$

   (C) $H_2$

   (D) $H_3O^+$

   (E) NaCl

38. About how many grams of sodium chloride whould be dissolved in water to form a 0.5 $m$ solution in 500 mL of solution?

   (A) 7

   (B) 29

   (C) 14.5

   (D) 58

   (E) 112

39. Which of the following is least likely to be found in nature in elemental form?

    (A) phosphorus          (D) sulfur

    (B) sodium              (E) helium

    (C) carbon

40. Which of the following is true of an electrochemical cell?

    (A) The cell voltage is independent of concentration.

    (B) The anode is negatively charged.

    (C) The cathode is the site of reduction.

    (D) Charge is carried from one electrode to the other by metal atoms passing through the solution.

    (E) Cathode is site of oxidation.

41. Hard water is characterized by

    (A) an unusually high $D_2O$ (D-deuterium) content

    (B) excessive hydrogen bonding due to dissolved solutes

    (C) a high salt and mineral content

    (D) high chloride and fluoride content

    (E) a phase change to ice at a temperature greater than 0 °C

42. An element of atomic number 17 has an atomic weight of 37. How many neutrons are in its nucleus?

    (A) 17                  (D) 37

    (B) 18                  (E) 54

    (C) 20

43. The most probable oxidation number of an element with an atomic number of 53 is

    (A) –5                  (D) +5

    (B) –1                  (E) +7

    (C) +1

**Questions 44–46** refer to the following diagram.

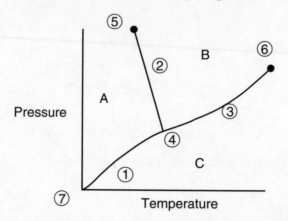

44. Which of the following represents a liquid and its vapor in equilibrium?

    (A) Region A

    (B) Region B

    (C) Region C

    (D) Line 2

    (E) Line 3

45. The critical point is indicated by

    (A) 4

    (B) 5

    (C) 6

    (D) 7

    (E) 3

46. A pure solid would be found

    (A) in Region A

    (B) in Region B

    (C) in Region C

    (D) along Line 1

    (E) along Line 2

47. The cathode reaction for $Cu^{2+} + Zn \rightleftharpoons Cu + Zn^{2+}$ is

    (A) $Zn \rightarrow Zn^{2+} + 2e^-$

    (B) $Zn^{2+} + 2e^- \rightarrow Zn$

    (C) $Cu \rightarrow Cu^{2+} + 2e^-$

    (D) $Cu^{2+} + 2e^- \rightarrow Cu$

    (E) $Cu^{2+} + 2e^- \rightarrow Zn$

48. How many grams of Cu could be produced from $CuSO_4$ by 0.5 fara-days of charge?

    (A) 15.9

    (B) 31.75

    (C) 63.5

    (D) 127.0

    (E) 252.0

49. The reaction $2H^+ + 2e^- \rightarrow H_2\,(g)$ is an example of

    (A) an oxidation

    (B) a reduction

    (C) an oxidation-reduction

    (D) the reaction at the hydrogen anode

    (E) an addition reaction

50. The ionization of salts in water is useful in explaining which of the following statements?

    I.   Their unusually large solubility in water.

    II.  Their electrical conductivity in solution.

    III. The lower freezing points and higher boiling points of their solutions.

    (A) I only

    (B) III only

    (C) II and III only

    (D) I and II only

    (E) I, II and III

51. The atomic weight of an element is calculated by considering which of the following?

    I.   A weighted average.

    II.  All naturally occurring isotopes.

    III. Electronic energy level populations.

    (A) III only

    (B) I and II only

    (C) I, II and III

    (D) II only

    (E) II and III only

52. Based on these standard reduction potentials

$$E^\circ_{red} (Fe^{2+}) = -0.44 \ V$$

$$E^\circ_{red} (Cu^{2+}) = +0.34 \ V$$

the reaction $Fe^{2+} + Cu \rightarrow Cu^{2+} + Fe$, will occur which of the following ways?

I.   Spontaneously.

II.  If the concentration of $Fe^{2+}$ is decreased.

III. If an electric current is applied to the cell.

(A) I only                    (D) II and III only

(B) II only                   (E) III only

(C) I and II only

53. Which of the following will cause the pressure of a gas to increase?

I.   Decreasing the volume while maintaining the temperature.

II.  Decreasing the volume while increasing the temperature.

III. Increasing the volume by 1 liter while increasing the temperature by 1K at STP.

(A) I only                    (D) II only

(B) I and II only             (E) I, II and III

(C) II and III only

54. Arrhenius would define a base as which of the following?

I.   Something which yields hydroxide ions in solution.

II.  A proton acceptor.

III. An electron pair donator.

(A) I and II only             (D) I only

(B) II only                   (E) I, II and III

(C) II and III only

55. Reacting $CO_2$ *(g)* with water results in the production of

    (A) methane and oxygen      (D) carbon and oxygen

    (B) carbonous acid          (E) sodium bicarbonate

    (C) carbonic acid

56. What is $K_b$ for a 0.1 *M* solution of $NH_3$ if $[OH^-] = 1.3 \times 10^{-3}$?

    (A) $7\,6 \times 10^{-1}$          (D) $3.7 \times 10^{-4}$

    (B) $1.1 \times 10^{-2}$          (E) $1.7 \times 10^{-5}$

    (C) $4.2 \times 10^{-3}$

57. What is the percent dissociation of this solution in the previous questions?

    (A) 0.093%                  (D) 1.3%

    (B) 0.073%                  (E) 13%

    (C) 0.73%

58. What is the concentration of $[OH^-]$ in a KOH solution if it has a pH of 11?

    (A) $10^{-1}$                (D) $10^{-9}$

    (B) $10^{-3}$                (E) $10^{-11}$

    (C) $10^{-5}$

59. How many grams of $HNO_3$ are required to produce a one liter aqueous solution with pH of 2?

    (A) 0.063                   (D) 1.26

    (B) 0.63                    (E) 12.6

    (C) 6.3

60. A 20% solution of NaOH will be produced by dissolving one mole of NaOH in

    (A) 160 mL of acetone       (D) 160 mL of carbon tetrachloride

    (B) 160 mL of water         (E) 20 mL of water

    (C) 160 mL of ammonia

61. How many grams of sodium sulfate can be produced by reacting 98g of $H_2SO_4$ with 40 g of NaOH?

   (A) 18 g                    (D) 142 g

   (B) 36 g                    (E) 150 g

   (C) 71 g

62. 20 mL of NaOH is needed to titrate 30 mL of a 6, $M$ HCl solution. The molarity of the NaOH is

   (A) 1 $M$                    (D) 9 $M$

   (B) 3 $M$                    (E) 11 $M$

   (C) 6 $M$

63. A one liter solution of 2 $M$ NaOH can be prepared with

   (A) 20 g of NaOH            (D) 80 g of NaOH

   (B) 40 g of NaOH            (E) 100 g of NaOH

   (C) 60 g of NaOH

64. This method is best suited for producing and collecting a gas which is

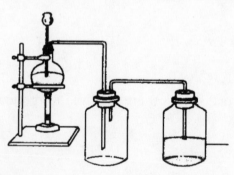

   (A) lighter than air         (D) nonsoluble in water

   (B) heavier than air         (E) toxic

   (C) soluble in water

65. Which of the following gases could not be effectively produced and collected using the method illustrated in the previous question?

   (A) HCl                      (D) $NH_3$

   (B) HBr                      (E) NaCl

   (C) $Cl_2$

66. This method is best suited for producing and collecting a gas which is

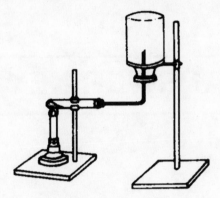

(A) lighter than air and soluble in water

(B) lighter than air and insoluble in water

(C) heavier than air

(D) heavier than air and soluble in water

(E) heavier than air and insoluble in water

67. What is/are the product gas/gases if $NH_4Cl$ and $Ca(OH)_2$ are used as reactants?

(A) $N_2$                    (D) $NH_3 + N_2$

(B) $NH_4$                   (E) $NH_3$

(C) $H_2O$

68. How many grams of water can be produced when 8 g of hydrogen reacts with 8 g of oxygen?

(A) 8 g                      (D) 27 g

(B) 9 g                      (E) 30 g

(C) 18 g

69. How many atoms are described by the formula $Na_2CO_3 \cdot 10H_2O$?

(A) 4                        (D) 60

(B) 16                       (E) 96

(C) 36

# SAT CHEMISTRY
# TEST 3

## ANSWER KEY

### PART A

| | | | | | | | |
|---|---|---|---|---|---|---|---|
| 1. | (E) | 7. | (E) | 13. | (B) | 19. | (A) |
| 2. | (A) | 8. | (E) | 14. | (A) | 20. | (C) |
| 3. | (C) | 9. | (B) | 15. | (C) | 21. | (A) |
| 4. | (C) | 10. | (C) | 16. | (C) | 22. | (E) |
| 5. | (A) | 11. | (C) | 17. | (B) | 23. | (B) |
| 6. | (D) | 12. | (E) | 18. | (D) | | |

### PART B

| | | | | | | | |
|---|---|---|---|---|---|---|---|
| 101. | T, T, CE | 105. | T, F | 109. | T, T | 113. | T, F |
| 102. | T, F | 106. | T, F | 110. | T, F | 114. | F, T |
| 103. | F, F | 107. | T, F | 111. | T, F | 115. | T, F |
| 104. | F, F | 108. | T, T, CE | 112. | F, F | 116. | F, T |

### PART C

| | | | | | | | |
|---|---|---|---|---|---|---|---|
| 24. | (B) | 36. | (B) | 48. | (A) | 60. | (B) |
| 25. | (C) | 37. | (D) | 49. | (B) | 61. | (C) |
| 26. | (B) | 38. | (C) | 50. | (C) | 62. | (D) |
| 27. | (A) | 39. | (B) | 51. | (B) | 63. | (D) |
| 28. | (D) | 40. | (C) | 52. | (E) | 64. | (B) |
| 29. | (B) | 41. | (C) | 53. | (B) | 65. | (D) |
| 30. | (B) | 42. | (C) | 54. | (D) | 66. | (A) |
| 31. | (D) | 43. | (B) | 55. | (C) | 67. | (E) |
| 32. | (D) | 44. | (E) | 56. | (E) | 68. | (B) |
| 33. | (B) | 45. | (C) | 57. | (D) | 69. | (C) |
| 34. | (B) | 46. | (A) | 58. | (B) | | |
| 35. | (B) | 47. | (D) | 59. | (B) | | |

# DETAILED EXPLANATIONS OF ANSWERS

## TEST 3

## PART A

1. **(E)**
The elements in the center of the table, dividing the metals and the non-metals are considered to be metalloids. B, Si, Ge, As, Sb, Te, Po, and At fall into this category. These elements have properties intermediate between those of metals and non-metals. (E) is therefore a metalloid, while (A) is a metal, (B) is a non-metal, (C) is an ion of a non-metal, and (D) is a metal.

2. **(A)**
Li has one electron in its $2s$ orbital. Its electron configuration is $1s^2 2s^1$. Br has the electron configuration

$$1s^2 2s^2 2p^6 3s^2 3p^6 4s^2 3d^{10} 4p^5.$$

$Cl^-$ has the electron configuration $1s^2 2s^2 2p^6$. Ge has the electron configuration

$$1s^2 2s^2 2p^6 3s^2 3p^6 4s^2 3d^{10} 4p^2.$$

3. **(C)**
As stated above, $Cl^-$ has the electron configuration $1s^2 2s^2 2p^6$ this is the same as that of a noble gas, with all occupied shells completely filled.

4. **(C)**
$PV = nRT$ is the combined law. It incorporates all of the relationships in Charles' Law, Avogadro's Law, and Boyle's Law.

5. **(A)**
$PV = k$ at constant $n$ and $T$ is Boyle's Law. This law states that at constant temperature, the pressure and volume of a given amount of a gas are inversely proportional.

6. **(D)**

$V = kT$ at constant $n$ and $P$ is Charles' and Gay-Lussac's Law. It states that at constant pressure, the volume and temperature of a given amount of gas are directly proportional.

7. **(E)**

$V = kn$ at constant $P$ and $T$ is Avogadro's Law. This law states that at constant pressure and temperature, the volume occupied by a gas is proportional to the number of moles it contains. Choice (B) is Dalton's Law and states that the total pressure of a gaseous system is given by the sum of the pressures of its component parts.

8. **(E)**

Amino acids are amphoteric: they may act as acids or bases.

$$\overset{\oplus}{H_3N} - \underset{\underset{R}{|}}{\overset{\overset{H}{|}}{C}} - COO^{\ominus}$$

9. **(B)**

Ammonia is a base: it can accept a proton (Brønsted theory).

$$NH_3 + H^+ \rightarrow NH_4^+$$

10. **(C)**

Ammonium sulfate is an acid salt: it yields a strong acid and a weak base upon hydrolysis.

$$(NH_4)_2SO_4 + 2H_2O \rightarrow H_2SO_4 + 2NH_4OH$$

11. **(C)**

Aluminum chloride is also an acid salt.

$$AlCl_3 + 3H_2O \rightarrow 3HCl + Al(OH)_3$$

12. **(E)**

Arsenic (Group VA) is amphoteric as are all the metalloids.

13. **(B)**

The alkali metals react with water to produce bases. For example

$$2Na + 2H_2O \rightarrow 2NaOH + H_2 \uparrow$$

14. **(A)**
   Carbon sulfide $S - C - S$ is shaped in a linear geometry.

15. **(C)**
   An $H_2O$ molecule is shaped like a regular tetrahedron since the two O-H bonds and the two lone electron pairs orient themselves at a maximum electron cloud distance from each other.

16. **(C)**
   The hydronium ion is identical to water except that a proton occupies the corner of the tetrahedron that was occupied by a lone electron pair.

17. **(B)**
   Boron trifluoride attains a trigonal planar geometry since boron has no lone electrons and this orientation maximizes the distance between the electron clouds of the three fluorine atoms.

18. **(D)**
   Maximization of the distance between the six electron clouds results in the fluorine atoms occupying the six corners of a regular octahedron.

19. **(A)**
   Mutual repulsion between the two electron clouds calls for a linear geometry (since there are no lone electron pairs on carbon).

20. **(C)**
   Ammonia assumes the shape of a regular tetrahedron due to mutual repulsion of the three electron clouds associated with N–H bonding and the lone electron pair on nitrogen.

21. **(A)**
   Organic compounds with double bonds are given names with *ene* in them. They are named so that the double bond is nearest the low numbered end of the carbon chain and is given the number of the lowest numbered carbon that it contains. Here it is between the first and the second carbon, so it receives the number 1. The four carbons in the chain give the carbon the base name *but*.

22. **(E)**

The four carbons in the chain give the compound the base name *but*. The double bond is located between carbons 2 and 3, so it is numbered 2. Because the groups attached to the double bond are on opposite sides, the compound is given the name *trans*. *cis*-2-butene would look like:

```
        H              H   H
        |              |   |
H  -  C  -  C  =  C  -  C  -  H
        |     |     |     |
        H     H     H     H
```

There is a difference because you can't rotate around a double bond.

23. **(B)**

Again there are 4 carbons in the main chain, and the compound is given the base name *but*. Note, that from whichever carbon atom you start from the longest chain possible is 4 carbons. It is convention to keep substituent carbon chain groups as short as possible. There is a methyl group attached to the second carbon and another to the third, hence the portion of the name 2,3-dimethyl.

# PART B

101. **T, T, CE**

An oxidation is defined by a substance losing electrons and a reduction by a substance gaining electrons.

102. **T, F**

Positive ions move toward a cathode because reduction occurs there and the ion can gain electrons, oxidation occurs at the anode.

103. **F, F**

Standard potential is a measure of the driving force of a particularly reaction, and it does not depend on total electrons transferred.

104. **F, F**

Carbon dioxide does not have any resonance structures that provide eight electrons around each carbon atom. The structure is

$$\ddot{O} = C = \ddot{O}$$

105. **T, F**

Hydrofluoric acid etches glass because it reacts with $SiO_2$ (the major constituent of glass). HF is a weak acid.

$$4HF + SiO_2 \rightarrow SiF_4\ (g) + 2H_2O$$

106. **T, F**

All the metalloids have similar characteristics but their electronic configuration ranges from $2p^1$ (boron) to $6p^5$ (astatine).

107. **T, F**

Cobalt nitrate is used in qualitative tests because it gives characteristic colors when added to hot samples of Al, Zn, or Mg.

108. **T, T,CE**

NaCl dissolved in $H_2O$ forms a solution that conducts an electric current. NaCl dissociates into $Na^+$ and $Cl^-$ ions in solution. These ions make this solution capable of carrying the electric current.

109. **T, T**

A catalyst alters the rate of a reaction by decreasing or increasing the activation energy.

110. **T, F**

An exothermic reaction, $\Delta H < 0$ does not necessarily go to completion spontaneously. The change in free energy, $\Delta G = \Delta H - T\Delta S$, determines if a reaction will occur or not. If $\Delta G < 0$ the reaction is spontaneous; if $\Delta G > 0$ the reaction is not spontaneous; if $\Delta G = 0$ the system is at equilibrium.

111. **T, F**

The forward and reverse reactions occur at the same rate at equilibrium, so the concentrations of the products and the reactants do not change. However, they do not change because forward and reverse reactions have stopped. They remain unchanged because the rate of the forward reaction equals the rate of the reverse reaction.

112. **F, F**

The equilibrium constant is dependent on temperature but independent of volume and pressure. The concentrations of the products and reactants at equilibrium are dependent on temperature, volume, and pressure.

### 113. **T, F**
A catalyst increases the rate of a reaction by lowering the activation energy, or energy barrier. It has no effect on the enthalpy or free energy charge of the reaction, nor does it change the equilibrium constant.

### 114. **F, T**
While Ge does contain $d$ electrons, it is not an excellent electrical conductor. Ge is considered a metalloid and a semi-conductor. Its electrical conductivity varies with temperature.

### 115. **T, F**
NO is paramagnetic, but it has only one unpaired electron. It is in the $\pi^*2p$ molecular orbital.

### 116. **F, T**
While it is true that NaCl contains two elements, Na and Cl, a substance is termed "pure" as long as it has no other *substance* (*i.e.*, besides NaCl) contaminating it.

# PART C

### 24. **(B)**
The only chemical change given is the burning of wood (which may be seen as the rapid oxidation of carbohydrates).

### 25. **(C)**
Water and carbon dioxide are the primary products of hydrocarbon combustion. These are the only products in the case of complete combustion. For example,

$$C_2H_6 + \tfrac{7}{2}O_2 \rightarrow 2CO_2 + 3H_2O$$

### 26. **(B)**
The following is a list of commonly used prefixes in the metric system

| | |
|---|---|
| $10^{-3}$ | *milli-* |
| $10^{-2}$ | *centi-* |
| $10^{-1}$ | *deci-* |
| $10^{1}$ | *deca-* |
| $10^{3}$ | *kilo-* |
| $10^{6}$ | *mega-* |

27. **(A)**

By simple unit conversion:

$$1.8 \times 10^{24} \text{ atoms} \times \frac{1 \text{ mole}}{6.02 \times 10^{23} \text{ molecules}} \times \frac{1 \text{ molecule}}{3 \text{ atoms}} = 1 \text{ mole}$$

since each $CO_2$ molecule is composed of three atoms.

28. **(D)**

Matter is conserved in terms of mass according to the Law of Conservation of Matter. All the other choices may change due to a chemical or physical change.

29. **(B)**

The critical point on a phase diagram indicates the temperature above which a liquid cannot exist regardless of the pressure. The triple point specifies the temperature and pressure at which gas, liquid and solid can coexist in equilibrium.

30. **(B)**

The alkali earth metals are found in Group IIA of the periodic table. Atomic number 11 designates an alkali metal (Group IA), 24 designates a transition metal (B-groups), and 32 and 52 are metalloids.

31. **(D)**

Hydrogenation using a metal catalyst is a common method of producing alkanes from alkenes.

$$C_2H_4 + H_2 \xrightarrow{\text{Pt}} C_2H_6$$

32. **(D)**

Water and most organic solvents are immiscible due to differences in polarity; water molecules are polar while most organic solvents are nonpolar (recall the principle of *like dissolves like*).

33. **(B)**

Water, the hydronium ion, and the ammonium ion have tetrahedral geometries; except lone electron pairs occupy two corners for a water molecule and there are no lone electrons in the ammonium ion.

Both $BF_3$ and $AlCl_3$ assume trigonal planar geometries since there are no lone electrons on boron or aluminum. (See the following figure.)

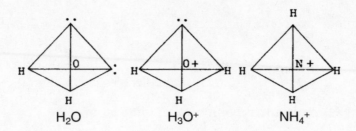

$H_2O$             $H_3O^+$             $NH_4^+$

34. **(B)**

The unequal sharing of electrons between two atoms is a polar covalent bond. Covalent (or nonpolar covalent) bonds are manifested by the equal sharing of bonding electrons. Coordinate covalent bonds are the result of one atom supplying both bonding electrons. Ionic bonds occur when one atom involved in the bond has control of both electrons (the atoms are bonded together by the attraction of one atom's positive charge to the other atom's negative charge). Metallic bonds are characterized by free electrons which travel from nucleus to nucleus.

35. **(B)**

A simple method for determining hybridization in carbon compounds is by determining how many atoms are attached to the carbon atom. If two atoms are attached, the hybridization is $sp$, if three; $sp^2$, and if four; $sp^3$. Thus,

$$H - C \equiv C - H \qquad \text{has } sp \text{ hybridization}$$

has $sp^2$ hybridization

has $sp^3$ hybridization

36. **(B)**

Hydrogen bonding between molecules increases their stability and thus increases the boiling point of water.

37. **(D)**

Coordinate covalent bonds result when one of the atoms supplies both bonding electrons

Electronegativity differences between the bonded atoms describes the type of bonding. Differences greater than 1.7 result in ionic bonds, those less than 0.5 result in nonpolar covalent bonds and those between result in polar covalent bonds. Thus, HCl and $H_2O$ are polar, $H_2$ is nonpolar and NaCl is ionic.

38. **(C)**

The formula weight of NaCl is about 58 grams, which forms a 1 $m$ solution in 1000 mL of solution. 29 grams forms a 0.5 $m$ solution in 1000 mL. In 500 mL, 14.5, or half this amount, is needed.

39. **(B)**

Elemental sodium is not found in nature since almost anything is capable of oxidizing it to $Na^+$. Phosphorus occurs mainly as phosphates in minerals. Carbon is found as diamond or as graphite. Sulfur is found as an elemental solid ($S_8$), and helium is a monoatomic gas.

40. **(C)**

The cathode of an electrochemical cell is defined as the site of reduction, and the anode is defined as the site of oxidation.

41. **(C)**

Hard water is characterized by a high salt and mineral content (particularly Ca).

42. **(C)**

The atomic number gives the number of protons in the nucleus and the atomic weight gives the sum of the number of protons and neutrons. Thus, the number of neutrons is given by the difference between the atomic number and the atomic weight.

43. **(B)**

Element 53 is iodine, a member of the halogens (Group VIIA). The halogens usually have an oxidation number of −1 although some other values sometimes (rarely) occur.

44. **(E)**

Region B represents the liquid and C the vapor, so the line separating them (Line 3) gives the temperature and pressure pairs where the liquid and vapor phases are in equilibrium.

45. **(C)**

Above the critical point (position 6), a liquid can no longer exist regardless of the pressure.

46. **(A)**

The pure phases are found in regions A (solid), B (liquid), and C (vapor).

47. **(D)**

The cathode is the reduction site and for this reaction, copper is being reduced from the +2 state to elemental copper. The anode reaction is the oxidation of elemental zinc to zinc in the +2 state:

$$Zn \rightarrow Zn^{2+} + 2e^-.$$

48. **(A)**

A faraday is the amount of electricity that allows the reaction of one mole of electrons. Each $Cu^{2+}$ ion requires two electrons to be reduced to elemental copper.

$$0.5\ F \times \frac{\text{one mole } Cu^2 \text{ reduced to Cu}}{2\ F}$$

$$= 0.25 \text{ mole of } Cu^{2+} \text{ reduced to Cu}$$

Since the atomic weight of copper is 63.5g/mol, we have

$$0.25 \text{ mol} \times \frac{63.5\text{ g}}{1\text{ mol}} = 15.9 \text{ g of Cu}.$$

49. **(B)**

This is an example of reduction since electrons are being gained by $H^+$ to produce $H_2$.

50. **(C)**

The ionization of salts in water does not explain their solubility. Just as sucrose has a large solubility in water without ionizing, some salts are extremely insoluble in water even though they are capable of ionizing.

51. **(B)**

The atomic weight of an element is the weighted average of the masses of all naturally occurring isotopes. This explains the occurrence of non-integral atomic weights. The mass of an atom's electrons are negligible and are thus omitted from the atomic weight calculation.

52. **(E)**

Using the standard half-cell voltages

$$Fe^{2+} + 2e^- \rightarrow Fe \qquad E° = -0.44\ V$$

$$\underline{Cu \rightarrow Cu^{2+} + 2e^- \qquad E° = -0.34\ V}$$

$$Fe^{2+} + Cu \rightarrow Cu^{2+} + Fe \qquad E° = -0.78\ V$$

we see that this reaction will not occur spontaneously. By examining the Nernst equation for the reaction $aA + bB \rightleftharpoons cC + dD$

$$E_{cell} = E°_{cell} - \frac{0.59}{n} \log \frac{[C]^c\ [D]^d}{[A]^a\ [B]^b}$$

where $n$ is the number of electrons we see that the reaction will occur if $[Fe^{2+}]$ is large. We determine the magnitude of $[Fe^{2+}]$ by solving the specific equation for this reaction

$$E_{cell} = E°_{cell} - \frac{0.59}{n} \log \frac{[Cu^{2+}]}{[Fe^{2+}]}$$

where $n = 2$ and $[Cu^{2+}] = 1$ (standard state)

The reaction will occur however if an electrical current is applied to the cell.

53. **(B)**

From the combined gas law

$$\frac{P_1 V_1}{T_1} = \frac{P_2 V_2}{T_2}$$

we obtain

$$P_2 = P_1 \times \frac{V_1}{V_2} \times \frac{T_2}{T_1}$$

Thus, we see that decreasing the volume ($V_1/V_2 > 1$) and maintaining the temperature increases the pressure. Decreasing the volume while increasing the temperature ($T_2/T_1 > 1$) also increases the pressure. Increasing $V$ by 1 liter and increasing $T$ by 1K at STP gives

$$P_2 = P_1 \times \frac{22.4}{23.4} \times \frac{274}{273} = 0.96 P_1$$

The pressure is decreased since for

$$\frac{P_2}{P_1} = 0.96 < 1.$$

54. **(D)**

The Arrhenius theory defines a base as a substance that gives hydroxide ions in aqueous solution. A base is defined as a proton acceptor by the Brønsted theory. This theory defines an acid as a proton donor. The Lewis theory defines an acid as an electron-pair acceptor and a base as an electron-pair donor.

55. **(C)**

$CO_2$ is an acid anhydride since an acid is produced upon reaction with water

$$CO_2\ (g) + H_2O \rightarrow H_2CO_3 \text{ (carbonic acid)}$$

56. **(E)**

$K_b$, the base dissociation constant, is defined as

$$K_b = \frac{[NH_4^+]\,[OH^-]}{[NH_3]}$$

Since $[OH^-] = 1.3 \times 10^{-3}$ we know that $[NH_4^+] = 1.3 \times 10^{-3}$ and that the original concentration of $NH_4OH$ is $0.1\ M$. Substituting values we obtain

$$K_b = \frac{(1.3 \times 10^{-3})(1.3 \times 10^{-3})}{(0.1 - 1.3 \times 10^{-3})} = \frac{1.69 \times 10^{-6}}{0.0987}$$

$$K_b = 1.7 \times 10^{-5}$$

57. **(D)**

The percent dissociation is given by

$$\frac{[OH^-]_{equilibium}}{[NH_3]_{initial}} \times 100\% = \frac{1.3 \times 10^{-3}}{0.1} \times 100\% = 1.3\%$$

58. **(B)**

A solution with pH of 11 has $[H^+] = 1 \times 10^{-11}$ by the equation $pH = -\log[H^+]$. Recalling that $K_w = [H^+][OH^-] = 10^{-14}$ we have

$$[OH^-] = \frac{K_w}{[H^+]} = \frac{10^{-14}}{[H^+]} = \frac{10^{-14}}{10^{-11}} = 10^{-3}$$

59. **(C)**

The pH of a solution is defined as

$$pH = -\log[H^+]$$

Solving for $[H^+]$, we obtain

$$[H^+] = 10^{-pH} = 10^{-2}$$

Nitric acid is assumed to dissociate completely in solution since it is a strong acid. In addition, nitric acid has only one proton so the concentration of hydronium ions is equal to the initial concentration of $HNO_3$. We are working with one liter of solution so the concentration is identical to the number of moles by

$$M = \frac{number\ of\ moles\ of\ solute}{liters\ of\ solution}$$

Thus we require $10^{-2}$ mole of $HNO_3$. Converting to grams:

$$10^{-2}\ mole\ of\ HNO_3 \times \frac{63\ g\ of\ HNO_3}{1\ mole\ of\ HNO_3} = 6.3\ g\ of\ HNO_3$$

60. **(B)**

One mole of NaOH has a weight of 40 g. We may determine that 40 g is 20% of 200 g from:

$$40 = (0.2)x$$

$$x = 200$$

Thus, we require 200 − 40 = 160 g of solvent. This condition is satisfied by water since it has a density of 1 g/cm$^3$ but not by acetone, ammonia, or carbon tetrachloride.

61. **(C)**

Converting the given quantities to moles:

$$98 \text{ g of } H_2SO_4 \times \frac{1 \text{ mole of } H_2SO_4}{98 \text{ g of } H_2SO_4} = 1 \text{ mole of } H_2SO_4$$

$$40 \text{ g of NaOH} \times \frac{1 \text{ mole of NaOH}}{40 \text{ g of NaOH}} = 1 \text{ mole of NaOH}$$

The reaction in question is

$$H_2SO_4 + 2NaOH \rightarrow Na_2SO_4 + 2H_2O$$

This shows that one mole of sulfuric acid reacts with two moles of sodium hydroxide to produce one mole of sodium sulfate. Since we only have one mole of sodium hydroxide, 0.5 mole of sulfuric acid reacts with it to produce 0.5 mole of sodium sulfate. Converting to grams:

$$0.5 \text{ mole of sodium sulfate} \times \frac{142 \text{ g of sodium sulfate}}{1 \text{ mole of sodium sulfate}}$$

$$= 71 \text{ g of sodium sulfate}$$

62. **(D)**

Using the formula $M_1V_1 = M_2V_2$ and rearranging we obtain

$$M_2 = \frac{M_1V_1}{V_2} = \frac{(6M)(30 \text{ mL})}{20 \text{ mL}} = 9M \text{ NaOH}$$

63. **(D)**

Molarity is defined as the number of moles of solute divided by the number of liters of solution. Thus,

$$M = \frac{\text{moles of solute}}{\text{liters of solution}}$$

Rearranging,

$$\text{moles of solute} = (M)\,(\text{liters of solution})$$
$$= (2)\,(1)$$
$$= 2$$

Converting to grams:

$$2 \text{ moles of NaOH} \times \frac{40 \text{ g of NaOH}}{1 \text{ mole of NaOH}} = 80 \text{ g of NaOH}$$

64. **(B)**

This setup is used to prepare gases such as $Cl_2$ and HCl which are heavier than air.

65. **(D)**

Ammonia could not be produced effectively with this setup since it is lighter than air and therefore would not be capable of displacing air from the first collection jar. NaCl is not a gas.

66. **(A)**

This setup is most effective in producing and collecting gases which are lighter than air and soluble in water.

67. **(E)**

The reaction is

$$2NH_4Cl \; (s) + Ca(OH)_2 \; (s) \rightarrow CaCl_2 + 2H_2O \; (g) + 2NH_3 \; (g)$$

68. **(B)**

The reaction in question is

$$2H_2 + O_2 \rightarrow 2H_2O$$

Converting the given quantities to moles:

$$8 \text{ g of } H_2 \times \frac{1 \text{ mole of } H_2}{2 \text{ g of } H_2} = 4 \text{ moles of } H_2$$

$$8 \text{ g of } O_2 \times \frac{1 \text{ mole of } O_2}{32 \text{ g of } O_2} = 0.25 \text{ mole of } O_2$$

Oxygen is the limiting reactant in this reaction. Multiplying all coefficients by 0.25 in order to obtain 0.25 $O_2$ we have

$$0.5H_2 + 0.25O_2 \rightarrow 0.5H_2O$$

Converting to grams:

$$0.5 \text{ mole of } H_2O \times \frac{18 \text{ g of } H_2O}{1 \text{ mole of } H_2O} = 9 \text{ g of } H_2O$$

69. **(C)**

The number of atoms in this compound is:

$$2(Na) + 1(C) + 3(O) + 20(H) + 10(O) = 36$$

# PRACTICE
# TEST 4

# SAT Chemistry
# Practice Test 4

**(Answer sheets appear in the back of this book.)**

## PART A

**TIME:**    1 Hour
            85 Questions

**DIRECTIONS**: Each set of questions below consists of five lettered choices followed by a list of numbered statements or questions. For each statement or question, select the answer choice that is most closely related to it. Each answer choice may be used once, more than once, or not at all.

*Note:* **For all questions involving solutions, assume that the solvent is water unless otherwise noted.**

**Questions 1–3** refer to the following number choices.

(A)  0          (D)  3

(B)  1          (E)  4

(C)  2

1.  Number of bonds predicted for $O_2$

2.  Number of bonds predicted for $N_2$

3.  Number of bonds predicted for $He_2$

**Questions 4–6** refer to the following electrochemical reaction.

In a $Zn \mid Zn^{2+} \parallel Cu^{2+} \mid Cu$ voltaic cell:

(A)  Zn $(s)$                    (D)  Cu $(s)$

(B)  $Cu^{2+}$ $(aq)$            (E)  $H_2O$

(C)  $Zn^{2+}$ $(aq)$

4.  Acts as the anode.

5.  Acts as the cathode.

6.  Is reduced.

**Questions 7–11** refer to the following:

Which group would the underlined element in the following compounds represent?

(A)  Group IA                    (D)  Group VIA

(B)  Group IIA                   (E)  Group VIIA

(C)  Group IIIA

7.  ____$_3(PO_4)_2$

8.  ____$_2O$ (oxidation state of oxygen is –2)

9.  Cu____$_2$

10.  Represented by the Lewis dot structure $\overset{\bullet}{\underset{\bullet}{X}} \bullet$

11.  Good reducing agents

**Questions 12–14** refer to the following equations.

(A)  $\pi = MRT$                 (D)  $C_g = KP_g$

(B)  $\Delta T_f = K_f m$        (E)  $P_A + P_B + P_C = P_T$

(C)  $P_1 = X_1 P_1^{\circ}$

12.  Equation which describes the lowering of the freezing point of a solution of a non-volatile solution as compared to the pure solvent.

13.  Equation which describes the relationship of osmotic pressure to solute concentration.

14.  Equation which describes the relationship between solvent vapor pressure and solute concentration.

**Questions 15–17** refer to the following compounds.

    (A) $BeF_2$             (D) $CH_2CH_2$

    (B) $BF_3$              (E) $CCl_4$

    (C) $CH_4$

15. Has $sp^2$ hybridized orbitals.

16. Has $sp$ hybridized orbitals.

17. Contains a *pi* bond.

**Questions 18–20** refer to the following methods.

    (A) Titration          (D) Spectrophotometry

    (B) Chromatography     (E) X-ray crystallography

    (C) Calorimetry

18. Used to separate pure substances out of mixtures

19. Used to determine the atomic structure of molecules

20. Used to measure heat changes that coincide with physical and chemical changes

**Questions 21–23** refer to the following conditions.

    (A) Gas at room temperature and pressure

    (B) Liquid at room temperature and pressure

    (C) Solid at room temperature and pressure

    (D) Does not ordinarily exist at room temperature and pressure

    (E) At equilibrium between two phases at room temperature and pressure

21. Hg

22. $CH_4$

23. $Cl_2$

# PART B

---

**DIRECTIONS:** Each question below consists of two Statements. Determine if Statement I is true or false and if Statement II is true or false and fill in the corresponding oval on your answer sheet. Fill in oval CE if Statement II is a correct explanation of the true Statement I.

---

| (I) | | (II) |
|---|---|---|
| 101. All matter is composed of small particles called atoms | *because* | these atoms suffer no loss of energy when they collide with each other. |
| 102. An electron cannot be described exactly | *because* | its position and momentum cannot be determined simultaneously. |
| 103. Benzene does not have true single and double bonds between its carbon atoms in the ring | *because* | of delocalized *pi* electrons in the ring giving rise to resonance structures. |
| 104. The alkali metals are extremely powerful oxidizing agents | *because* | the one electron in their valence shell is easily lost. |
| 105. Sulfur dioxide is used to bleach paper products | *because* | it oxidizes the colored material present. |
| 106. Paper chromatography may not be used to separate solutions of transition metal ions but it may be for other metals | *because* | the transition metals have electrons that occupy *d*-shells. |
| 107. The chemical behavior of nitrogen atoms is different from that of helium atoms | *because* | atoms of different elements have different properties. |

108. A proton is lighter (in mass) than an electron        *because*   an electron carries a negative charge and a proton does not.

109. One mole of carbon contains Avogadro's number ($6.023 \times 10^{23}$) of atoms whereas one mole of hydrogen does not        *because*   hydrogen is lighter and therefore one mole must contain a smaller number of atoms.

110. Enthalpy ($H$) is known as a state property        *because*   its magnitude is dependent both upon the state of a substance as well as the path it took to get there.

111. Heat flowing into a reaction lowers its enthalpy        *because*   $\Delta H$ is <0 in this situation.

112. A spontaneous redox reaction must have a negative voltage        *because*   a spontaneous reaction has a negative $\Delta G$.

113. The reaction is a beta emission reaction        *because*   a beta particle has mass $\cong$ 0 and charge = +1.

114. $H_2SO_4$ is a stronger acid than $HNO_3$        *because*   $H_2SO_4$ has more protons than $HNO_3$.

115. NaCl(*s*) is soluble in water        *because*   it is an ionic compound.

116. $He_2$ is not known to commonly form        *because*   He is lighter than air.

# PART C

---

**DIRECTIONS:** For each question in this section, select the best answer from among the given choices and fill in the corresponding oval on the answer sheet.

---

24. A change of phase is never accompanied by

    (A) a change in volume     (D) a change in density

    (B) a change in pressure     (E) a change in structure

    (C) a change in temperature

25. Baking soda is best described as

    (A) an element

    (B) a compound

    (C) a homogeneous mixture

    (D) a heterogeneous mixture

    (E) an aggregate of homogeneous mixtures.

26. A molecule may be described as

    (A) an element

    (B) an atom

    (C) protons and electrons

    (D) an aggregate of elements, each with different properties

    (E) the smallest unit of a substance that retains that compound's properties

27. The relation $P_1V_1 = P_2V_2$ is known as

    (A) Boyle's Law     (D) the combined gas law

    (B) Charles' Law     (E) the ideal gas law

    (C) Van der Waals' Law

28. Which of the following indicates a basic solution?

    (A) $[H^+] > 10^{-7}$          (D) $pH = 7$

    (B) $[OH^-] < 10^{-4}$          (E) $pH = 9$

    (C) $pH = 5$

29. Which of the following is incorrect?

    (A) 1 liter = 1,000 $cm^3$          (D) 1 liter = 1 $meter^3$

    (B) 1 meter = 100 cm          (E) 1 milliliter = $10^{-6}$ $meter^3$

    (C) 1 milliliter = 1 $cm^3$

30. The number of electrons in sulfur atom associated with the primary quantum number, $n = 3$, is

    (A) 2          (D) 8

    (B) 4          (E) 16

    (C) 6

31. Amphoteric substances are best described as

    (A) having the same number of protons and electrons but different numbers of neutrons

    (B) having the same composition but occurring in different molecular structures

    (C) being without definite shape

    (D) having both acid and base properties

    (E) having the same composition but occurring in different crystalline form

32. The oxidizing agent in the reaction

    $$Pb + HgSO_4 \rightarrow PbSO_4 + Hg$$

    is

    (A) Pb          (D) $Hg^0$

    (B) $PbSO_4$          (E) $SO_4^{2-}$

    (C) $Hg^{+2}$

33. The ratio of the rates of effusion of oxygen to hydrogen is

    (A) 1:2            (D) 1:16

    (B) 1:4            (E) 1:32

    (C) 1:8

34. Standard conditions using a Kelvin thermometer are

    (A) 760 torr, 273 K           (D) 0 torr, 0 K

    (B) 760 torr, 273 K, 1 liter  (E) 0 torr, 273 K, 1 liter

    (C) 760 torr, 0 K

35. What is the resulting volume if 10 liters of a gas at 546 K and 2 atm is brought to standard conditions?

    (A) 5 liters       (D) 20 liters

    (B) 10 liters      (E) 25 liters

    (C) 15 liters

36. How many grams of $C_6H_{12}O_6$ need to be dissolved in water to make 2.0 L of a 2.0 $M$ solution?

    (A) 90             (D) 720

    (B) 180            (E) 360

    (C) 270

37. Which of the following occurs when a sample of sodium is added to water?

    (A) The solution changes color.

    (B) The solution becomes acidic.

    (C) A gas is evolved.

    (D) Phenolphthalein indicator remains colorless.

    (E) It forms a precipitate.

38. The electrolysis of 34 g of ammonia has a theoretical yield of

(A) 14 g of $N_2$, 6 g of $H_2$      (D) 14 g of $N_2$, 3 g of $H_2$

(B) 14 g of N, 3 g of H      (E) 28 g of $N_2$, 6 g of $H_2$

(C) 28 g of N, 6 g of H

39. Which of the following is an example of a gas dissolved in a liquid?

(A) shaving cream      (D) silicon chip

(B) aerosol room freshener      (E) coffee

(C) toothpaste

40. The Fahrenheit temperature corresponding to 303 K is

(A) −15 °F      (D) 86 °F

(B) 22 °F      (E) 1,069 °F

(C) 49 °F

41. What is the density of bromine vapor at STP?

(A) 2.5 g/L      (D) 4.9 g/L

(B) 2.9 g/L      (E) 7.1 g/L

(C) 3.6 g/L

42. The relation between the pressure and volume of a gas at constant temperature is given by

(A) Boyle's Law      (D) the ideal gas law

(B) Charles' Law      (E) conservation of energy

(C) the combined gas law

43. The relation between the absolute temperature and volume of a gas at constant pressure is given by

(A) Boyle's Law      (D) the ideal gas law

(B) Charles' Law      (E) conservation of energy

(C) the combined gas law

44. The relation between the pressure, volume, and absolute temperature is given by

   (A) Boyle's Law
   (B) Charles' Law
   (C) the combined gas law
   (D) the ideal gas law
   (E) conservation of energy

45. Which of the following would produce an aqueous solution that most easily conducts electricity?

   (A) cyclohexane
   (B) hydrochloric acid
   (C) benzene
   (D) sucrose
   (E) acetic acid

46. Which of the following describe water?

   I.   Universal solvent

   II.  Polar molecule

   III. Good electrical conductor

   (A) I only
   (B) I and II only
   (C) II and III only
   (D) III only
   (E) I, II and III

47. Which of the following are correct?

   I.   $NaNO_2 + H_2SO_4 \rightarrow$ no fumes

   II.  $Co(NO_3)_2 + Zn \rightarrow$ yellow color

   III. $Ni + H_2S \rightarrow$ black precipitate

   (A) I only
   (B) II and III only
   (C) II only
   (D) I, II and III
   (E) III only

48. Which of the following exhibit hydrogen bonding?

    I.   $NH_3$

    II.   $CH_4$

    III.  $BH_3$

(A) II and III only        (D) I only

(B) II only             (E) I, II and III

(C) I and III only

49. $6.02 \times 10^{23}$ molecules of $H_2O$ is identical to which of the following?

    I.   1 mole of hydrogen atoms

    II.  1 mole of $H_2O$

    III. 18 g of $H_2O$

(A) I only             (D) I and III only

(B) II only             (E) I, II and III

(C) II and III only

50. Which of the following should be reacted with sodium hydroxide to produce sodium chlorite?

(A) $Cl_2$             (D) $HClO_2$

(B) HCl            (E) $HClO_3$

(C) HClO

51. Which of the following elements can form bonds with $sp^3$ hybridization?

(A) sodium         (D) oxygen

(B) nitrogen       (E) fluorine

(C) carbon

52. The yield of AB $(g)$

$$A\ (g) + B\ (g) \rightleftharpoons AB\ (g) + heat$$

would be increased by

(A) decreasing the pressure

(B) adding additional AB to the reaction mixture

(C) decreasing the temperature

(D) adding a nonreactive liquid to the reaction mixture

(E) decreasing the volume of the reaction container

53. The functional group shown below represents

$$O$$
$$||$$
$$R - C - H$$

(A) an alcohol

(D) a ketone

(B) an ether

(E) an organic acid derivative

(C) an aldehyde

54. How many grams of $CH_4$ are required to produce 425.6 kcal of heat by the reaction below?

$$CH_4 + 2O_2 \rightarrow CO_2 + 2H_2O + 212.8 \text{ kcal}$$

(A) 8 g

(D) 32 g

(B) 16 g

(E) 64 g

(C) 24 g

55. All of the following are spontaneous reactions EXCEPT:

| | | | | |
|---|---|---|---|---|
| $Co^{+2} + 2e^- \rightarrow Co$; | $E° = -0.28\ V$ | | $Sn^{+2} + 2e^- \rightarrow Sn$; | $E° = -0.14\ V$ |
| $Zn^{+2} + 2e^- \rightarrow Zn$; | $E° = -0.76\ V$ | | $Fe^{+2} + 2e^- \rightarrow Fe$; | $E° = -0.44\ V$ |
| $Mg^{+2} + 2e^- \rightarrow Mg$; | $E° = -2.37\ V$ | | $F_2 + 2e^- \rightarrow 2F^-$; | $E° = +2.87\ V$ |
| $Cn^{+2} + 2e^- \rightarrow Mn$; | $E° = -1.18\ V$ | | $Li^+ + e^- \rightarrow Li$; | $E° = -3.00\ V$ |
| $2\ (Ag^+ + e^- \rightarrow Ag)$ | $E° = +0.80\ V$ | | | |

(A) $Co^{2+} + Zn \rightarrow Zn^{2+} + Co$   (D) $Sn^{2+} + Fe \rightarrow Fe^{2+} + Sn$

(B) $Mg^{2+} + Mn \rightarrow Mn^{2+} + Mg$   (E) $F_2 + 2Li \rightarrow 2Li^+ + 2F^-$

(C) $2Ag^+ + H_2 \rightarrow 2H^+ + 2Ag$

56. How many faradays of charge are required to electroplate 127 g of copper from a cuprous chloride solution?

(A) 1    (D) 6
(B) 2    (E) 8
(C) 4

57. What is $X$ in the reaction $X + {}^1_0n \rightarrow {}^{14}_6C + {}^1_1H$ ?

(A) ${}^{15}_7O$    (D) ${}^{17}_9O$
(B) ${}^{15}_7N$    (E) ${}^{15}_9F$
(C) ${}^{17}_9H$

58. What is the molarity of a 10 mL solution in which 3.7 g of KCl are dissolved?

(A) 0.05 $M$    (D) 5 $M$
(B) 0.1 $M$    (E) 10 $M$
(C) 1 $M$

59. A 10% solution of $HNO_3$ would be produced by dissolving 63 g of $HNO_3$ in ___ ml of water.

(A) 100    (D) 630
(B) 300    (E) 1,000
(C) 567

60. A saturated solution of $KNO_3$ contains 63 g $KNO_3$ at 40 °C. If a solution at the same temperature is found to contain more than 63 g of $KNO_3$, but with no precipitation, then the solution is probably

(A) dilute    (D) saturated
(B) concentrated    (E) supersaturated
(C) unsaturated

61. Which of the following terms also describes this particular solution?

(A) dilute

(D) saturated

(B) concentrated

(E) supersaturated

(C) unsaturated

62. How many moles of ions are present in one liter of a 2 $M$ solution of NaCl?

(A) 0.2

(D) 4.0

(B) 1.0

(E) 8.0

(C) 2.0

63. An example of an acid salt is

(A) NaCl

(D) $MgCO_3$

(B) $Na_2SO_4$

(E) $Mg(HSO_4)_2$

(C) $NaHCO_3$

64. At a certain temperature and pressure, ice, water, and steam are found to coexist at equilibrium. This pressure and temperature corresponds to

(A) the critical temperature

(D) the triple point

(B) the critical pressure

(E) the freezing point

(C) the sublimation point

65. How many moles of ions are present in a saturated one liter solution of $BaSO_4$ ($K_{sp} = 1.1 \times 10^{-10}$)?

(A) $1 \times 10^{-10}$

(D) $1 \times 10^{-5}$

(B) $2 \times 10^{-10}$

(E) $2 \times 10^{-5}$

(C) $4 \times 10^{-10}$

66. What is the boiling point of an aqueous solution containing 117 g of NaCl in 1,000 g of $H_2O$?

   $K_b$ $(H_2O)$ = 0.52 °C · kg/mol

   (A)  98.96 °C          (D)  101.04 °C

   (B)  99.48 °C          (E)  102.08 °C

   (C)  100.52 °C

67. The high boiling point of water considering its low molecular weight could best be explained in terms of

   (A)  polar covalent bonding     (D)  Van der Waals' forces

   (B)  hydrogen bonding           (E)  London forces

   (C)  dipole attraction

68. What is the hydronium ion concentration of an HCl solution at pH of 3?

   (A)  0.001 $M$          (D)  0.3 $M$

   (B)  0.003 $M$          (E)  3 $M$

   (C)  0.1 $M$

69. How many grams of Na are present in 30 grams of NaOH?

   (A)  10 g              (D)  20 g

   (B)  15 g              (E)  22 g

   (C)  17 g

# SAT CHEMISTRY
# TEST 4

## ANSWER KEY

### PART A

| | | | | | | | |
|---|---|---|---|---|---|---|---|
| 1. | (C) | 7. | (B) | 13. | (A) | 19. | (E) |
| 2. | (D) | 8. | (A) | 14. | (C) | 20. | (C) |
| 3. | (A) | 9. | (E) | 15. | (B) | 21. | (B) |
| 4. | (A) | 10. | (C) | 16. | (A) | 22. | (A) |
| 5. | (D) | 11. | (A) | 17. | (D) | 23. | (A) |
| 6. | (B) | 12. | (B) | 18. | (B) | | |

### PART B

| | | | | | | | |
|---|---|---|---|---|---|---|---|
| 101. | T, T | 105. | T, F | 109. | F, F | 113. | T, F |
| 102. | T, T, CE | 106. | F, T | 110. | T, F | 114. | F, T |
| 103. | T, T, CE | 107. | T, T, CE | 111. | F, F | 115. | T, T |
| 104. | F, T | 108. | F, T | 112. | F, T | 116. | T, T |

### PART C

| | | | | | | | |
|---|---|---|---|---|---|---|---|
| 24. | (C) | 36. | (D) | 48. | (D) | 60. | (E) |
| 25. | (B) | 37. | (C) | 49. | (C) | 61. | (B) |
| 26. | (E) | 38. | (E) | 50. | (D) | 62. | (D) |
| 27. | (A) | 39. | (A) | 51. | (C) | 63. | (E) |
| 28. | (E) | 40. | (D) | 52. | (C) | 64. | (D) |
| 29. | (D) | 41. | (E) | 53. | (C) | 65. | (E) |
| 30. | (C) | 42. | (A) | 54. | (D) | 66. | (E) |
| 31. | (D) | 43. | (B) | 55. | (B) | 67. | (B) |
| 32. | (C) | 44. | (C) | 56. | (B) | 68. | (A) |
| 33. | (B) | 45. | (B) | 57. | (B) | 69. | (C) |
| 34. | (A) | 46. | (B) | 58. | (D) | | |
| 35. | (B) | 47. | (E) | 59. | (C) | | |

# DETAILED EXPLANATIONS
# OF ANSWERS
## TEST 4
## PART A

1.  **(C)**

    $O_2$ is considered to have 2 bonds, or a double bond. This can be predicted using the formula,

    number of bonds =

    $$\frac{\text{Number of electrons} - \text{number of electrons in}}{\text{in bonding orbitals} \quad \text{non-binding orbitals}}{2}$$

Using the idea of molecular bonding orbitals, oxygen has 8 electrons in bonding orbitals and 4 electrons in non-bonding orbitals. Thus $O_2$ will have 2 bonds.

2.  **(D)**

    Using the same formula as in #1 above, N having 8 electrons in bonding orbitals and 2 electrons in non-bonding orbitals, will cause $N_2$ to have 3 bonds, or a triple bond.

3.  **(A)**

    $He_2$ has 8 electrons in bonding orbitals and 8 electrons in non-bonding orbitals. This predicts that He will not form any bonds with itself. This is in general the case with the noble gases.

4.  **(A)**

5.  **(D)**

6.  **(B)**

Explanations for questions 4–6:

A voltaic cell, which is also known as a galvanic cell, is one in which a spontaneous oxidation-reduction reaction is used as a source of electrical energy. In the diagram below,

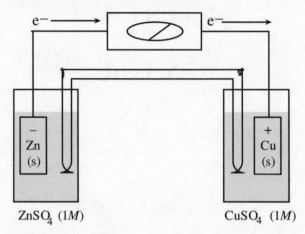

$$ZnSO_4 \ (1M) \qquad CuSO_4 \ (1M)$$

electrons are produced at the zinc anode, which is the negative electrode. The electrons are produced by their half reaction

$$Zn(s) \rightarrow Zn^{2+}(aq) + 2e^-.$$

Because $Zn(s)$ loses electrons, it is said to have been oxidized. The electrons travel through the wire at the top, and an electric current is created. This puts a positive charge at the copper cathode. The electrons then participate in the half reaction

$$Cu^{2+}(aq) + 2e^- \rightarrow Cu \ (s).$$

Because $Cu^{2+}$ gains electrons, it is said that it has been reduced. The circuit is completed by ions moving through the salt bridge.

7. **(B)**
The overall charge on a neutral molecule must be zero. Since the phosphate group has a charge of –3, we have an overall negative charge of –6 which must be divided between three cations each of charge +2. The elements of Group IIA are most likely to have this oxidation state.

8. **(A)**
The overall negative charge on the molecule is $1 \times (-2) = -2$. Thus, we must have an overall positive charge of +2 divided among two atoms. Group IA is most likely to exhibit a +1 oxidation state.

9. **(E)**

Copper usually has a +2 oxidation state but a +1 species also exists. However, since two anions are bonded to it, the copper must be +2 (a $-\frac{1}{2}$ oxidation state is not possible). Thus, each of the two anions must have an oxidation state of −1. This is seen to occur among the elements of Group VIIA.

10. **(C)**

The Lewis dot structure shows an element with three electrons in its valence shell. Thus, we must have an element representing Group IIIA.

11. **(A)**

A good reducing agent is easily oxidized. The elements of Group IA lose an electron most easily as seen by their small ionization energies.

12. **(B)**

The equation in choice (B) indicates that the change in the freezing point of a solution is directly proportional to the concentration of the solute. The more of a solute added to a solution, the lower the freezing point of the solution will be relative to that of the pure solvent.

13. **(A)**

The equation in choice (A) indicates that the osmotic pressure of a solution is proportional to the concentration of the solute and the temperature. Osmosis is the process by which a solvent, but not the solute, will pass through a membrane. Osmotic pressure, which is a colligative property, is the pressure which is sufficient to prevent this passage. The more solute there is in the solution, the greater will be the pressure which is needed to prevent osmosis.

14. **(C)**

This equation, known as Raoult's Law, states that the vapor pressure of a pure solution is directly proportional to the concentration of the solute. The more solute there is in a solution, the lower its vapor pressure will be compared to that of the pure solvent. Vapor pressure is also a colligative property because it depends only on concentration of the solute and not any property of solute. Choice (D) states that the solubility of a gas in a liquid is directly proportional to its partial pressure above the solution. Choice (E) is Dalton's Law that states that the total pressure of a gaseous system is equal to the sum of the pressures of its component parts.

15. **(B)**

$BF_3$ has $sp^2$ hybridized orbitals. This allows for three equivalent atomic bonding orbitals for each of the three F atoms attached to the B.

16. **(A)**

$BeF_2$ has $sp$ hybridized orbitals. This allows for two equivalent atomic bonding orbitals for both of the F atoms. Both $CCl_4$ and $CH_4$ have $sp^3$ hybridized orbitals.

17. **(D)**

$CH_2CH_2$ contains a *pi* bond. The two carbons are bonded by a double bond. One of these bonds is a *sigma* bond and the second is a *pi* bond, formed by the combination of two *p* orbitals which are not symmetric around the C-C axis. All of molecules in the other responses contain only *sigma* bonds.

18. **(B)**

Chromatography is a technique that is used to separate pure substances out of a mixture. There are various types of chromatography: gas, paper, column. Each involves a mobile phase and a stationary phase. In paper chromatography, a piece of paper acts as the stationary phase and a solvent acts as the mobile phase. Compounds are separated out by their differing adhesion to the paper and solubility in the solvent.

19. **(E)**

X-ray crystallography is used to determine the atomic structure of molecules. By measuring the way X-rays are diffracted from a solid crystal, information about the way atoms in the molecule are arranged may be deduced.

20. **(C)**

Calorimetry is used to measure heat changes that coincide with physical and chemical changes. A calorimeter is ideally used in a closed system in which heat can neither escape or enter and the only heat change measured comes from the reaction of interest.

21. **(B)**

Mercury is one of the only metals that is a liquid at room temperature and pressure.

22. **(A)**

Methane is commonly a gas at room temperature and pressure.

23. **(A)**

Chlorine is commonly a gas as well at room temperature and pressure. Many non-polar diatomic molecules, such as $N_2$, $Br_2$, and $O_2$, are gases at room temperature and pressure.

# PART B

101. **T, T**

Both the assertion and the reason are assumptions of the Kinetic-Molecular Theory but the reason does not explain the assertion.

102. **T, T, CE**

This is the theory of the Heisenberg Uncertainty Principle.

103. **T, T, CE**

Benzene does not have localized and alternating single and double bonds between its carbon atoms, but rather a delocalized electron cloud giving rise to resonance structures. This also gives great thermodynamical stability to the molecule.

104. **F, T**

The alkali metals are good reducing agents since they are easily oxidized (their one valence electron is easily removed).

105. **T, F**

Sulfur dioxide bleaches paper products by reducing the colored material. Yellowing of paper is due to the reoxidation of the colored material by the environment.

106. **F, T**

Paper chromatography *can* be used to separate and identify solutions of transition metals. While it is true that transition metals possess *d*-electrons, this in no way hinders chromatography as a tool where they are involved.

107. **T, T, CE**

Both statements are true and the second is a correct explanation of the first. This notion arises out of Dalton's Atomic Theory which contains three main tenets. The first, that matter is composed of very small particles called atoms; the second, that these atoms have different properties depending on the element to which they belong; the third, that when atoms of more than one element combine, compound substances are formed.

108. **F, T**

A proton is heavier than an electron. A proton weighs about the same as a hydrogen atom; electrons weigh much less. An electron does carry a negative charge, while a proton carries a positive charge, but this is not the reason for a proton being heavier.

109. **F, F**

A mole of any element or compound contains Avogadro's number of atoms or molecules. If an atom is lighter, one mole of it simply weighs less.

110. **T, F**

$H$ is a state property, but this means that its magnitude is dependent only upon the state of the substance and not how it got there.

111. **F, F**

When heat flows into a reaction it is known as endothermic. Enthalpy is said to increase when a reaction is endothermic and $\Delta H$ is therefore $> 0$.

112. **F, T**

A spontaneous reaction must have a positive voltage. The relation between free energy and voltage is $\Delta G = -nFE$.

113. **T, F**

A beta particle has mass $\cong 0$ and charge $= -1$. It arises when a neutron (of mass $= 1$ and charge $= 0$) is transformed to a proton (mass $= 1$ and charge $= +1$) at the surface of the nucleus.

114. **F, T**

$HNO_3$ is a stronger acid than $H_2SO_4$ by the oxyacid *m-n* rule. $HNO_3$ has a higher ratio of double bonded oxygens to OH than does $H_2SO_4$.

115. **T, T**

Ionic compounds are any that contain an element from the right side of the periodic table and another from the left. Ionic compounds are soluble in polar solvents such as water.

116. **T, T**

$He_2$ is not known to commonly form. While He is lighter than air, the reason it doesn't form $He_2$ is that He is a noble gas and has its outer electron shell filled. It, thus, has no need and is incapable of accepting or sharing another electron.

# PART C

24. **(C)**

Phase changes always occur at constant temperature (for example, water freezing to ice at $0°$ C). Changes in volume, pressure, and density usually occur during a phase change: consider a liquid vaporizing to a gas. In most cases the gas will exhibit a larger volume, a greater pressure, and a lower density. Changes in structure also occur as is obvious from the highly organized structure of ice as compared to the random orientations of water molecules in the vapor phase.

25. **(B)**

Baking soda (sodium bicarbonate) is an example of a compound since it is composed of a number of different elements in specified proportions. Mixtures are a conglomerate of individual compounds. Homogeneous mixtures (for example, solutions) result when the constituent compounds are evenly interspersed. Heterogeneous mixtures (granite) are indicated when the compounds present are unevenly interspersed.

26. **(E)**

A molecule is defined as the smallest unit of a compound that retains that compound's properties. A specific arrangement of protons and electrons defines an atom of a particular element while a specific aggregate of elements defines a compound.

27. **(A)**

Boyle's Law shows that the volume of a gas varies inversely with the pressure at constant temperature.

28. **(E)**

A basic (alkaline) solution is indicated by a hydronium ion concentration less than $10^{-7}$ or identically, pH > 7 since pH = $-\log[H^+]$.

29. **(D)**

The correct expression would be

$$1 \text{ liter} = 1,000 \text{ cm}^3 \times \left( \frac{1 \text{ m}}{100 \text{ cm}} \right)^3$$

$$1 \text{ liter} = 1,000 \text{ cm}^3 \times \frac{1 \text{ m}^3}{1 \times 10^6 \text{ cm}}$$

$$1 \text{ liter} = 1 \times 10^{-3} \text{ m}^3$$

30. **(C)**

The electronic configuration of sulfur is $1s^2\, 2s^2\, 2p^6\, 3s^2\, 3p^4$ as given by the periodic table. Thus, we have 2 electrons in the first energy level, 8 in the second, and 6 in the third.

31. **(D)**

An amphoteric substance has both acid and base properties. Isotopes of an element have the same number of protons and electrons but different numbers of neutrons.[1] Isomers of a compound are indicated by the same molecular formulas but different structures.[2] Amorphous substances are designated as having no definite shape.[3] Allotropes of a substance have the same composition but have different crystalline structures.[4]

[1]  (for example, $^{12}_{6}C$ and $^{13}_{6}C$)

[2]  (for example, 1-propanol and 2-propanol)

[3]  (for example, the product obtained when liquid sulfur is poured in water)

[4]  (for example, rhombic and monoclinic sulfur)

32. **(C)**

The oxidizing agent in the reaction is the reagent that gains electron oxidizing another element or compound in a redox reaction.

$$Pb + HgSO_4 \rightarrow PbSO_4 + Hg$$
$$\quad 0 \quad +2\ -2 \quad\ \ +2\ -2 \quad\ 0$$

We see that $Hg^{+2}$ served as an oxidizing agent by oxidizing Pb, while also becoming reduced.

33. **(B)**

Graham's law of effusion states that the rate of effusion of a gas is inversely proportional to the square root of its molecular weight. Thus, we have

$$\frac{\text{rate } O_2}{\text{rate } H_2} = \sqrt{\frac{\text{mol. wt. of } H_2}{\text{mol. wt. of } O_2}} = \sqrt{\frac{2}{32}} = \sqrt{\frac{1}{16}} = \frac{1}{4}$$

34. **(A)**

Standard conditions are 1 atm or 760 torr and 273 K or 0 °C.

35. **(B)**

Using the combined gas law

$$\frac{P_1 V_1}{T_1} = \frac{P_2 V_2}{T_2}, \text{ and knowing STP} = 273 \text{ K and 1 atm,}$$

and rearranging

$$V_2 = V_1 \times \frac{P_1}{P_2} \times \frac{T_2}{T_1}$$

we obtain

$$V_2 = 10 \text{ L} \times \frac{2 \text{ atm}}{1 \text{ atm}} \times \frac{273 \text{ K}}{546 \text{ K}}$$

$$V_2 = 10 \text{ L}$$

36. **(D)**

One mole of $C_6H_{12}O_6$ is 180 grams. The mass needed to make 2.0 liters of a 2.0 molar solution is 720 grams.

$$\text{Molarity } (M) = \frac{\text{moles of solute}}{\text{liters of solution}}$$

Substituting the given information and solving for moles of solute:

$$2M = \frac{\text{moles of solute}}{\text{2 L of solution}}$$

moles of solute = (2) (2) = 4

moles of solute = 4; thus we have 4 moles of $C_6H_{12}O_6$; each mole of $C_6H_{12}O_6$ is 180 grams, thus

$$4 \text{ moles of } C_6H_{12}O_6 = \frac{180 \text{ g of } C_6H_{12}O_6}{1 \text{ mole of } C_6H_{12}O_6} = 720 \text{ grams of } C_6H_{12}O_6$$

37. **(C)**
The reaction which occurs when sodium is added to water

$$2Na + 2H_2O \rightarrow 2NaOH + H_2$$

shows that a basic solution and a gas are the products. Phenolphthalein indicator is colorless in acidic solution and pink in basic solution. Thus, the solution remains colorless.

38. **(E)**
The electrolysis of ammonia gives:

$$2NH_3 \rightarrow N_2 + 3H_2$$

Converting to moles:

$$34 \text{ g of } NH_3 \times \frac{1 \text{ mole of } NH_3}{17 \text{ g of } NH_3} = 2 \text{ moles of } NH_3$$

We see that 2 moles of $NH_3$ are available to undergo electrolysis. From the reaction equation, the respective theoretical yields of $N_2$ and $H_2$ are 1 and 3 moles. Converting to grams

$$1 \text{ mole of } N_2 \times \frac{28 \text{ g of } N_2}{1 \text{ mole of } N_2} = 28 \text{ g of } N_2$$

$$3 \text{ moles of } H_2 \times \frac{2 \text{ g of } H_2}{1 \text{ mole of } H_2} = 6 \text{ g of } H_2$$

39. **(A)**
Shaving cream is an example of a gas dissolved in a liquid. Aerosol room freshener is a liquid using a gas as a dispersant. Toothpaste is an example of a solid dispersed in a viscous liquid.

40. **(D)**
Converting to the Celsius scale ($t = T - 273$) we have

$$t = 303 - 273 = 30\,°$$

Converting to the Fahrenheit scale:

$$°F = \frac{9}{5}\,(°C) + 32$$

$$°F = \frac{9}{5}\,(30) + 32$$

$$°F = 86$$

41. **(E)**
Since the volume of one mole of an ideal gas is 22.4 liters, we have

$$\frac{160 \text{ g of Br}_2}{1 \text{ mol of Br}_2} \times \frac{1 \text{ mol of Br}_2}{22.4 \text{ L}} = \frac{7.1 \text{ g of Br}_2}{\text{L}}$$

42. **(A)**
Boyle's Law states that the volume of a gas varies inversely with the pressure at constant temperature.

43. **(B)**
Charles' Law states that the volume of a gas varies directly with the absolute temperature at constant pressure.

44. **(C)**
The combined gas law is a combination of Boyle's Law and Charles' Law, taking the form

$$\frac{P_1 V_1}{T_1} = \frac{P_2 V_2}{T_2}$$

45. **(B)**
    The conductivity of a solution is directly related to the number of ions in solution. Hydrochloric acid, being a strong acid, dissociates completely while acetic acid, a weak acid, is only slightly dissociated. Cyclohexane, benzene, and sucrose are undissociated in solution.

46. **(B)**
    Water is known as the universal solvent since it is the most widely occurring in nature. It is a polar molecule due to oxygen's large electronegativity but it is a poor electrolyte since it is only barely dissociated ($[H^+][OH^-] = 10^{-14}$).

47. **(E)**
    All three of the reactions given are qualitative tests to indicate the presence of $NO_2^-$, Zn, and Ni, respectively. The reaction

$$Ni + H_2S \rightarrow NiS$$

results in the production of black nickel sulfide.

48. **(D)**
    Only compounds containing nitrogen, oxygen, or fluorine in addition to hydrogen exhibit hydrogen bonding, which refers to the attractive forces between one molecule and another. The geometry of $NH_3$ lends itself to hydrogen bonding.

49. **(C)**
    Avogadro's number of water molecules indicates 1 mole of water molecules which is equivalent to 18 grams of water. It also indicates 2 moles or 2 grams of hydrogen atoms and 1 mole or 16 grams of oxygen atoms.

50. **(D)**
    The nomenclature of salts is based upon the names of the acids used to produce them. This system is based upon the following rules: *-ic* acids form *-ate* salts, *-ous* acids form *-ite* salts, and *hydro- -ic* acids form *-ide* salts. Thus, in reacting with sodium hydroxide, HCl, hydrochloric acid, produces sodium chloride; HClO, hypochlorous acid, produces sodium hypochlorite; $HClO_2$, chlorous acid, produces sodium chlorite, and $HClO_3$, chloric acid, produces sodium chlorate.

51. **(C)**
    The element in question must be able to engage in four covalent bonds if it is to have $sp^3$ hybridization. The only element given which

fulfills this criteria is carbon (for example, in $CH_4$). Nitrogen may also form four bonds, as in $NH_4^+$, but one of these bonds is coordinate covalent, with nitrogen donating both bonding electrons.

52. **(C)**
According to Le Chatelier's Principle, if a stress is placed on an equilibrium system, the equilibrium is shifted in the direction which reduces the effect of that stress. This stress may be in the form of changes in pressure, temperature, concentrations, etc. By decreasing the pressure on the system, the system shifts in a direction so as to increase the pressure. For our reaction, the reverse reaction rate would increase since a larger volume (hence a greater pressure) results. This is due to the fact that two moles of gaseous product will result as opposed to one mole if the forward reaction were favored. Note that only gaseous products are accounted for when considering pressure effects. Adding AB to the reaction mixture would also serve to favor the reverse reaction since the system reacts to this stress by producing more A and B. Decreasing the temperature favors the forward reaction since heat (which will counteract the stress by increasing the temperature) is liberated in this process. The addition of a nonreactive liquid to the reaction mixture has no effect on the reaction rates (assuming pressure and temperature to remain constant). Decreasing the volume of the reaction mixture has the same effect as increasing the pressure (Boyle's Law) if temperature is constant.

53. **(C)**
The functional group of an alcohol is indicated by

$$R - OH;$$

that of an ether is

$$R - O - R^1;$$

an aldehyde is indicated by

$$\overset{\displaystyle O}{\overset{\displaystyle \|}{R - C - H}};$$

while that of a ketone is

$$\overset{\displaystyle O}{\overset{\displaystyle \|}{R - C - R^1}}$$

Derivatives of organic acids; esters, amides, and acid anhydrides for example, have the following functional groups:

carboxylic acid

$$
\begin{array}{c}
O \\
\parallel \\
R - C - OH
\end{array}
$$

ester

$$
\begin{array}{c}
O \\
\parallel \\
R - C - O - R^1
\end{array}
$$

amide

$$
\begin{array}{c}
O \\
\parallel \\
R - C - NH_2
\end{array}
$$

acid anhydride

$$
\begin{array}{c}
O \qquad\ O \\
\parallel \qquad \parallel \\
R - C - O - C - R^1
\end{array}
$$

54. **(D)**

The heat of combustion of methane is −212.8 kcal/mole according to the reaction equation. To determine how many grams of $CH_4$ are required to produce 425.6 kcal, we have

$$
-425.6 \text{ kcal} \times \frac{1 \text{ mol of } CH_4}{-212.8 \text{ kcal}} \times \frac{16 \text{ g of } CH_4}{1 \text{ mol of } CH_4} = 32 \text{ g of } CH_4
$$

Note the negative values used for $\Delta H_c$ to indicate that heat is evolved (exothermic) when methane undergoes combustion.

55. **(B)**

Using the standard electrode potentials and recalling that if the sum of the potentials is a positive value, the reaction is spontaneous and will run on its own while a negative value means that energy has to be supplied to make the reaction go:

$$Co^{2+} + 2e^- \rightarrow Co \qquad\qquad E^\circ_{red} = -0.28V$$

$$\underline{Zn \rightarrow Zn^{2+} + 2e^- \qquad\qquad E^\circ_{ox} = +0.76V}$$

$$Co^{2+} + Zn \rightarrow Zn^{2+} + Co \qquad E^\circ_{Redox} = +0.48V$$

$$Mg^{2+} + 2e^- \rightarrow Mg \qquad\qquad E^\circ_{red} = -2.37V$$

$$\underline{Mn \rightarrow Mn^{2+} + 2e^- \qquad\qquad E^\circ_{ox} = +1.18V}$$

$$Mg^{2+} + Mn \rightarrow Mn^{2+} + Mg \qquad E^\circ_{Redox} = -1.19V$$

$$2(Ag^+ + e^- \rightarrow Ag) \qquad\qquad E^\circ_{red} = +0.80V$$

$$\underline{H_2 \rightarrow 2H^+ + 2e^- \qquad\qquad E^\circ_{ox} = 0.00V}$$

$$2Ag^+ + H_2 \rightarrow 2H^+ + 2Ag \qquad E^\circ_{Redox} = +0.80V$$

$$Sn^{2+} + 2e^- \rightarrow Sn \qquad\qquad E^\circ_{red} = -0.14V$$

$$\underline{Fe \rightarrow Fe^{2+} + 2e^- \qquad\qquad E^\circ_{ox} = +0.44V}$$

$$Sn^{2+} + Fe \rightarrow Fe^{2+} + Sn \qquad E^\circ_{Redox} = +0.30V$$

$$F_2 + 2e^- \rightarrow 2F^- \qquad\qquad E^\circ_{red} = +2.87V$$

$$\underline{2(Li \rightarrow Li^+ + e^-) \qquad\qquad E^\circ_{ox} = +3.00V}$$

$$F_2 + 2Li \rightarrow 2Li^+ + 2F^- \qquad E^\circ_{Redox} = +5.87V$$

56. **(B)**

Using the following conversions and recalling that cuprous chloride is CuCl and cupric chloride is $CuCl_2$ we have

$$127 \text{ g of Cu} \times \frac{1 \text{ mol of Cu}}{63.5 \text{ g of Cu}} = 2 \text{ moles of Cu}$$

Since one faraday of charge corresponds to one mole of electrons we require

$$2 \text{ moles of Cu}^+ \times \frac{1 \text{ mole of electrons}}{1 \text{ mole of Cu}^+ \rightarrow Cu} = 2 \text{ moles of electrons}$$

$$= 2 \text{ faradays}$$

57. **(B)**
The total number of protons and neutrons of the products must equal that of the reactants. Summing the number of protons and the atomic masses of the products we have $6 + 1 = 7$ protons and an atomic mass of $14 + 1 = 15$. Subtracting $_0^1 n$, we have $_7^{15}X$. The atomic number 7 corresponds to nitrogen, so we have $_7^{15}N$.

58. **(D)**
Converting to moles:

$$37 \text{ g of KCl} \times \frac{1 \text{ mol of KCl}}{74 \text{ g of KCl}} = 0.05 \text{ mol of KCl}$$

Converting to liters of solution:

$$10 \text{ mL} \times \frac{1 \text{ L}}{1{,}000 \text{ mL}} = 0.01 \text{ L of solution}$$

Molarity is defined as the number of moles of solute dissolved in one liter of solution. Thus,

$$M = \frac{0.05 \text{ mole of KCl}}{0.01 \text{ liter of solution}} = 5$$

59. **(C)**
Percent solutions are based on the mass of the solute rather than the number of moles. Since a 10% solution is produced with 63 g of $HNO_3$, we know that $10(10\%) = 100\%$ of the solution has a mass of $10(63 \text{ g}) = 630$ g. This gives the mass of the water as $630 - 63 = 567$ g. Using the density of water: $d = 1 \text{ g/cm}^3$ and the conversion factor

$$1 \text{ mL} = 1 \text{ cm}^3$$

we have

$$567 \text{ g of H}_2\text{O} = \frac{1 \text{ cm}^3}{1 \text{ g}} = \frac{1 \text{ mL}}{1 \text{ cm}^3} = 567 \text{ mL of H}_2\text{O}$$

60. **(E)**

Converting to grams

$$1.3 \text{ mol of KNO}_3 \times \frac{101 \text{ g of KNO}_3}{1 \text{ mol of KNO}_3} = 131 \text{ g of KNO}_3$$

A solution that contains more solute than necessary for saturation but without precipitation is an example of supersaturation.

61. **(B)**

A less specific term to describe this solution is concentrated since a large amount of $KNO_3$ is dissolved.

62. **(D)**

One liter of a 2 *M* solution contains two moles of solute. Sodium chloride dissociates completely to $Na^+$ and $Cl^-$ ions so a 2 *M* sodium chloride solution contains two moles of $Na^+$ and two moles of $Cl^-$ for a total of four moles of ions.

63. **(E)**

An acid salt yields an acidic solution upon hydrolysis.

$$NaCl + H_2O \rightarrow HCl + NaOH$$

The solution produced by NaCl is neutral since HCl is a strong acid and NaOH is a strong base.

$$Na_2SO_4 + 2H_2O \rightarrow H_2SO_4 + 2NaOH$$

This is also a neutral solution since $H_2SO_4$ is a strong acid.

$$NaHCO_3 + H_2O \rightarrow H_2CO_3 + NaOH$$

A basic solution is produced by hydrolysis of $NaHCO_3$ since $H_2CO_3$ is a weak acid. Therefore $NaHCO_3$ is a basic salt.

$$MgCO_3 + 2H_2O \rightarrow H_2CO_3 + Mg(OH)_2$$

This solution is approximately neutral since $Mg(OH)_2$ is a weak base (slightly soluble only in acid solution).

$$Mg(HSO_4)_2 + 2H_2O \rightarrow H_2SO_4 + Mg(OH)_2$$

$Mg(HSO_4)_2$ is an acid salt since hydrolysis produces a strong acid and a weak base.

64. **(D)**

The existence of all three phases at equilibrium occurs at a temperature and pressure pair known as the triple point. The critical temperature refers to the temperature above which a liquid cannot exist regardless of the pressure applied.

65. **(E)**

The solubility product of $BaSO_4$ is given by

$$K_{sp} = [Ba^{2+}] [SO_4^{2-}] = 1.1 \times 10^{-10}$$

where $[Ba^{2+}]$ and $[SO_4^{2-}]$ are the concentrations of $Ba^{2+}$ and $SO_4^{2-}$ in solution, respectively. It is necessary, stoichiometrically, that $[Ba^{2+}] = [SO_4^-]$ so if we let $x = [Ba^{2+}] = [SO_4^{2-}]$, we have

$$K_{sp} = x^2 = 1.1 \times 10^{-10}$$

and $\quad x = \sqrt{1.1 \times 10^{-10}} = 1 \times 10^{-5}$

The total number of ions present in a saturated one liter solution is given by the sum of the concentrations of the individual species present. Note that this is true only if the solution is of one liter volume. Since the molarity is the number of moles per liter of total solution, then for one liter of total solution, the total number of ions is given by:

$$[Ba^{2+}] + [SO_4^{2-}] = 1 \times 10^{-5} + 1 \times 10^{-5} = 2 \times 10^{-5}$$

66. **(E)**

Converting to moles:

$$117 \text{ g of NaCl} \times \frac{1 \text{ mol of NaCl}}{58.5 \text{ g of NaCl}} = 2 \text{ mol of NaCl}$$

The molality of a solution is defined as the number of moles of dissolved solute per 1,000g of solvent. Therefore the molality of the solution is 2 $m$ in NaCl. However, since NaCl dissociates completely to $Na^+$ and $Cl^-$, the molality of the solution is 4 $m$ in particles. It has been found that a 1 $m$ aqueous solution freezes at $-1.86$ °C and boils at 100.52 °C, a change of $-1.86$ °C and $+0.52$ °C, respectively. Thus, the boiling point increase for a 4 $m$ solution (since boiling point elevation is a colligative property) is

$$4 \, m \times \frac{0.52 \text{ °C}}{1 \, m} = 2.08 \text{ °C}$$

Therefore, the boiling point of the solution is

$$100 \text{ °C} + 2.08 \text{ °C} = 102.08 \text{ °C}$$

67. **(B)**

The abnormally high boiling point of water is due to hydrogen bonding. This mutual attraction between the hydrogens of one water molecule and the oxygen of another water molecule represent a significant attractive force that must be overcome if water is to be converted to steam.

68. **(A)**

The pH of a solution is defined as

$$pH = -\log[H^+]$$

where $[H^+]$ is the hydronium ion concentration. Rearranging this equation, we obtain

$$[H^+] = 10^{-pH}$$

Substituting the given pH, we have $[H^+] = 10^{-3} = 0.001$.

69. **(C)**

We find that there are 23 g of sodium (its atomic weight) in 40g of NaOH (its formula weight). Using this as a conversion factor

$$30 \text{ g of NaOH} \times \frac{23 \text{ g of Na}}{40 \text{ g of NaOH}} = 17 \text{ g of Na}$$

Another method for determining this quantity is to convert 30 g of NaOH to moles

$$30 \text{ g of NaOH} \times \frac{1 \text{ mol of NaOH}}{40 \text{ g of NaOH}} = 0.75 \text{ mol of NaOH}$$

and calculating the weight of sodium corresponding to 0.75 mole

$$0.75 \text{ mol of Na} \times \frac{23 \text{ g of NaOH}}{1 \text{ mol of NaOH}} = 17 \text{ g of Na}$$

since one mole of Na is present in one mole of NaOH.

# PRACTICE
# TEST 5

# SAT Chemistry
# Practice Test 5

**(Answer sheets appear in the back of this book.)**

## PART A

**TIME:**    1 Hour
             85 Questions

**DIRECTIONS**: Each set of questions below consists of five lettered choices followed by a list of numbered statements or questions. For each statement or question, select the answer choice that is most closely related to it. Each answer choice may be used once, more than once, or not at all.

*Note:* **For all questions involving solutions, assume that the solvent is water unless otherwise noted.**

**Questions 1–4** refer to the following graph.

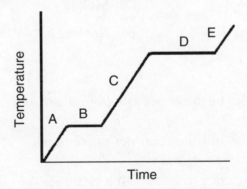

1.    Which region indicates the material is entirely solid?

2.    Which region indicates the material is entirely liquid?

3.    Which region indicates the material is entirely gas?

4.    Which region indicates the material is a combination of liquid and a gas?

**Questions 5–7** refer to the following diagram.

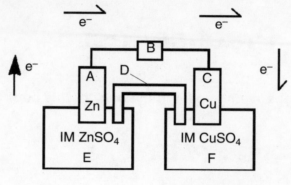

(A) A

(B) C

(C) A and F

(D) C and E

(E) E and F

5.  Which region is the anode?

6.  Which region is responsible for maintaining electrical neutrality?

7.  Which region(s) is(are) eventually depleted by the cell reaction?

**Questions 8 and 9** refer to the following terms.

(A) Molarity

(B) Mass percent

(C) Density

(D) Molality

(E) Normality

8.  Is defined as moles of solute per kilogram of solvent

9.  Is defined as moles of solute per liter of solution

**Questions 10 and 11** refer to the following elements.

(A) O

(B) Na

(C) S

(D) B

(E) Sr

10.  Is the most electronegative of the atoms listed

11. Has the electron configuration $1s^2 2s^2 2p^4$

**Questions 12–14** refers to the equation NaCl $(s) \rightarrow$ Cl$^-$ $(g)$ + Na$^+$ $(s)$.

    (A) the concentration of Cl$^-$ will decrease

    (B) more NaCl $(s)$ will dissolve

    (C) the concentration of Cl$^-$ will be increased

    (D) the concentration of Na$^+$ will be increased

    (E) the equilibrium will remain where it is

12. If additional NaCl $(s)$ is added to the system

13. If Na$^+$ is removed from the system

14. If solid lead chloride is added to the system

**Questions 15–17** refer to the reaction and rate data below:

    A $(g)$ + B $(g) \rightarrow$ products

| Experiment | Conc. of A (in mol/lit) | Conc. of B (in mol/lit) | initial rate (in mol/lit sec) |
|:---:|:---:|:---:|:---:|
| 1 | .060 | .010 | 0.040 |
| 2 | .030 | .010 | 0.040 |
| 3 | .030 | .020 | 0.080 |

    (A) 0           (D) 3

    (B) 1           (E) 4

    (C) 2

15. What is the order with respect to A?

16. What is the order with respect to B?

17. What is the rate constant (in liter/mole sec)?

**Questions 18–20** refer to the following species.

(A) $_4^2\text{He}$

(D) $_1^0\text{e}$

(B) $_0^1\text{n}$

(E) $\text{H}^+$

(C) $_{-1}^0\text{e}$

18. A beta particle

19. A positron

20. An electron

**Questions 21–23** refer to the illustrations below.

(A)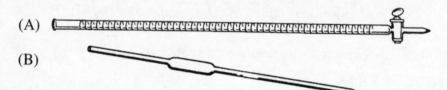

(B)

(C)

(D)

(E)

21. Erhlenmeyer flask

22. Florence flask

23. Buret

# PART B

**DIRECTIONS:** Each question below consists of two statements. Determine if Statement I is true or false and if Statement II is true or false and fill in the corresponding ovals on your answer sheet. Fill in oval CE if Statement II is a correct explanation of the true Statement I.

|  (I)  |  | (II) |
|---|---|---|

101. Elements along the heavy line in the periodic table are amphoteric     *because*     they have both acid and base properties.

102. A highly exothermic reaction is not easily reversed     *because*     a large amount of energy is required.

103. Elements in a group have similar properties     *because*     their valence shells have the same energy.

104. $AgCl$ is more soluble in $0.1\,M$ $NaCl$ than in pure water     *because*     of the common ion effect.

105. Equilibrium is characterized by constant reactant and product concentrations     *because*     the forward and reverse reaction rates have decreased.

106. Brownian motion is observed to occur in suspensions     *because*     solvent molecules interact electronically with the suspension particles.

107. The reaction of $CaCO_3$ with HCl is favored by increased pressure     *because*     a gas is evolved by the reaction.

108. Increasing the pressure    *because*    a system subjected
     for the reaction                        to a stress will shift in a
     $2H_2(g) + O_2(g) \rightleftharpoons 2H_2O(g)$    direction so as to relieve
     will result in a greater amount          that stress.
     of product being formed

109. A calorimeter can          *because*    a calorimeter allows
     be used to measure                      any heat produced or
     the amount of heat                      absorbed in a reaction to
     lost or absorbed in                     escape into the
     a process                               surroundings.

110. At a particular temperature    *because*    in a gas the distances
     it is easier to compress a                  between molecules
     gas than a liquid                           are greater than in
                                                 a liquid.

111. The vapor pressure of a        *because*    this would mean
     substance can never                        that the atmosphere
     be equal to atmospheric                    was entirely composed
     pressure                                   of that substance in
                                                its gaseous state.

112. At constant pressure,          *because*    temperature and
     a certain amount of gas                    volume are inversely
     will double in volume                      proportional.
     as the temperature is
     halved

113. Carbon's electron             *because*    $3s$ electrons are
     configuration is $1s^2 2s^2 2p^2$          lower in energy than
     rather than $1s^2 2s^2 3s^2$               $2p$ electrons.

114. The first ionization energy    *because*    the closer an
     for an atom is greater than                electron is to the
     the second ionization energy               nucleus, the
                                                more difficult it
                                                is to remove.

115. The halogens, in Group      *because*      they each need one
     VIIA, all form stable diatomic              electron to fill
     molecules                                   their outer shells.

116. Sodium has a              *because*      sodium atoms do
     smaller atomic                            not have as many
     radius than chlorine                      valence electrons as
                                               chlorine atoms do.

# PART C

**DIRECTIONS:** For each question in this section, select the best answer from among the given choices and fill in the corresponding oval on your answer sheet.

24. The sum of the coefficients of the reaction

    ___ $C_6H_6$ + ___$O_2$ → ___$CO_2$ + ___$H_2O$

    when it is balanced is

    (A)  7

    (B)  14

    (C)  28

    (D)  35

    (E)  42

25. Which of the following sequences lists the relative sizes of particles in a water mixture from smallest to largest?

    (A)  solutions, suspensions, colloids

    (B)  solutions, colloids, suspensions

    (C)  colloids, solutions, suspensions

    (D)  colloids, suspensions, solutions

    (E)  suspensions, colloids, solutions

26. All of the following are characteristics of the Group IIA elements except

    (A)  They form bases with water.

    (B)  They form oxides with the formula XO.

    (C)  The ionic radius is larger than the atomic radius.

    (D)  They are good reducing agents.

    (E)  They are highly electropositive.

27. How many atoms are represented by the formula, $K_3Fe(CN)_6$?

    (A) 6                    (D) 18

    (B) 10                   (E) 20

    (C) 16

28. The compound, $Na_2CO_3 \cdot 10H_2O$, is an example of

    (A) a hydrate            (D) an amorphous solid

    (B) an anhydride         (E) dispersion

    (C) a solution

29. How many protons would be found in a nucleus of atomic weight 80 if it contains 43 neutrons?

    (A) 37                   (D) 80

    (B) 43                   (E) 123

    (C) 60

30. Which of the following is an ionic compound?

    (A) bleach               (D) baking soda

    (B) air                  (E) graphite

    (C) oxygen gas

31. What volume would 16 g of oxygen gas occupy at STP?

    (A) 5.6 liters           (D) 33.6 liters

    (B) 11.2 liters          (E) 44.8 liters

    (C) 22.4 liters

32. The most effective reducing agents are found among

    (A) the alkali metals        (D) the transition metals

    (B) the alkaline earth metals (E) the halogens

    (C) the amphoteric elements

33. How many orbitals can one find in a $p$ subshell?

    (A) 2                          (D) 7

    (B) 3                          (E) 14

    (C) 6

34. Which elements form oxides with the formula $X_2O_3$?

    (A) Group IA                   (D) Group IVA

    (B) Group IIA                  (E) Group VA

    (C) Group IIIA

35. Twenty-two grams of $CO_2$ at STP, is identical to

    (A) 1 mole of $CO_2$           (D) 11.2 liters

    (B) $6 \times 10^{23}$ atoms   (E) 22.4 liters

    (C) $6 \times 10^{23}$ molecules

36. Which of the following pairs would result in a combination of elements in the ratio 1:2?

    (A) Group IA with Group VIIA

    (B) Group IA with Group VIA

    (C) Group IIA with Group VIIA

    (D) Group IIA with Group VIA

    (E) Group IIIA with Group VIA

37. Which of the following is a chemical property?

    (A) melting point              (D) mass

    (B) density                    (E) burning

    (C) viscosity

38. How many atoms are present in 22.4 liters of oxygen gas at STP?

    (A) $3 \times 10^{23}$         (D) $12 \times 10^{23}$

    (B) $6 \times 10^{23}$         (E) $15 \times 10^{23}$

    (C) $9 \times 10^{23}$

39. Which of the following is a poor electrolyte?

    (A) a dilute hydrochloric acid solution

    (B) a dilute sodium hydroxide solution

    (C) a dilute sucrose solution

    (D) a dilute sodium chloride solution

    (E) fused sodium chloride

40. Isomers differ in

    (A) the number of neutrons in their nuclei

    (B) their atomic compositions

    (C) their molecular weights

    (D) their molecular structures

    (E) number of protons

41. Which of the following indicates an ether functional group?

    (A) $R - OH$

    (B) $R - O - R^1$

    (C) $$R - \overset{\displaystyle O}{\overset{\displaystyle \|}{C}} - H$$

    (D) $$R - \overset{\displaystyle O}{\overset{\displaystyle \|}{C}} - R^1$$

    (E) $$R - \overset{\displaystyle O}{\overset{\displaystyle \|}{C}} - OH$$

42. Which of the following would you expect to precipitate first if a $AgNO_3$ solution is added to an aqueous solution containing NaCl, NaBr, and NaI?

    (A) Ag

    (B) AgCl

    (C) AgBr

    (D) AgI

    (E) NaI

43. The observation that the atom is mostly empty space was first made by

    (A) Avogadro

    (B) Rutherford

    (C) Moseley

    (D) Boyle

    (E) Charles

44. Which of the following represents the ground state of the process,

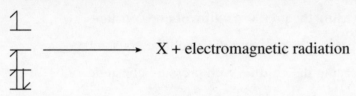

X + electromagnetic radiation

(A)

(D)

(B)

(E)

(C)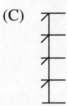

45. Each element has an individual emission spectra because of different

   (A) atomic numbers

   (B) numbers of electrons

   (C) electronic energy-level separations

   (D) bonding structures

   (E) electronegativities

46. A triple bond may best be described as

   (A) two *sigma* bonds and one *pi* bond

   (B) one *sigma* bond and two *pi* bonds

   (C) two *sigma* bonds and two *pi* bonds

   (D) three *sigma* bonds

   (E) three *pi* bonds

47. Water could be made to boil at 90 °C by

    (A) increasing the pressure with volume constant

    (B) decreasing the pressure with volume constant

    (C) increasing the volume with pressure constant

    (D) decreasing the volume with pressure constant

    (E) increasing the pressure while decreasing the volume

48. *sp* bond hybridization for carbon is characteristic in

    (A) alkanes                (D) alkynes

    (B) alkenes                (E) aromatics

    (C) dienes.

49. Given

$$Zn^{+2} + 2e^- \rightarrow Zn; \quad E° = -0.76 \quad | \quad Cr^{+3} + 3e^- \rightarrow Cr; \quad E° = -0.74$$

$$Mn^{+2} + 2e^- \rightarrow Mn; \quad E° = -1.03 \quad | \quad Ni^{+2} + 2e^- \rightarrow Ni; \quad E° = -0.14$$

$$Al^{+3} + 3e^- \rightarrow Al; \quad E° = -1.66 \quad |$$

    Which of the following is most easily oxidized?

    (A) Zn                (D) Cr

    (B) Mn                (E) Ni

    (C) Al

50. A compound that when dissolved in water barely conducts electrical current can probably be

    (A) a strong electrolyte        (D) a strong base

    (B) an ionic salt               (E) a weak base

    (C) a strong acid

51. Which of the following best describes four equivalent bonds having $^1/_4$ *s* character and $^3/_4$ *p* character?

    (A) *sp*                (D) *sp³d*

    (B) *sp²*               (E) *sp³d²*

    (C) *sp³*

52. The equilibrium expression, $K = [Ag^+] [Cl^-]$ describes the reaction

    (A) $AgCl \rightarrow Ag^+ + Cl^-$       (D) $Ag + Cl \rightarrow Ag^+ + Cl^-$

    (B) $Ag^+ + Cl^- \rightarrow AgCl$       (E) $Ag \rightarrow Cl$

    (C) $Ag^+ + Cl^- \rightarrow Ag + Cl$

53. What would be the concentration of $Ag^+$ at equilibrium if $K_{sp} = 1.6 \times 10^{-10}$?

    (A) $1 \times 10^{-10}$       (D) $1.3 \times 10^{-5}$

    (B) $1.6 \times 10^{-10}$       (E) $1 \times 10^{-2}$

    (C) $1 \times 10^{-5}$

54. How many grams of HCl must be added to 500 mL of water to produce a solution that freezes at −1.86 °C? (Molal freezing constant = 1.86 °C kg/mole.)

    (A) 4.6       (D) 36.5

    (B) 9.1       (E) 73.0

    (C) 18.3

55. What is the pOH of a solution with $[H^+] = 1 \times 10^{-3}$?

    (A) −3       (D) 11

    (B) 1       (E) 14

    (C) 3

56. Which of the following is produced at the anode of an electrolytic cell containing a solution of HCl?

    (A) $H_2O$       (D) $H_2$

    (B) $O_2$       (E) $N_2$

    (C) $Cl_2$

57. Which of the following acids is capable of dissolving gold?

    (A) hydrochloric       (D) a combination of A and B

    (B) nitric       (E) a combination of A and C

    (C) sulfuric

58. What volume does 8.5 g of ammonia occupy at STP?

    (A) 2.8 L                (D) 22.4 L

    (B) 5.6 L                (E) 44.8 L

    (C) 11.2 L

59. What is the formula of a hydrocarbon composed of 86% carbon and 14% hydrogen by weight?

    (A) $CH_4$                (D) $C_3H_8$

    (B) $C_2H_4$                (E) $C_4H_6$

    (C) $C_2H_6$

60. How many grams of $CO_2$ are produced by the complete reaction of 180 g of $CaCO_3$ with excess HCl?

    (A) 22 g                (D) 110 g

    (B) 44 g                (E) 132 g

    (C) 79 g

61. To what final volume should 100 mL of 4 $N$ $H_2SO_4$ be diluted to produce a 1 $M$ solution?

    (A) 100 mL                (D) 700 mL

    (B) 300 mL                (E) 900 mL

    (C) 800 mL

62. How much chromium can be electroplated out of 100 mL of a solution 0.5 $M$ in $CrCl_3$?

    (A) 1.3 g                (D) 26 g

    (B) 2.6 g                (E) 52 g

    (C) 10 g

63. A student tritrates 100 mL of acid with 5 $M$ NaOH. Phenolphthalein indicator changes color after 50 mL of NaOH have been added. What is the molarity of the monoprotic acid?

    (A) 0.1 $M$                     (D) 2.5 $M$

    (B) 1 $M$                       (E) 25 $M$

    (C) 1.5 $M$

64. Which of the following is a correct order for decreasing strength as reducing agents?

    (A) Li, Ca, Pb, Cr, Zn          (D) Li, Al, Zn, Co, $Sn^{2+}$

    (B) Ca, Mg, Mn, Fe, Sr          (E) Mg, $Sn^{2+}$, Co, Al, Ni

    (C) Rb, Sn, Cu, Al, Fe

65. A mixture of water, ether, and sulfuric acid is distilled. In what order would these appear in the distillate?

    (A) water, ether, sulfuric acid

    (B) water, sulfuric acid, ether

    (C) ether, water, sulfuric acid

    (D) ether, sulfuric acid, water

    (E) sulfuric acid, water, ether

66. Which of the following tests would you perform to confirm the presence of the first material to appear in the distillate?

    (A) immerse a flaming splint in the distillate

    (B) attempt to dissolve naphthalene in the distillate

    (C) immerse litmus paper in the distillate

    (D) add phenolphthalein to the distillate

    (E) chromatography

67. 28 mL of nitrogen are reacted with 15 mL of hydrogen. How many milliliters of which gas is left unreacted?

   (A) 5 mL of $H_2$        (D) 11 mL of $N_2$

   (B) 5 mL of $N_2$        (E) 23 mL of $N_2$

   (C) 7 mL of $H_2$

68. What is the total volume of the gases present after reaction in the previous question?

   (A) 11 mL        (D) 33 mL

   (B) 17 mL        (E) 42 mL

   (C) 27 mL

69. Which odor would be detected upon completion of the following reaction?

   $$C_3H_7COOH + C_2H_5OH + H^+ \rightarrow$$

   (A) bitter        (D) rotten egg

   (B) sour        (E) no odor

   (C) sweet

# SAT CHEMISTRY
# TEST 5

## ANSWER KEY

### PART A

| | | | | | | | |
|---|---|---|---|---|---|---|---|
| 1. | (A) | 7. | (C) | 13. | (B) | 19. | (D) |
| 2. | (C) | 8. | (D) | 14. | (C) | 20. | (C) |
| 3. | (E) | 9. | (A) | 15. | (A) | 21. | (C) |
| 4. | (D) | 10. | (A) | 16. | (B) | 22. | (D) |
| 5. | (A) | 11. | (A) | 17. | (E) | 23. | (A) |
| 6. | (D) | 12. | (E) | 18. | (C) | | |

### PART B

| | | | | | | | |
|---|---|---|---|---|---|---|---|
| 101. | T, T, CE | 105. | T, F | 109. | T, F | 113. | T, F |
| 102. | T, T, CE | 106. | F, F | 110. | T, T, CE | 114. | F, T |
| 103. | T, F | 107. | F, T | 111. | F, F | 115. | T, T, CE |
| 104. | F, T | 108. | T, T, CE | 112. | F, F | 116. | F, T |

### PART C

| | | | | | | | |
|---|---|---|---|---|---|---|---|
| 24. | (D) | 36. | (C) | 48. | (D) | 60. | (C) |
| 25. | (B) | 37. | (E) | 49. | (C) | 61. | (C) |
| 26. | (C) | 38. | (D) | 50. | (E) | 62. | (B) |
| 27. | (C) | 39. | (C) | 51. | (C) | 63. | (D) |
| 28. | (A) | 40. | (D) | 52. | (A) | 64. | (D) |
| 29. | (A) | 41. | (B) | 53. | (D) | 65. | (C) |
| 30. | (D) | 42. | (D) | 54. | (B) | 66. | (B) |
| 31. | (B) | 43. | (B) | 55. | (D) | 67. | (E) |
| 32. | (A) | 44. | (E) | 56. | (C) | 68. | (D) |
| 33. | (B) | 45. | (C) | 57. | (D) | 69. | (C) |
| 34. | (C) | 46. | (B) | 58. | (C) | | |
| 35. | (D) | 47. | (B) | 59. | (B) | | |

# DETAILED EXPLANATIONS
# OF ANSWERS
## TEST 5
## PART A

1. **(A)**
Region A indicates a solid being heated.

2. **(C)**
Region C indicates a liquid being heated.

3. **(E)**
Region E indicates a gas being heated.

4. **(D)**
Region D indicates a liquid undergoing a phase change to a gas at a constant temperature.

5. **(A)**
The anode is the site of oxidation. An electrochemical cell consisting of Zn and Cu will result in Zn being oxidized to $Zn^{2+}$ and Cu being reduced from $Cu^{2+}$. Thus, zinc is the anode.

6. **(D)**
The salt bridge contains a concentrated soluble electrolyte such as KCl. As electrons are removed from the anode and are transported to the cathode, $Cl^-$ moves towards the anode and $K^+$ towards the cathode to maintain electrical neutrality.

7. **(C)**
The half cell reactions are

$$Zn \rightarrow Zn^{2+} + 2e^- \qquad \text{oxidation}$$
$$Cu^{2+} + 2e^- \rightarrow Cu \qquad \text{reduction}$$

Thus, the Zn electrode and the $Cu^{2+}$ electrolyte will eventually be depleted.

8.  **(D)**
    Molality is a measure of concentration that is defined as moles of the solute per kilogram of solvent.

9.  **(A)**
    Molarity is a measure of concentration that is defined as moles of solute per liter of solution. Choice (C) density is defined as mass per volume. Choice (E) normality is a measure of concentration that is defined as the number of equivalents of solute per liter of solution.

10. **(A)**
    Since electronegativity increases going from left to right and from bottom to top along the periodic table, the most electronegative atoms will appear in the upper right corner of the table. Of the atoms given O is the closest to this corner and is hence the most electronegative. Sr would have the lowest electronegativity because it appears nearest to the bottom left corner of the table.

11. **(A)**
    O has the electron configuration of $1s^2 2s^2 2p^4$. The electron configuration of Na is

    $$1s^2 2s^2 2p^6 3s^1.$$

    The electron configuration of S is

    $$1s^2 2s^2 2p^6 3s^2 3p^4.$$

    The electron configuration of B is

    $$1s^2 2s^2 2p^1.$$

    The electron configuration of Sr is

    $$1s^2 2s^2 2p^6 3s^2 3d^{10} 3p^6 4s^2 4p^6 5s^2.$$

Questions 12–14
    These three questions all relate to Le Chatelier's principle, which states that any time a stress is added to a system, the system will react in such a way as to minimize that stress.

12. **(E)**
    If additional solid NaCl is added to the saturated system, the equilibrium will remain where it is because the solution already has as much $Na^+$ and $Cl^-$ as it can hold. The additional solid NaCl will just add to the solid NaCl already at the bottom of the vessel.

13. **(B)**

If $Na^+$ is removed from the system, more NaCl *(s)* will dissolve to replace the $Na^+$ that was removed and restore the equilibrium.

14. **(C)**

If solid lead chloride is added to the system, the concentration of $Cl^-$ will increase. This is known as the common ion effect. The addition of the lead chloride disturbs the equilibrium. NaCl will precipitate out, but the final concentration of $Cl^-$ is higher than it was before the lead chloride was added.

15. **(A)**

To find the order of the reaction with respect to A, write the general rate equation for two different concentrations. To eliminate the affects of B, choose the two conditions where the concentration of B remains the same. This occurs in experiments 1 and 2.

$$rate_1 = k \, (concentration_1)^n$$

$$rate_2 = k \, (concentration_2)^n$$

Writing these two equations as ratios:

$$\frac{rate_1}{rate_2} = \left[ \frac{concentration_1}{concentration_2} \right]^n$$

$$\frac{0.040}{0.040} = \left( \frac{0.060}{0.030} \right)^n$$

$$1 = 2^n$$

Therefore, $n$ must be 0 and the reaction is 0th order in A, meaning that the rate of the reaction does not depend on the concentration of A.

16. **(B)**

Here, the same technique is used only choosing the experiments where the concentration of A is held constant. This occurs in experiments 2 and 3. Writing as ratios:

$$\frac{rate_1}{rate_2} = \left[ \frac{concentration_3}{concentration_2} \right]^m$$

$$\frac{0.080}{0.040} = \left[ \frac{0.020}{0.010} \right]^m$$

$$2 = 2^m$$

$$m = 1$$

Therefore, the reaction is 1st order in B.

17. **(E)**

Using the equation:

$$rate = k\,[A]^0\,[B]^1$$

and rearranging to

$$k = \frac{rate}{[A]^0[B]^1}$$

we can substitute in from any one of the experiments:

$$k = \frac{0.080}{(.030)^0(.02)^1} = 4 \text{ L/mol} \cdot \text{sec}$$

18. **(C)**

A beta particle is an electron. Choice (C) is correct.

19. **(D)**

A positron has the same mass of an electron but a positive charge. Choice (D) is correct.

20. **(C)**

Beta radiation is made up of negatively charged particles. They have a mass of 0 and a charge of −1. This is the same as that of an electron. Convention dictates that the nuclear charge is written to the left of the symbol as a subscript and the mass as a superscript. Thus, choice (C) is both an electron and a beta particle. Choice (D) is a positron which has the same mass as an electron but a charge of +1. Choice (A) is an alpha particle which has a charge of +2 and a mass of four (the same mass as an atom of helium). Choice (B) is a neutron, a particle with a mass of 1 and a charge of 0. Choice (E) is a proton, having a mass of 1 and a charge of +1. This is the same as the positive ion of hydrogen, and is generally written as such.

21. **(C)**

Choice C is an Erhlenmeyer flask.

22. **(D)**

Choice (D) is a Florence flask.

23. **(A)**

Choice (A) is a picture of a buret. It is used to release specific quantities of a liquid or a solution. It is often used in acid-base titrations. Choice (B) is a volumetric pipet. It is used to deliver an accurate volume of a liquid or a solution. Choice (C) is an Erhlenmeyer flask. Choice (D) is a Florence flask. Choice (E) is a beaker.

# PART B

101. **T, T, CE**

The elements along the heavy line in the periodic table are called metalloids. The metalloids have both acidic and basic properties; hence, they are amphoteric.

102. **T, T, CE**

The reverse reaction of an exothermic process is endothermic; it requires the addition of heat if it is to occur.

103. **T, F**

Elements in the same group have similar properties because their valence shells have the same number of electrons. However, these electrons do not have the same energy: the $6s$ electron of cesium has much more energy than the $2s$ electron of lithium.

104. **F, T**

AgCl is less soluble in 0.1 $M$ NaCl than in pure water because of the common ion effect.

105. **T, F**

The forward and reverse reactions of a system in equilibrium are occurring at the same rate resulting in unchanging product and reactant concentrations.

106. **F, F**

Brownian motion is observed in colloids due to collisions of the solvent molecules with the colloid particles. The particles of a suspension are too large to be buffeted about by the solvent.

107. **F, T**

The reaction of $CaCO_3$ with HCl is hindered by increased pressure because a gas $(CO_2)$ is evolved.

108. **T, T, CE**

Increasing the pressure causes the reaction to shift in the direction where a smaller volume of gaseous product is produced.

109. **T, F**

A calorimeter can be used to measure the heat flow of a reaction, but it is because it is a good insulator and does not permit any heat transfer to or from the surroundings.

110. **T, T, CE**

Both statements are true and the second is a good explanation of the first. A gas can be compressed and molecules will come closer together; this is not as easy in a liquid. In general, the volume of a gas varies inversely with the pressure applied to it.

111. **F, F**

Both statements are false. When a substance's vapor pressure is equal to atmospheric pressure, the substance has reached its boiling point.

112. **F, F**

At constant pressure, an amount of gas will double in volume as the temperature is doubled. By Charles' and Gay-Lussac's Law $P$ and $V$ are directly proportional to temperature.

113. **T, F**

Carbon's electronic configuration is $1s^2 2s^2 2p^2$ because $2p$ electrons are at a lower energy than $3s$ electrons and the lower energy levels must be filled first.

114. **F, T**

The first ionization energy of an atom is always less than the second and the second less than the third, and so on. The first ionization energy refers to removal of the electron furthest away from the nucleus and is therefore easiest to remove and will require the least amount of energy to do so.

115. **T, T, CE**

Both statements are true and the latter is a good explanation of the former. Halides have 7 electrons in their outer shells, by sharing one electron with another atom of its own kind both outer shells can be filled.

116. **F, T**

Sodium has a larger atomic radius than chlorine because chlorine has a higher effective nuclear charge and, as a result, the electrons surrounding chlorine are drawn-in more tightly leading to a smaller atomic radius.

# PART C

24. **(D)**

The balanced reaction is

$$C_6H_6 + \frac{15}{2}O_2 \rightarrow 6CO_2 + 3H_2O$$

Since the carbon in $CO_2$ can only be obtained from benzene, which has 6 carbons, we know that the coefficient of $CO_2$ will be 6. In a similar fashion, the coefficient of $H_2O$ will be 3 since benzene has 6 hydrogens. There are 12 oxygens in $6CO_2$ and 3 oxygens in $3H_2O$ so the coefficient of $O_2$ is $^{15}/_2$. Multiplying by 2 to remove the fraction, we obtain

$$2C_6H_6 + 15O_2 \rightarrow 12CO_2 + 6H_2O$$

25. **(B)**
These terms describe the relative sizes of the particles in a water mixture. Solutions involve the smallest particles, which are invisible and do not settle on standing. The particles of a colloid are visible with an ultramicroscope, exhibit Brownian motion, and do not settle on standing. Suspensions may be visible with the naked eye, show no Brownian motion, and settle upon standing.

26. **(C)**
The ionic radius of the Group IIA elements is smaller than the atomic radius because they form ions with a +2 charge. The loss of electrons results in the nucleus attracting the remaining electrons to a greater extent. These elements produce bases with water by the reaction:

$$M + 2H_2O \rightarrow M(OH)_2 + H_2$$

Oxygen, having an oxidation state of $-2$ forms oxides with the formula MO when M has an oxidation state of +2. The Group IIA elements are easily oxidized, hence they are good reducing agents. They are also highly electropositive since they easily give up their valence electrons.

27. **(C)**
> 3 K atoms
> 1 Fe atom
> 6 C Atoms
> 6 N atoms,
> thus
>
> $3 + 1 + (6 \times 2) = 16$ atoms

28. **(A)**
Hydrates are salts that contain a definite proportion of water in their crystal structure.

29. **(A)**
The atomic weight gives the number of protons plus the number of neutrons. Thus, the number of protons (atomic number) is $80 - 43 = 37$.

30. **(D)**
Baking soda, or sodium bicarbonate, is the only ionic compound given. Bleach is a dilute solution of sodium hypochlorite, air is a mixture of gases, oxygen is an element, and graphite is one of the several naturally occurring forms of carbon.

31. **(B)**

Oxygen, $O_2$, has a molecular weight of 32 g/mole. Taking the volume of one mole of an ideal gas to occupy 22.4 liters, we have

$$16 \text{ g } \times \frac{1 \text{ mol}}{32 \text{ g}} \times \frac{22.4 \text{ L}}{1 \text{ mol}} = 11.2 \text{ L}$$

32. **(A)**

The most effective reducing agents are those species which are most easily oxidized. These elements will have the smallest electronegativities and the lowest ionization energies. The Group IA elements (alkali metals) fulfill these criteria. The alkaline earth metals are also good reducing agents but they are not nearly as effective as the alkali metals. The amphoteric elements are named as such because they have both acid and base properties. These as well as the transition metals are not as effective as oxidizing agents or reducing agents. The halogens, characterized by their large electronegativities, are extremely effective oxidizing agents.

33. **(B)**

The number of orbitals in a subshell is described by the quantum number $m_1$ in the following manner:

| subshell | 1 | $m_1 = 21 + 1$ |
|---|---|---|
| s | 0 | 1 |
| p | 1 | 3 |
| d | 2 | 5 |
| f | 3 | 7 |

34. **(C)**

Recalling that oxygen normally has an oxidation number of $-2$, we find that the overall negative charge on the molecule is $3(-2) = -6$. Thus, in order to produce a stable compound, two atoms of X must have a combined charge of $+6$. This gives each X a charge of $+3$, indicating an element from Group IIIA.

35. **(D)**

Using the information that the molecular weight of $CO_2$ is 44 g/mole and that one mole of an ideal gas occupies a volume of 22.4 liters at STP, we have

$$22 \text{ g} \times \frac{1 \text{ mol}}{44 \text{ g}} \times \frac{22.4 \text{ L}}{1 \text{ mol}} = 11.2 \text{ L}$$

36. **(C)**

To combine in a 1:2 ratio, the oxidation number of the negative species must be twice that of the positive species. We have a combination ratio of 1:1 for IA:VIIA since Group IA has an oxidation state of +1 and Group VIIA has an oxidation state of –1. Group IA and Group VIA combine 2:1 since they have oxidation states of +1 and –2, respectively. Group IIA and Group VIIA combine 1:2, whereas Group IIA and Group VIA combine 1:1 and Group IIIA and Group VIA combine 2:3.

37. **(E)**

A chemical property is one which refers to the way in which a substance is able to change into other substances, its reactivity. Burning is the process of uncontrolled oxidation. Choices A through D are physical properties, those that do not involve a change in the chemical identity of the substance.

38. **(D)**

For $O_2$ we have 2 atoms of oxygen present, thus

$$22.4 \text{ liters} \times \frac{1 \text{ mole}}{22.4 \text{ liters}} \times \frac{6 \times 10^{23} \text{ molecules}}{1 \text{ mole}} \times \frac{2 \text{ atoms}}{\text{molecule}}$$

$$= 12 \times 10^{23} \text{ atoms}$$

39. **(C)**

An electrolytic solution is characterized by mobile ions. Sucrose does not dissociate into ions in solution. Therefore, it is a poor electrolyte.

40. **(D)**

Isomers differ only in their molecular structures. Isotopes vary in the number of neutrons in the nucleus and thus have different weights.

41. **(B)**

| | |
|---|---|
| R — OH | alcohol |
| R — O — R$^1$ | ether |
| $\begin{matrix} O \\ \parallel \\ R - C - H \end{matrix}$ | aldehyde |
| $\begin{matrix} O \\ \parallel \\ R - C - R^1 \end{matrix}$ | ketone |
| $\begin{matrix} O \\ \parallel \\ R - C - OH \end{matrix}$ | carboxylic acid |

42. **(D)**

The most insoluble of the salts would precipitate out of the solution. AgI is the least soluble salt present. In general, solubility of the AgI is less than the solubility of AgBr and AgCl. AgI < AgBr < AgCl. In general, the larger salts will be less soluble.

43. **(B)**

Rutherford bombarded a thin gold foil with $\alpha$-particles and found that most passed straight through the foil, a few were deflected from their original path, and a very small amount were deflected back. This showed that atoms are mostly empty space (most $\alpha$-particles passed straight through), that the nucleus is positively charged (the $\alpha$-particles were slightly deflected), and that the gold nucleus is more massive than an $\alpha$-particle (some $\alpha$-particles were deflected back). Avogadro's law states that equal numbers of molecules are contained in equal volumes of different gases if the pressure and the temperature are constant. Moseley determined the concept of atomic number using X-rays to conclude that positive charge (number of protons) increases unit-wise from element to element. Boyle showed that the pressure of a gas is inversely related to its volume if temperature is constant ($P_1V_1 = P_2V_2$). Charles determined that the volume of a gas is directly related to the absolute temperature at constant pressure ($V_1/T_1 = V_2/T_2$).

44. **(E)**

An excited electron always falls back to the lowest unfilled energy level upon emission of light (electromagnetic radiation). The ground state will have two electrons of opposite spin in the orbitals of lowest energy level.

45. **(C)**

Unique emission spectra occur because of different electronic energy-level separations. Only specific wavelengths of light may be absorbed or emitted by an element due to the quantization of its electronic energy levels.

46. **(B)**

A single bond consists of one *sigma* bond while double and triple bonds consist of one *sigma* bond and one and two *pi* bonds, respectively.

47. **(B)**

Boiling occurs when the vapor pressure of a liquid is equal to the atmospheric pressure. Therefore, decreasing the pressure would lower the boiling point of water.

48. **(D)**

*sp* bond hybridization of carbon is characteristic of the triple bonds found in alkynes. The double bonds of alkenes, dienes, and aromatics give rise to $sp^2$ hybridization of carbon while the single bonds of the alkanes characterize $sp^3$ bond hybridization.

49. **(C)**

Aluminum is the least readily reduced metal of the given choices. Therefore, it is the most easily oxidized.

50. **(E)**

Most common ionic salts, strong acids (HCl, nitric acid, sulfuric acid, etc.), and strong bases (most hydroxides of IA and IIA metals, except Be) are strong electrolytes because they can conduct electrical current when dissolved in water.

51. **(C)**

Two *sp* hybrid bonds are produced by the combination of one *s* orbital and one *p* orbital. Three $sp^2$ hybrid orbitals result from the combination of one *s* orbital and two *p* orbitals. Four $sp^3$ hybrid orbitals are produced from one *s* orbital and three *p* orbitals. In a likewise manner, the combination of one *s* orbital, three *p* orbitals, and two *d* orbitals give six equivalent $sp^3d^2$ orbitals.

52. **(A)**

The equilibrium constant is given by the product of the concentrations of the products divided by the product of the reactant concentrations. Recall that the concentrations of solid products or reactants and water are omitted since they are assumed to be constant. This gives:

$$K = [Ag^+] [Cl^-] \text{ for AgCl} \rightarrow Ag^+ + Cl^-$$

Atomic chlorine does not exist in nature, so the reactions proposed for it are irrelevant.

53. **(D)**

$$K_{sp} = [Ag^+] [Cl^-] = 1.6 \times 10^{-10}$$

Letting $x = [Ag^+] = [Cl^-]$ since the concentrations of silver and chloride are necessarily equal, we have

$$x^2 = 1.6 \times 10^{-10}$$

$$x = [Ag^+] = [Cl^-] = 1.3 \times 10^{-5}$$

54. **(B)**

If $\Delta T$ is the change in the melting point, $K_m$ is the melting or freezing point constant, and $m$ = molality, then

$$\Delta T = m \times K_m \times \text{number of effective particles.}$$

Since HCl dissociates into $H^+$ and $Cl^-$ then substituting we obtain:

$$1.86(°C) = m \text{ (mole/kg)} \times 1.86 \text{ ( °C kg/mole)} \times 2$$

therefore, $m = 0.5$ = moles of HCl (solute)/kg of water (solvent). Since we have 0.5 kg of water then, 0.5 (mol/kg) × 0.5 kg = 0.25 mole HCl. Finally, converting 0.25 mole to grams, 0.25 mole × 36.5 g/mole = 9.1 g HCl.

55. **(D)**

Using the definition of pH, we find that

$$pH = -\log[H^+] = 3$$

Since pH + pOH = 14, we have pOH = 11.

56. **(C)**

Hydrochloric acid dissociates in solution to give $H^+$ and $Cl^-$. Since the anode is the oxidation site and the cathode is the reduction site, we have

$$2Cl^- \rightleftharpoons Cl_2 + 2e^- \quad \text{for the anode reaction and}$$

$$2H^+ + 2e^- \rightleftharpoons H_2 \quad \text{for the cathode reaction.}$$

57. **(D)**

Aqua regia, a combination of hydrochloric acid and nitric acid, is capable of dissolving gold.

58. **(C)**

$$8.5 \text{ g of NH}_3 \times \frac{1 \text{ mol}}{17 \text{ g of NH}_3} \times \frac{22.4 \text{ liters at STP}}{1 \text{ mol}}$$

$$= 11.2 \text{ liters at STP}$$

59. **(B)**

We would find 86 g of carbon and 14 g of hydrogen in a 100 g sample of the unknown. Dividing each of these terms by their respective atomic weights gives the number of moles of each in the unknown.

$$86 \text{ g} \times \frac{1 \text{ mol}}{12 \text{ g}} = 7.2 \approx 7 \text{ moles of carbon}$$

$$14 \text{ g} \times \frac{1 \text{ mol}}{1 \text{ g}} = 14 \text{ moles of hydrogen}$$

This gives the formula $C_7H_{14}$. Dividing by the smallest coefficient gives us the empirical formula $CH_2$. The only compound in the list with this empirical formula is $C_2H_4$.

60. **(C)**

The reaction in question is

$$CaCO_3 + 2HCl \rightarrow CaCl_2 + H_2O + CO_2.$$

Converting grams of $CaCO_3$ to moles:

$$180 \text{ g of CaCO}_3 \times \frac{1 \text{ mol}}{100 \text{ g of CaCO}_3} = 1.8 \text{ mol of CaCO}_3$$

Since one mole of $CaCO_3$ reacts to produce one mole of $CO_2$, 1.8 moles of $CO_2$ are produced. Converting to grams:

$$1.8 \text{ mol of CO}_2 \times \frac{44 \text{ g of CO}_2}{1 \text{ mol}} = 79 \text{ g of CO}_2$$

61. **(C)**

From the expression $M_1V_1 = M_2V_2$ we have,

$$(8 \, M^*) \, (100 \text{ mL}) = (1 \, M) \, (V_2) : V_2 = 800 \text{ mL}$$

(*) Note that we are required to change normality to molarity before we substitute. With $4 \, N \, H_2SO_4$ being equal to $8 \, M \, H_2SO_4$.

62. **(B)**
    Converting from molarity to moles:

$$\frac{0.5 \text{ mole}}{\text{liter}} \times 0.1 \text{ liter} = 0.05 \text{ mole of } Cr^{3+}$$

Now converting to grams of chromium:

$$0.05 \text{ mole} \times \frac{52 \text{ g of Cr}}{1 \text{ mole}} = 2.6 \text{ g of Cr}$$

63. **(D)**
    Since $M_1 V_1 = M_2 V_2$, we have

$$M_2 = \frac{M_1 V_1}{V_2} = \frac{(5 \ M \ \text{NaOH})(50 \text{ mL NaOH})}{100 \text{ mL acid}} = 2.5$$

64. **(D)**
    When referring to a standard table of reduction potentials, it can be seen that the elements are listed in order of decreasing strength as reducing agents. Therefore, as we read down a standard table the strength of the elements as oxidizing agents increases. The correct order for each of the species in the choices given is:

    | | |
    |---|---|
    | Li, Ca, Zn, Cr, Pb | for (A) |
    | Sr, Ca, Mg, Mn, Fe | for (B) |
    | Rb, Al, Fe, Sn, Cu | for (C) |
    | Li, Al, Zn, Co, $Sn^{2+}$ | for (D) |
    | Mg, Al, Co, Ni, $Sn^{2+}$ | for (E) |

65. **(C)**
    The compounds present in the mixture will appear in order of increasing boiling point; that is ether, water, and finally sulfuric acid.

66. **(B)**
    Naphthalene, an organic compound, will dissolve in ether but not in water or sulfuric acid. Acid/base indicators would give decisive results only if sulfuric acid were present in the distillate.

67. **(E)**

The reaction is

$$N_2 + 3H_2 \rightarrow 2NH_3.$$

Multiplying each coefficient by 5 gives

$$5N_2 + 15H_2 \rightarrow 10NH_3.$$

This leaves $28 - 5 = 23$ mL of $N_2$ unreacted.

68. **(D)**

The total volume is

$$10 \text{ mL of } NH_3 + 23 \text{ mL of } N_2 = 33 \text{ mL}$$

69. **(C)**

The combination of a carboxylic acid and an alcohol will result in the formation of an ester, which is sweet-smelling. The particular ester formed in this reaction is ethyl-butyrate, which has the characteristic sweet smell.

# PRACTICE
# TEST 6

# SAT Chemistry
# Practice Test 6

**(Answer sheets appear in the back of this book.)**

# PART A

**TIME:**   1 Hour
             85 Questions

---

**DIRECTIONS**: Each set of questions below consists of five lettered choices followed by a list of numbered statements or questions. For each statement or question, select the answer choice that is most closely related to it. Each answer choice may be used once, more than once, or not at all.

---

*Note:* **For all questions involving solutions, assume that the solvent is water unless otherwise noted.**

For questions 1–10, the following information may be useful.

$MW_{carbon} = 12.01$ g/mole

$MW_{oxygen} = 16.00$ g/mole

$MW_{hydrogen} = 1.008$ g/mole

$MW_{phosphorous} = 10.97$ g/mole

$MW_{nitrogen} = 14.01$ g/mole

$MW_{sodium} = 22.99$ g/mole

$MW_{chlorine} = 35.45$ g/mole

**Questions 1–3** refer to the following possible compounds.

(A) $N_2O_5$

(B) $N_2O_3$

(C) $NO_2$

(D) $NO$

(E) $N_2O$

1. The empirical formula for a compound containing 63.8% N and 36.2% O.

2. The empirical formula for a compound containing 36.7% N and 63.3% O.

3. The empirical formula for a compound containing 25.9% N and 74.1% O.

**Questions 4–6**

For the following questions, consider the reaction:

$$4NH_3\,(g) + 5O_2\,(g) \rightarrow 4NO\,(g) + 6H_2O\,(g)$$

(A)  2.294                    (D)  25.3

(B)  36.51                    (E)  2.513

(C)  1.409

4. If you begin with 16.00 grams of ammonia, and an excess of oxygen, how many grams of water will be obtained?

5. If you begin with 66.00 grams of ammonia, and 54.00 grams of oxygen, how many grams of water will be obtained?

6. How many moles of $NH_3$ are needed to produce 2.513 moles of NO?

**Questions 7–10** refer to the following values.

(A)  $1.807 \times 10^{24}$                (D)  $1.204 \times 10^{24}$

(B)  $3.476 \times 10^{-2}$                (E)  $2.414 \times 10^{-1}$

(C)  $1.171 \times 10^{-2}$

7. Number of phosphine molecules in two moles of phosphine.

8. Number of moles in 1.53 grams of carbon dioxide.

9. Number of atoms in one mole of water.

10. Number of moles in 4.35 grams of water.

**Questions 11–13**

(A)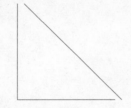

(D)

(B)

(E)

(C)

Which of these plots would be obtained if one were to experimentally investigate

11. Boyle's Law?

12. Charles' Law?

13. the relationship of $P$ and $T$?

**Questions 14–19** refer to the following processes.

   (A) Single replacement     (D) Hydrolysis

   (B) Double replacement   (E) Decomposition

   (C) Neutralization

14. $NaCl + AgNO_3 \rightarrow NaNO_3 + AgCl$

15. $2HgO \rightarrow 2Hg + O_2$

16. $Zn + H_2SO_4 \rightarrow ZnSO_4 + H_2$

17. $Zn + CuSO_4 \rightarrow Cu + ZnSO_4$

18. $NaCl + H_2O \rightarrow HCl + NaOH$

19. $HCl + NaOH \rightarrow H_2O + NaCl$

**Questions 20–23** refer to the following conditions.

(A) $\Delta G$ is negative      (D) $\Delta G$ is positive

(B) $\Delta H$ is positive      (E) $\Delta H$ is negative

(C) $\Delta S$ is positive

20. A reaction is said to be exothermic when

21. A reaction is said to be spontaneous when

22. A reaction is said to increase randomness when

23. A reaction is said to be able to perform useful work when

# PART B

**DIRECTIONS:** Each question below consists of two statements. Determine if Statement I is true or false and if Statement II is true or false and fill in the corresponding ovals on your answer sheet. Fill in oval CE if Statement II is a correct explanation of the true Statement I.

|   | (I) |   | (II) |
|---|---|---|---|

101. Sodium chloride has a high melting point — *because* — it is an ionic compound.

102. Strong acids are good electrolytes — *because* — they are completely dissociated at high concentrations.

103. The reaction between an alkali metal and water does not go to completion — *because* — a gas is produced.

104. Atoms of different elements may either form polar covalent or ionic bonds with each other — *because* — different elements have different electronegativity values.

105. Chloride ions, Cl⁻ are easily reacted to produce chlorine gas, $Cl_2$, — *because* — chloride easily gives up an electron.

106. Pure HCl is a strong acid — *because* — it is completely dissociated.

107. The properties of phosphorous should be closer to those of sulfur than to those of nitrogen — *because* — phosphorous and nitrogen are in the same row of the periodic table.

108. An aqueous solution of NaCl would be a good conductor of electricity    *because*    $Na^+$ and $Cl^-$ ions are free to move about.

109. Hydrogen fluoride (HF) is considered to be a polar molecule    *because*    the electron density cloud surrounding the molecule is shifted toward the H atom.

110. Ethylene ($C_2H_4$) has a higher carbon-carbon bond energy than acetylene ($C_2H_2$)    *because*    ethylene contains a double bond and acetylene has only a single bond between the carbons.

111. $NO_3^-$ cannot be described by the use of resonance structures    *because*    $NO_3^-$ can be described accurately by only one structure.

112. $H_2O$ adopts a bent rather than linear structure    *because*    $H_2O$ is diamagnetic.

113. Water has a high specific heat in relation to other liquids and solids    *because*    water has a large number of hydrogen bonds.

114. Metals are good conductors of electricity    *because*    they are held together by ionic bonds.

115. Long chain hydrocarbons are insoluble in water    *because*    "like dissolves like" and water contains oxygen and no carbon and long chain hydrocarbons contain carbon, but no oxygen.

116. At high altitudes water takes less time to boil    *because*    of the lower atmospheric pressure at high altitudes.

# PART C

**DIRECTIONS:** For each question in this section, select the best answer from among the given choices and fill in the corresponding oval on the answer sheet.

24. The normal Lewis Dot structure of chlorine gas is

    (A) Cl : Cl                    (D) : Cl : : Cl :

    (B) : C̈l : C̈l :              (E) : Cl : : : Cl :

    (C) Cl : : Cl

25. Which of the following has the greatest charge?

    (A) proton                     (D) alpha particle

    (B) electron                   (E) beta particle

    (C) neutron

26. Which of the following states of a compound has the greatest kinetic energy?

    (A) a solid

    (B) a liquid

    (C) a gas

    (D) a solid changing to a liquid at the melting point

    (E) a liquid changing to a gas at the boiling point

27. How many protons are there in the nucleus of an uncharged atom containing 13 electrons and 14 neutrons?

    (A) 1                          (D) 14

    (B) 12                         (E) 27

    (C) 13

28. Molecules of sodium chloride

    (A) display ionic bonding

    (B) display polar covalent bonding

    (C) are polar

    (D) dissociate in water solution

    (E) do not exist

29. Which of the following salts is produced when chlorous acid is neutralized with sodium hydroxide?

    (A) sodium chloride           (D) sodium hypochlorite

    (B) sodium chlorite           (E) sodium perchlorate

    (C) sodium chlorate

30. The lanthanide and actinide series are characterized by incomplete

    (A) $s$ subshells             (D) $f$ subshells

    (B) $p$ subshells             (E) $d$ and $f$ subshells

    (C) $d$ subshells

31. Which of the following shifts the equilibrium of the following reaction to the right?

    $$A\ (g) + B\ (g) + C\ (g) \rightleftharpoons A\ (g) + BC\ (g)$$

    (A) addition of more A         (D) decreasing the temperature

    (B) removal of B               (E) increasing the temperature

    (C) increasing the pressure

32. Which of the following salts will hydrolyze in water to produce a neutral solution?

    (A) $BaSO_4$                   (D) $Na_2CO_3$

    (B) $AlCl_3$                   (E) $Na_3PO_4$

    (C) $NaNO_3$

33. Based on the following information, which will be the most effective oxidizing agent?

$$Na^+ + e^- \rightarrow Na; \qquad E° = -2.71$$

$$O_2 + 4e^- + 2H_2O \rightarrow 4OH^-; \quad E° = +0.40$$

$$Cl_2 + 2e^- \rightarrow 2Cl^-; \qquad E° = +1.36$$

(A) Na (D) $Cl^-$

(B) $Na^+$ (E) $Cl_2$

(C) $O_2$

34. Which of the following is an example of a chemical change?

(A) rusting of iron

(B) crumbling a piece of paper

(C) melting ice

(D) density

(E) mass

35. How many atoms are there in the empirical formula of magnesium acetate?

(A) 3 (D) 15

(B) 7 (E) 16

(C) 8

36. Organic compounds of substantial molecular weight are generally insoluble in water because

(A) They contain large amounts of carbon.

(B) They do not ionize in solution.

(C) They do not dissociate in solution.

(D) They are nonpolar.

(E) They are polar.

37. The atomic number 20 describes

    (A) an alkali metal          (D) an inert gas

    (B) an alkaline earth metal  (E) a transition metal

    (C) a halogen

38. A 1 molal solution of NaCl results when 58.5 g of sodium chloride is dissolved in

    (A) one liter of water       (D) 100 g of water

    (B) 100 mL of water          (E) one cubic meter of water

    (C) one kilogram of water

39. An element, A, forms a sulfide with the formula AS. Which of the following formulas is correct?

    (A) ABr                      (D) $A_2O_3$

    (B) $AO_2$                   (E) $AH_4$

    (C) $AH_2$

40. Which of the following is a nonelectrolyte in water?

    (A) sodium nitrate           (D) carbon tetrachloride

    (B) sulfuric acid            (E) potassium acetate

    (C) sodium bicarbonate

41. An atom of calcium has the same number of electrons as all of the following except

    (A) $K^-$                    (D) $Cl^{3-}$

    (B) $Sc^+$                   (E) $V^{3+}$

    (C) $Kr^{2-}$

42. A substance will boil at a lower temperature if

    (A) the volume of the system is decreased.

    (B) the pressure of the system is decreased.

    (C) an additional amount of the substance is added.

    (D) the substance is dissolved in water.

    (E) A and B.

43. Which of the following reactions goes to completion because a gas is evolved?

    (A) $2H_2 + O_2 \rightarrow 2H_2O$          (D) $Zn + 2HCl \rightarrow ZnCl_2 + H_2$

    (B) $N_2 + 3H_2 \rightarrow 2NH_3$          (E) $NO + 2O_2 \rightarrow 2NO_2$

    (C) $2CO + O_2 \rightarrow 2CO_2$

44. A reaction is said to be at equilibrium when

    (A) $\Delta H = 0$          (D) $\Delta H < 0$

    (B) $\Delta G = 0$          (E) $\Delta H > 0$

    (C) $\Delta S = 0$

45. A suspension of particles in solution will

    (A) not settle upon standing

    (B) exhibit Brownian movement

    (C) pass through filter paper

    (D) have a cloudy or opaque color

    (E) not be visible with a microscope

46. Rutherford's experiment indicated that

    (A) Alpha particles are helium nuclei

    (B) Beta particles are electrons

    (C) Atoms are mostly empty space

    (D) Electrons have both particle and wave properties

    (E) Electronic energy levels are quantized

SAT Chemistry

47. A sample of $Br_2$ was analyzed and it was found that molecules of three different masses were present. This is an example of the

(A) Law of Definite Composition.

(B) Law of Multiple Proportions.

(C) existence of isomers.

(D) existence of isotopes.

(E) amphoteric nature of $Br_2$.

48. How much does 1 liter of a gas weigh if its molecular weight is 254 g/mole?

(A) 11.3 g
(D) 76.5 g

(B) 25.4 g
(E) 254 g

(C) 30.6 g

49. A stock solution of 10 $M$ NaOH was used to prepare 2 liters of 0.5 $M$ NaOH. How many milliliters of sodium hydroxide stock solution were used?

(A) 10 mL
(D) 200 mL

(B) 100 mL
(E) 2,000 mL

(C) 1,000 mL

50. How many moles of sulfate ions are there in 500 mL of a 5 $M$ sulfuric acid solution?

(A) 0.5
(D) 5.0

(B) 1.0
(E) 10.0

(C) 2.5

51. Which is the empirical formula of a compound consisting of 70% iron and 30% oxygen?

(A) FeO
(D) $Fe_2O_3$

(B) $FeO_2$
(E) $Fe_3O_5$

(C) $Fe_2O$

52. Predict the theoretical voltage of an electrochemical cell consisting of a zinc anode in 1 $M$ $ZnSO_4$ and a copper cathode in 1$M$ $CuSO_4$ if

$$Zn \rightarrow Zn^{+2} + 2e^-, \qquad E° = +0.76V$$

$$Cu \rightarrow Cu^{+2} + 2e^-, \qquad E° = -0.34V$$

(A) −0.76 $V$          (D) +0.42 $V$

(B) −0.42 $V$          (E) +1.10 $V$

(C) +0.34 $V$

53. In the previous question, what is the site where oxidation takes place?

(A) the zinc electrode          (D) the $CuSO_4$ solution

(B) the $ZnSO_4$ solution       (E) the salt bridge

(C) the copper electrode

54. The salt bridge in the electrochemical cell serves to

(A) increase the rate at which equilibrium is attained

(B) increase the voltage of the cell

(C) maintain electrical neutrality

(D) increase the oxidation/reduction rate

(E) supply a pathway for electrons to travel along

55. How many moles of electrons must pass through the cell to change the weight of the zinc electrode by 3.2 grams?

(A) 0.025          (D) 0.5

(B) 0.05           (E) 1.0

(C) 0.1

56. What is the heat of combustion of octane at 25 °C if $\Delta H_f$ for octane is −49.4 kcal/mole?

$$C_6H_{18} + \frac{25}{2}O_2 \rightarrow 8CO_2 + 9H_2O$$

$\Delta H_f$ for $H_2O$ (1) = −68.3 kcal/mol

$\Delta H_f$ for $CO_2$ (g) = −94.1 kcal/mol

(A) −1,318.1 kcal/mol      (D) −543.6 kcal/mol

(B) −963.6 kcal/mol      (E) −232.7 kcal/mol

(C) −795.9 kcal/mol

57. How many grams of sodium must be reacted with water to produce 22.4 liters of $H_2$? ($Na + H_2O \rightarrow NaOH + H_2$)

(A) 11.5      (D) 46.0

(B) 23.0      (E) 57.5

(C) 34.5

58. What are the lowest possible whole number coefficients for the reaction of the previous question?

(A) 1, 1, 1, 1      (D) 2, 2, 2, 1

(B) 1, 2, 2, 1      (E) 1, 2, 1, 2

(C) 2, 1, 2, 1

59. How many moles of water can be produced by the reaction of 5 moles of hydrogen with 5 moles of oxygen?

(A) 1.0 moles      (D) 10.0 moles

(B) 2.5 moles      (E) 15.0 moles

(C) 5.0 moles

60. What is the gram-molecular weight of $CH_3COOH$?

(A) 42      (D) 60

(B) 44      (E) 72

(C) 48

61. Which molecule among the following has the lowest molecular weight?

(A) 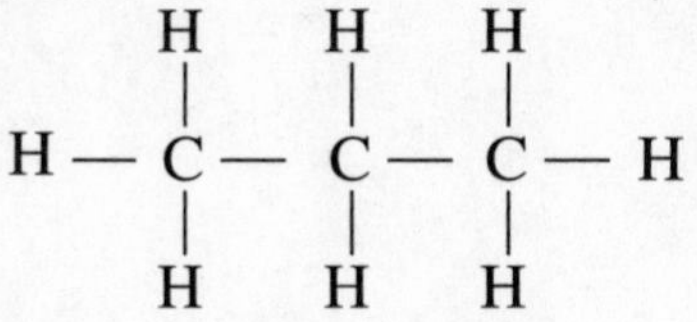

(B) 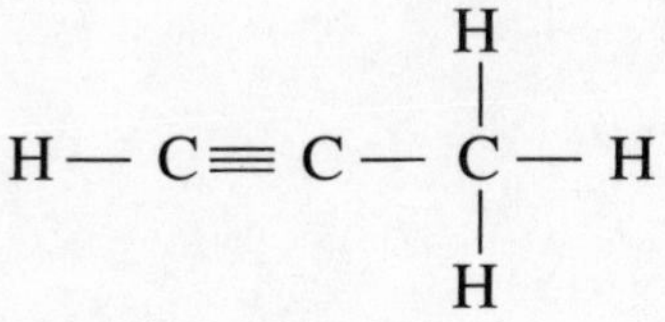

(C) 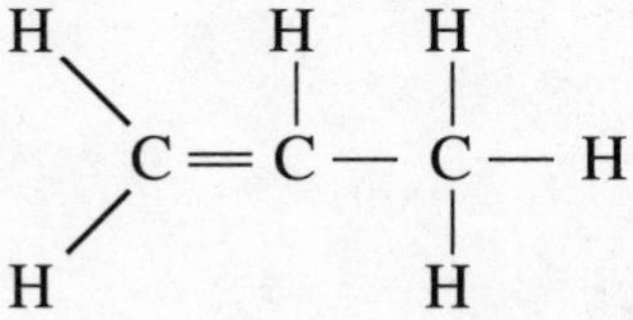

(D) H—C C—C C—H

(E) 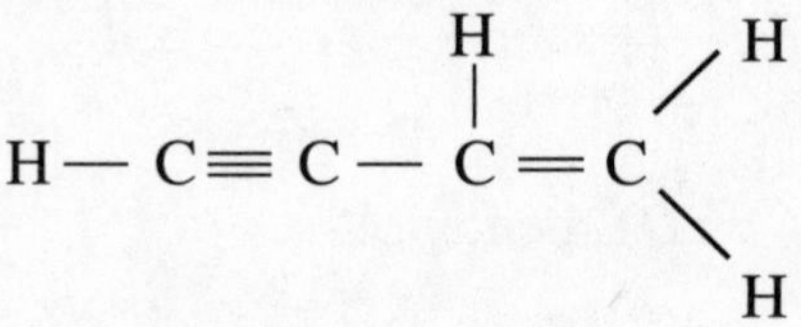

62. Which of the following structures indicates a component of an unsaturated fat?

(A) 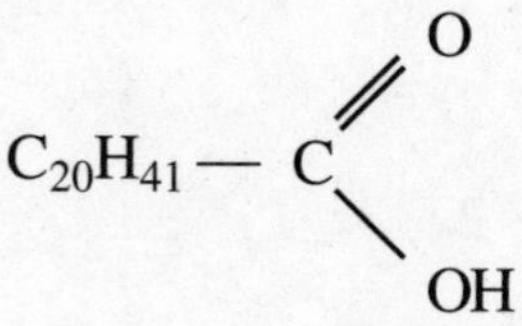

(B) 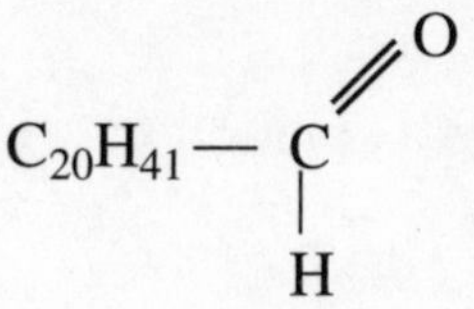

(C) $C_{20}H_{39}$ — C $\overset{O}{\underset{OH}{\diagdown}}$

(D) $C_{20}H_{39}$ — C $\overset{O}{\underset{OCH_3}{\diagdown}}$

(E) $C_{21}H_{41}$ — C $\overset{O}{\underset{CH_3}{\diagdown}}$

63. What is the IUPAC name for the structure below?

$$H-\underset{\underset{H}{|}}{\overset{\overset{H}{|}}{C}}-\underset{\underset{H}{|}}{\overset{\overset{H}{|}}{C}}-\underset{\underset{H}{|}}{\overset{\overset{H}{|}}{C}}-\underset{\underset{H}{|}}{\overset{\overset{H}{|}}{C}}-C\overset{O}{\underset{H}{\diagdown}}$$

(A) butanal

(B) pentanal

(C) butanol

(D) pentanol

(E) butanoic acid

64. What is the electronic configuration of sulfur?

(A) $1s^2\,2s^2\,2p^8\,3s^2\,3p^2$

(B) $1s^2\,2s^2\,2p^6\,3s^2\,3p^4$

(C) $1s^2\,2s^2\,3s^2\,2p^8\,3p^2$

(D) $1s^2\,2s^2\,2p^8\,3s^2\,3p^8$

(E) $1s^2\,2s^2\,3s^2\,2p^8\,3p^8$

65. What is the hydroxide ion concentration in a solution with a pH of 5?

(A) $10^{-3}$

(B) $10^{-5}$

(C) $10^{-7}$

(D) $10^{-9}$

(E) $10^{-11}$

66. What correction factor must be applied to the volume of a gas if it is heated from 10 °C to 200 °C and the pressure is changed from 1 atmosphere to 0.1 atmosphere?

(A) $\dfrac{760}{76} \times \dfrac{473}{283}$

(D) $\dfrac{76}{760} \times \dfrac{200}{10}$

(B) $\dfrac{760}{76} \times \dfrac{283}{473}$

(E) $\dfrac{76}{760} \times \dfrac{10}{200}$

(C) $\dfrac{76}{760} \times \dfrac{283}{473}$

67. What is the solubility of AgCl in water if $K_{sp} = 1.6 \times 10^{-10}$?

(A) $1.6 \times 10^{-10}$
(D) $1.6 \times 10^{-5}$

(B) $3.2 \times 10^{-10}$
(E) $3.2 \times 10^{-5}$

(C) $1.3 \times 10^{-5}$

68. The equilibrium constant for the reaction

$$CO\,(g) + O_2\,(g) \rightarrow CO_2\,(g)\,(\text{not balanced})$$

may be expressed as

(A) $K = \dfrac{[CO_2]}{[CO][O_2]}$

(D) $K = \dfrac{[CO]^2\,[O_2]}{[CO]}$

(B) $K = \dfrac{[CO][O_2]}{[CO_2]}$

(E) $K = \dfrac{[CO_2]^2}{[CO]^2\,[O_2]}$

(C) $K = [CO]^2\,[O_2]\,[CO_2]^2$

69. Which of the following is the usual bond hybridization exhibited by carbon in alkanes?

(A) $sp$
(D) $sp^3 d$

(B) $sp^2$
(E) $sp^3 d^2$

(C) $sp^3$

# SAT CHEMISTRY
# TEST 6

# ANSWER KEY

## PART A

| | | | | | | | |
|---|---|---|---|---|---|---|---|
| 1. | (E) | 7. | (D) | 13. | (C) | 19. | (C) |
| 2. | (B) | 8. | (B) | 14. | (B) | 20. | (E) |
| 3. | (A) | 9. | (A) | 15. | (E) | 21. | (A) |
| 4. | (D) | 10. | (E) | 16. | (A) | 22. | (C) |
| 5. | (B) | 11. | (B) | 17. | (A) | 23. | (A) |
| 6. | (E) | 12. | (C) | 18. | (D) | | |

## PART B

| | | | | | | | |
|---|---|---|---|---|---|---|---|
| 101. | T, T, CE | 105. | F, F | 109. | T, F | 113. | F, T |
| 102. | T, F | 106. | F, F | 110. | F, F | 114. | T, F |
| 103. | F, T | 107. | F, T | 111. | F, F | 115. | T, F |
| 104. | T, T, CE | 108. | T, T, CE | 112. | T, T | 116. | T, T, CE |

## PART C

| | | | | | | | |
|---|---|---|---|---|---|---|---|
| 24. | (B) | 36. | (D) | 48. | (A) | 60. | (D) |
| 25. | (D) | 37. | (B) | 49. | (B) | 61. | (C) |
| 26. | (C) | 38. | (C) | 50. | (C) | 62. | (C) |
| 27. | (C) | 39. | (C) | 51. | (D) | 63. | (B) |
| 28. | (E) | 40. | (D) | 52. | (E) | 64. | (B) |
| 29. | (B) | 41. | (C) | 53. | (A) | 65. | (D) |
| 30. | (D) | 42. | (B) | 54. | (C) | 66. | (A) |
| 31. | (C) | 43. | (D) | 55. | (C) | 67. | (C) |
| 32. | (C) | 44. | (B) | 56. | (A) | 68. | (E) |
| 33. | (E) | 45. | (D) | 57. | (D) | 69. | (C) |
| 34. | (A) | 46. | (C) | 58. | (D) | | |
| 35. | (D) | 47. | (D) | 59. | (C) | | |

# DETAILED EXPLANATIONS OF ANSWERS

## TEST 6

## PART A

For questions 1–10 we must determine the relative numbers of atoms of N and O. To do this you must calculate the number of gram atomic weights of each in a given sample. We will, for ease of calculation, make this amount 100 g.

1. **(E)**

In 100 g of the sample there are 63.8% or 63.8 g of N and 36.2% or 36.2 g of O. To convert to number of gram atomic weights, we divide each of these by the atomic mass of the element.

$$63.8 \text{ g N} / 14.01 \text{ g/mol} = 4.55 \text{ mol of N}$$

$$36.2 \text{ g O} / 16.00 \text{ g/mol} = 2.26 \text{ mol of O}$$

These numbers represent the relative numbers of atoms of N and O in the compound. N and O are present in the compound in the ratio 4.55:2.26. To find the simplest ratio between these numbers, we divide through by the smallest number.

For O, 2.26/2.26 = 1. For N, 4.55/2.26 = 2.01, or essentially 2. Therefore, N and O are in the ratio 1:2 in the compound. $N_2O$, or choice (E) matches this result.

2. **(B)**

This question can be handled similarly. Here, in 100 g of a sample, there would be 36.7 g of N and 63.3 g of O. Converting to gram atomic weights:

$$36.7 \text{ g N} / 14.01 \text{ g/mol} = 2.62 \text{ mol of N}$$

$$63.3 \text{ g O} / 16.00 \text{ g/mol} = 3.96 \text{ mol of O}$$

N and O are in the ratio 2.62:3.96. Dividing through by 2.62, for every 1 N atom in the compound, there are 1.51 O atoms. Multiplying by 2 to get whole numbers, N and O are in the ratio 2:3. Choice (B) or $N_2O_3$ corresponds to this result.

3.   **(A)**

Here, in 100 g of a sample, there would be 25.9 g of N and 74.1g of O. Converting to gram atomic weights:

25.9 g N / 14.01 g/mol = 1.85 mol of N

74.1 g O / 16.00 g/mol = 4.63 mol of O

N and O are in the ratio 1.85:4.63. Dividing through by 1.85, there are 2.50 O atoms for every 1 N atom in the compound. Multiplying by 2 to get whole numbers, N and O are in the ratio 2:5. Choice (A) or $N_2O_5$ corresponds to this result.

4.   **(D)**

In the reaction given, since there is an excess of oxygen, it is the amount only of ammonia put in that will determine how much product there will be. For every 4 moles of ammonia put into the reaction, 6 moles of water will be obtained. The first step is to determine how many moles are in 16.00 grams of ammonia. Dividing 16.00 by the molecular weight of ammonia:

$$\frac{16.00 \text{ g}}{17.03 \text{ g/mole}} = 0.9395 \text{ moles of } NH_3$$

Using cross multiplication, if for every 4 moles of $NH_3$ you get 6 moles of water:

$$\frac{4 \text{ moles ammonia}}{6 \text{ moles water}} = \frac{0.9395 \text{ moles ammonia}}{x \text{ moles water}}$$

$x = 1.409$ moles of water. To convert this to grams, we multiply by the molecular weight of water:

1.409 moles $H_2O \times 18.02$ g/mol = 25.39 g $H_2O$.

This corresponds to choice D.

5.   **(B)**

Here you must determine which is the limiting reagent. First you must convert the masses of both the ammonia and the oxygen to number of moles by dividing by the molecular weights.

$$\frac{66.00 \text{ g}}{17.04 \text{ g/mole}} = 3.873 \text{ moles of } NH_3$$

$$\frac{54.00 \text{ g O}_2}{32.00 \text{ g/mole}} = 1.688 \text{ moles of O}_2$$

Oxygen is therefore the limiting reagent.

For every 5 moles of oxygen put in, you get 6 moles of water out. Using cross multiplication:

$$\frac{5 \text{ moles oxygen}}{6 \text{ moles water}} = \frac{1.688 \text{ moles oxygen}}{x \text{ moles water}}$$

$x = 2.026$ moles water. Converting to grams by multiplying by the molecular weight of water:

$$2.026 \text{ moles} \times 18.02 = 36.51 \text{ grams O}_2$$

This corresponds to choice (B).

6. **(E)**
For every 4 moles of $NH_3$ that are put into the reaction, 4 moles of NO are produced. Therefore, if 2.513 moles of $NH_3$ are reacted, 2.513 moles will be produced.

7. **(D)**
In one mole of anything there are always Avogadro's number, or $6.023 \times 10^{23}$, of that thing. So, in two moles of phosphine, there are (2) $(6.023 \times 10^{23}) = 1.204 \times 10^{24}$ molecules of phosphine.

8. **(B)**
To get to the number of moles, divide the number of grams by the molecular mass of carbon dioxide:

$$\frac{1.53 \text{ grams}}{44.01 \text{ g/mole}} = 0.03476 \text{ moles}$$

9. **(A)**
In one mole of $H_2O$ there are $6.023 \times 10^{23}$ $H_2O$ molecules. Because each water molecule has 3 atoms, there are (3) $(6.023 \times 10^{23}) = 1.807 \times 10^{24}$ atoms in each mole.

10. **(E)**

This is similar to question 8. To get to the number of moles, divide the number of grams by the molecular mass of water:

$$\frac{4.35 \text{ grams}}{18.02 \text{ g/mole}} = 0.2414 \text{ moles}$$

11. **(B)**

Boyle's Law states that the product of $P$ and $V$ is a constant (at a constant temperature). Since $P \times V$ = constant, then a plot of $P$ vs. $V$ (and of $V$ vs. $P$) will result in a graph as displayed in B.

12. **(C)**

Charles' Law states that the ratio of $V/T$ is a constant (at constant pressure). Since $V/T$ = constant, then a plot of $V$ vs. $T$, and of $T$ vs. $V$, will result in a graph similar to C.

13. **(C)**

The pressure of a gas at constant volume varies directly with the absolute temperature. Therefore $P/T$ = constant and a plot of $P$ vs. $T$ or $T$ vs. $P$ gives a graph similar to C.

14. **(B)**

This is an example of a double replacement: $Na^+$ replaces $Ag^+$ in $AgNO_3$ to produce $NaNO_3$ and $Ag^+$ replaces $Na^+$ in $NaCl$ to produce $AgCl$.

15. **(E)**

This is a decomposition reaction in which mercuric oxide decomposes to mercury and oxygen.

16. **(A)**

This is a single replacement reaction in which $Zn^{2+}$ replaces $2H^+$ in $H_2SO_4$ to produce $ZnSO_4$.

17. **(A)**

This is also a single replacement reaction: $Zn^{2+}$ replaces $Cu^{2+}$ in $CuSO_4$ to produce $ZnSO_4$.

18. **(D)**

Hydrolysis reactions concern the reaction of a salt with water to produce an acid and a base.

19. **(C)**
     The opposite of hydrolysis, neutralization reactions involve the reaction of an acid with a base to produce water and a salt.

20. **(E)**
     A reaction is said to be exothermic, when it releases heat, which is when the change in enthalpy, $\Delta H$ is negative. This is the common convention. A reaction in which $\Delta H$ is positive, is termed endothermic and requires heat to be put in for the reaction to run.

21. **(A)**
     By convention, a reaction is said to be spontaneous, when the free-energy change, or $\Delta G$, is negative. When $\Delta G$ is positive, a given reaction will not proceed without the addition of energy.

22. **(C)**
     By convention, a reaction is said to increase randomness when the entropy change, or $\Delta S$, is positive.

23. **(A)**
     A reaction is said to be able to perform useful work when it is spontaneous, or when $\Delta G$ is negative. If work has to be supplied from the surroundings, the reaction is not spontaneous.

# PART B

101. **T, T, CE**
     Sodium chloride has a high melting point due to the strength of its ionic crystal lattice.

102. **T, F**
     Strong acids are good electrolytes because they are completely dissociated in dilute solutions. An increasing amount of acid remains undissociated as the acid concentration is increased.

103. **F, T**
     The reaction of an alkali metal with water goes to completion because a gas is evolved. For example,

$$\text{Na} + \text{H}_2\text{O} \rightarrow \text{NaOH} + \frac{1}{2}\text{H}_2\,(g)$$

### 104. **T, T, CE**

Atoms of different elements form either polar covalent or ionic bonds depending upon the electronegativity difference of the atoms. An electronegativity difference greater than 0.5 and less than 1.7 results in a polar covalent bond while one greater than 1.7 gives an ionic bond.

### 105. **F, F**

Chloride ions react to produce $Cl_2$ extremely reluctantly since chlorine is highly electronegative. This may be seen by the large negative reduction potential for the reaction.

$$2Cl^- \rightarrow Cl_2 + 2e^- \qquad E° = -1.36 \ V$$

### 106. **F, F**

Pure HCl, hydrogen chloride, is not the same as hydrochloric acid. HCl exhibits acid properties when dissolved in solution but remains undissociated when pure.

### 107. **F, T**

In the periodic table similar behavior is generally divided by columns, not rows. P should behave more closely to N.

### 108. **T, T, CE**

NaCl solutions are good conductors of electricity because the mobility of ions allows electricity to be transmitted easily through the solution.

### 109. **T, F**

HF is a polar molecule, but because of its large electronegativity the electron cloud is more concentrated around the fluorine.

### 110. **F, F**

Ethylene has a double bond between carbons and acetylene has a triple bond. Triple bonds are always stronger than double bonds and therefore have higher bond energies. Thus, acetylene has a higher C-C bond energy than ethylene.

111. **F, F**

$NO_3^-$ can be described by the following three resonance structures.

112. **T, T**

$H_2O$ does adopt a bent structure and it is diamagnetic, but the reason it is bent is a due to electron-pair repulsion pushing the hydrogens and the electron pairs on the oxygen as far apart as possible.

113. **F, T**

Specific heat is the energy required to raise one gram of a substance one degree Kelvin. The more tightly a compound is held together, the greater its specific heat will be. As water has a large number of hydrogen bonds to hold it together it will require a lot of energy to break these bonds. Water will thus have a higher specific heat than other similar substances that have a lesser degree of hydrogen bonding.

114. **T, F**

Metallic bonding is generally described by the "electron-sea" model wherein there is a lattice of positively charged metal cations through which the valence electrons may freely travel. This leads to good conductivity.

115. **T, F**

The phase "like dissolves like" refers to polar compounds dissolving polar compounds and non-polar compounds dissolving non-polar compounds. As water is polar and long chain hydrocarbons are non-polar, they will not be soluble in each other.

116. **T, T, CE**

At high altitudes the atmospheric pressure is lower. Since boiling point is defined as the temperature at which vapor pressure equals atmospheric pressure, less heat (and time) will be required to reach the lower pressures.

# PART C

24. **(B)**

The most stable electronic configuration of a molecule is that in which each atom has a complete octet of electrons surrounding it. Chlorine, being in Group VIIA has seven electrons in its valence shell. Therefore, $Cl_2$ has 14 electrons. This leads to the structure

$$: \overset{..}{\underset{..}{Cl}} : \overset{..}{\underset{..}{Cl}} :$$

25. **(D)**

A proton has a charge of +1, an electron a charge of –1, and a neutron is uncharged. An alpha particle is identical to a helium nucleus; since a helium nucleus has two protons, an alpha particle has a charge of +2. A beta particle is identical to an electron.

26. **(C)**

Temperature is a direct measure of the kinetic energy of a species. Thus, the state of the species at the highest temperature has the greatest kinetic energy.

27. **(C)**

The number of protons in the nucleus of an uncharged atom is the same as the number of electrons.

28. **(E)**

Molecules of sodium chloride do not exist individually. Rather sodium and chloride ions occupy points in a crystal lattice structure.

29. **(B)**

Binary acids such as hydrochloric acid form chloride salts. Ternary acids such as hypochlorous, chlorous, chloric, and perchloric form hypochlorite, chlorite, chlorate, and perchlorate salts, respectively.

30. **(D)**

The lanthanide and actinide series are characterized by incomplete $f$ subshells. Transition metals have incomplete $d$ subshells. Elements in Groups IIIA—VIIA are characterized by incomplete $p$ subshells while elements in Group IA have incomplete $s$ subshells.

31. **(C)**

Addition of more A does not affect the equilibrium because A appears both as a reactant and a product. Removal of B causes the equilibrium to shift to the left. Increasing the pressure causes the system to move to the right in an effort to reduce the number of moles of gas present. Changes in temperature will not affect the equilibrium since there is no heat released to or absorbed from the environment during the reaction. The previous explanations are all based on Le Chatelier's Principle: a system when subjected to a stress will shift in a direction so as to minimize that stress.

32. **(C)**

A salt hydrolyzes to produce a neutral solution if a strong acid and a strong base or a weak acid and a weak base are the hydrolysis products.

$$NaNO_3 + H_2O \rightarrow \underset{\substack{\text{strong} \\ \text{base}}}{NaOH} + \underset{\substack{\text{strong} \\ \text{acid}}}{HNO_3}$$

An acidic solution results when a strong acid and a weak base are produced.

$$BaSO_4 + 2H_2O \rightarrow \underset{\substack{\text{weak} \\ \text{base}}}{Ba(OH)_2} + \underset{\substack{\text{strong} \\ \text{acid}}}{H_2SO_4}$$

$$AlCl_3 + 3H_2O \rightarrow \underset{\substack{\text{weak} \\ \text{base}}}{Al(OH)_3} + \underset{\substack{\text{strong} \\ \text{acid}}}{3HCl}$$

A basic solution is produced in cases where a weak acid and a strong base are the result:

$$Na_2CO_3 + 2H_2O \rightarrow \underset{\substack{\text{strong} \\ \text{base}}}{2NaOH} + \underset{\substack{\text{weak} \\ \text{acid}}}{H_2CO_3}$$

$$Na_3PO_4 + 3H_2O \rightarrow \underset{\substack{\text{strong} \\ \text{base}}}{3NaOH} + \underset{\substack{\text{weak} \\ \text{acid}}}{H_3PO_4}$$

33. **(E)**

The strongest oxidizing agent is the one most easily reduced. Based on the reactions given, $Cl_2$ should be the most easily reduced. *Notice:* Based in the reactions given, $O_2$ requires the presence of $H_2O$ for reduction.

34. **(A)**

Rusting of iron is the chemical process of producing iron oxide. All the other choices are physical changes.

35. **(D)**

The formula for magnesium acetate is

$$Mg \left( \begin{matrix} O \\ \| \\ OCCH_3 \end{matrix} \right)$$

Thus, we have $1Mg + 4C + 6H + 4O = 15$ atoms.

36. **(D)**

Water, being highly polar, cannot dissolve nonpolar compounds (most organic compounds). Recall that "like dissolves like."

37. **(B)**

The atomic number 20 represents calcium which is an alkaline earth metal (Group IIA). The other choices and their respective groups are alkali metals (Group IA), halogens (Group VIIA), inert gases (Group O), and transition metals (B Groups).

38. **(C)**

Converting 58.5 g of sodium chloride to moles of sodium chloride:

$$58.5 \text{ g} \times \frac{1 \text{ mole}}{58.5 \text{ g}} = 1 \text{ mole of NaCl}$$

The molality of a solution, $m$, is defined as the number of moles of solute dissolved in one kilogram of solvent. Therefore, we have

$$m = 1 = \frac{1 \text{ mole}}{x \text{ kg}}$$

and     $x = 1$ kg of water

39. **(C)**

Sulfur in the sulfide ion has an oxidation state of $-2$. Therefore, A must have an oxidation state of $+2$. The bromide of A would be $ABr_2$ since bromine has an oxidation state of $-1$. The oxide of A would have the same formula as the sulfide. The hydrogens in a hydride have an oxidation state of $-1$ so the hydride of A would have the formula $AH_2$.

40. **(D)**

A nonelectrolyte is characterized by not dissociating in water solution. Of the choices given, only carbon tetrachloride satisfies this requirement.

41. **(C)**

Calcium, atomic number 20, has 20 electrons. Potassium has 19 electrons, so $K^-$ has 20. Scandium has 21 electrons, so $Sc^+$ has 20. Krypton has 36 electrons so $Kr^{2-}$ has 38. Chlorine has 17 electrons so $Cl^{3-}$ has 20. Vanadium has 23 electrons so $V^{3+}$ has 20.

42. **(B)**

The boiling point of a substance is defined as the temperature at which its vapor pressure equals the external pressure. Since the vapor pressure of a substance increases with temperature, the boiling point may be depressed by decreasing the external pressure.

43. **(D)**

The addition of hydrochloric acid to zinc is a reaction which can be made to go to completion if the product (which in this case happens to be the only gas involved in the reaction) is removed or allowed to escape as the reaction proceeds (Le Chatelier).

In the other cases such as in the formation of ammonia, the reaction will go also close to completion but by the removal *specifically* of $NH_3$, since the reactants nitrogen and hydrogen are also in the gas phase. The same is true for the other reactions, they will require the removal of the product not just the gas because there are gases both as reactants and products.

44. **(B)**

A reaction is said to be at equilibrium when the Gibbs' free energy change, $\Delta G$, is equal to zero. A reaction is spontaneous when $\Delta G < 0$ and not spontaneous when $\Delta G > 0$. An enthalpy change, $\Delta H$, of zero indicates that heat is neither released nor absorbed by the system. $\Delta H < 0$ indicates that the reaction evolves heat while $\Delta H > 0$ indicates absorption of heat. The change in entropy, $\Delta S$, is zero when the randomness of the system remains unchanged by the reaction, while $\Delta S > 0$ indicates an increase in randomness and $\Delta S < 0$, a decrease.

45. **(D)**

A suspension will have a cloudy or opaque color. It will settle upon standing, will not exhibit Brownian motion, will not pass through filter paper, and the particles will be visible with a microscope.

46. **(C)**

Rutherford bombarded a thin gold foil with alpha particles and observed that most passed through the foil without being deflected. This indicated that the atom consisted of mostly empty space.

47. **(D)**

Isotopes of an element have different numbers of neutrons which results in different atomic weights. The atomic masses given by the periodic table are a result of a weighted average of all naturally occurring isotopes of an element.

48. **(A)**

Recalling that one mole of an ideal gas occupies a volume of 22.4 liters, we calculate

$$\frac{254 \text{ g}}{1 \text{ mol}} \times \frac{1 \text{ mol}}{22.4 \text{ L}} = \frac{11.3 \text{ g}}{\text{L}}$$

49. **(B)**

Since $M_1 V_1 = M_2 V_2$, we have:

$$(0.5)\,(2,000) = (10)\,V_2$$

Upon rearranging the equation:

$$V_2 = \frac{(0.5)(2,000)}{10} = 100 \text{ mL}$$

Note that 2 liters was converted to 2,000 mL.

50. **(C)**

Using the following conversion factors:

$$500 \text{ mL} \times \frac{1 \text{ L}}{1,000 \text{ mL}} \times \frac{5 \text{ mol}}{\text{L}} \times \frac{1 \text{ mol of SO}_4^{2-}}{1 \text{ mol of H}_2\text{SO}_4}$$

we find that there are 2.5 moles of sulfate ion present.

51. **(D)**

A 100 g sample of this compound would contain 70 g of iron and 30 g of oxygen. Converting these weights to moles

$$70 \text{ g of FE} \times \frac{1 \text{ mol of Fe}}{56 \text{ g of Fe}} = 1.25 \text{ mol of Fe}$$

$$30 \text{ g of O} \times \frac{1 \text{ mol of O}}{16 \text{ g of O}} = 1.9 \text{ mol of O}$$

This gives an empirical formula of $Fe_{1.25} O_{1.9}$. We convert to whole numbers by dividing each subscript by the smallest subscript:

$$Fe_{\frac{1.25}{1.25}} O_{\frac{1.9}{1.25}} = FeO_{1.5}$$

Multiplying each subscript by 2 to obtain integer values, we obtain $Fe_2O_3$.

52. **(E)**

The half cell reactions and their corresponding electrode potentials are

$$Zn \rightarrow Zn^{2+} + 2e^-; \quad E° = +0.76 \text{ V}$$

$$Cu^{2+} + 2e^- \rightarrow Cu; \quad E° = +0.34 \text{ V}$$

The half cells were written in these directions because Zn is oxidized (definition of the anode) and Cu is reduced. The cell reaction is the sum of the half cell reactions

$$Zn + Cu^{2+} \rightarrow Zn^{2+} + Cu \qquad E° = +1.10 \text{ V}$$

53. **(A)**

The anode is, by definition, the site of oxidation in an electrochemical cell. Zinc is being oxidized so the zinc electrode is the anode.

54. **(C)**

The salt bridge prevents mixing of the electrolyte solutions but allows ions to flow through in order to maintain electrical neutrality.

55. **(C)**

Converting to moles

$$3.2 \text{ g of Zn} \times \frac{1 \text{ mol of Zn}}{65.4 \text{ g of Zn}} = 0.05 \text{ mol of Zn}$$

Examining the half cell reaction for zinc

$$Zn \rightarrow Zn^{2+} + 2e^-$$

we see that two moles of electrons are liberated for each mole of Zn that is oxidized. Therefore, $2 \times 0.05 = 0.1$ mole of electrons is required.

56. **(A)**

The heat of combustion of octane is given by

$$\Delta H_c = (8\Delta H_{f(CO_2)} + 9\Delta H_{f(H_2O)}) - (\Delta H_{f(C_8H_{18})} + \frac{25}{2}\Delta H_{f(O_2)})$$

Substituting the values given ($H_2O$ ($l$) is used because $t = 25$ °C):

$$\Delta H_c = (8(-94.1) + 9(-68.3)) - (-49.4 + 25/2(0))$$

$$\Delta H_c = -1318.1 \text{ kcal/mole}$$

Note that $\Delta H_f$ of an element ($O_2$) is zero.

57. **(D)**

The balanced reaction in question is

$$2Na + 2H_2O \rightarrow 2NaOH + H_2$$

Recalling that one mole of an ideal gas occupies a volume of 22.4 liters at STP, we find that we require 2 moles of Na to produce 1 mole of $H_2$. Converting to grams

$$2 \text{ moles of Na} \times \frac{23 \text{ g of Na}}{1 \text{ mole of Na}} = 46 \text{ g of Na}$$

58. **(D)**

$$Na + H_2O \rightarrow NaOH + H_2$$

In balancing the equation, we see that there are equal amounts of Na and O on both sides but that there are 2H reacting and 3H produced. Placing a $^1/_2$ in front of $H_2$ gives

$$Na + H_2O \rightarrow NaOH + \frac{1}{2}H_2$$

Now we multiply each term by 2 to remove the fraction, giving

$$2Na + 2H_2O \rightarrow 2NaOH + H_2$$

or 2, 2, 2, 1 as the respective coefficients.

59. **(C)**

The reaction is

$$2H_2 + O_2 \rightarrow 2H_2O$$

Multiplying each coefficient by 2.5 gives

$$5H_2 + 2.5O_2 \rightarrow 5H_2O$$

Therefore, we find that 5 moles of $H_2$ reacts with 2.5 moles of $O_2$ to produce 5 moles of $H_2O$.

60. **(D)**

Consulting the periodic table we find that

$$2C + 4H + 2O =$$

$$2(12 \text{ g/mol}) + 4(1 \text{ g/mol}) + 2(16 \text{ g/mol}) = 60 \text{ g/mole}$$

61. **(C)**

It has only three carbon atoms and six hydrogen atoms.

C: $3 \times 12$ g/mol = 36 g/mol
H: $6 \times 1$ g/mol = 6 g/mol
36 g/mol + 6 g/mol = 42 g/mol, which is the molecular weight.

62. **(C)**

Fats are composed of glycerol and three long chain carboxylic acids. B is an aldehyde, D is an ester, and E is a ketone. A and C are both long chain acids. An unsaturated carboxylic acid contains one or more double and/or triple bonds. The general formula for an alkane is $C_nH_{2n+2}$. With C = 20, we find that H = 42. Since we have a carboxy group attached to the carbon skeleton, the saturated fatty acid with C = 20 would have the formula $C_{20}H_{41}$ – COOH. Thus, A is a saturated carboxylic acid. C, having two fewer hydrogens than A must have one double bond and therefore be unsaturated.

63. **(B)**

The carbon skeleton of this molecule contains five carbons so we name it with the prefix *pentan-*. The molecule contains the functional group of an aldehyde which gives us the suffix *-al*. Thus, the structure is named pentanal. The correct structures associated with the other choices are

butanal

$$H - \overset{\displaystyle H}{\underset{\displaystyle H}{C}} - \overset{\displaystyle H}{\underset{\displaystyle H}{C}} - \overset{\displaystyle H}{\underset{\displaystyle H}{C}} - C \overset{\displaystyle O}{\underset{\displaystyle H}{\diagup}}$$

butanol

$$H - \overset{\displaystyle H}{\underset{\displaystyle H}{C}} - \overset{\displaystyle H}{\underset{\displaystyle H}{C}} - \overset{\displaystyle H}{\underset{\displaystyle H}{C}} - \overset{\displaystyle H}{\underset{\displaystyle H}{C}} - OH$$

pentanol

$$H - \overset{\displaystyle H}{\underset{\displaystyle H}{C}} - \overset{\displaystyle H}{\underset{\displaystyle H}{C}} - \overset{\displaystyle H}{\underset{\displaystyle H}{C}} - \overset{\displaystyle H}{\underset{\displaystyle H}{C}} - \overset{\displaystyle H}{\underset{\displaystyle H}{C}} - OH$$

butanoic acid

$$H - \overset{\displaystyle H}{\underset{\displaystyle H}{C}} - \overset{\displaystyle H}{\underset{\displaystyle H}{C}} - \overset{\displaystyle H}{\underset{\displaystyle H}{C}} - \overset{\displaystyle O}{\overset{\displaystyle \|}{C}} - OH$$

64. **(B)**

Consulting the periodic table, we find that sulfur (atomic number 16) has the electronic configuration

$$1s^2\, 2s^2\, 2p^6\, 3s^2\, 3p^4$$

65. **(D)**

Since pH = $-\log$ H$^+$ we find that $[H^+] = 10^{-pH}$.

Substituting our value gives

$$[H^+] = 10^{-5}$$

Recalling that $[H^+][OH^-] = 10^{-14}$ we have

$$[OH^-] = \frac{10^{-14}}{[H^+]} = \frac{10^{-14}}{10^{-5}} = 10^{-9}$$

66. **(A)**

Rearranging the combined gas law

$$\frac{P_1 V_1}{T_1} = \frac{P_2 V_2}{T_2}$$

to give

$$V_2 = V_1 \times \frac{P_1}{P_2} \times \frac{T_2}{T_1}$$

allows us to substitute

$$V_2 = V_1 \times \frac{760 \text{ torr}}{76 \text{ torr}} \times \frac{473 \text{ K}}{283 \text{ K}}$$

using 1 atm = 760 torr and T = $t$ + 273 K.

67. **(C)**

The solubility product of AgCl is

$$K_{sp} = [Ag^+][Cl^-] = 1.6 \times 10^{-10}$$

Letting $x$ = $[Ag^+]$ and since $[Ag^+] = [Cl^-]$, we have

$$x^2 = 1.6 \times 10^{-10}$$

and $x = 1.3 \times 10^{-5}$

Since $[Ag^+] = [Cl^-] = [AgCl]$, the solubility of silver chloride is $1.3 \times 10^{-5}$ mole/liter.

68. **(E)**

The equilibrium expression of a reaction is specified as the concentrations of the products divided by the concentrations of the reactants each being raised to the power of the corresponding stoichiometric coefficient. For the general reaction

$$aA + bB \rightarrow cC + dD$$

the equilibrium expression is

$$K = \frac{[C]^c [D]^d}{[A]^a [B]^b}$$

The concentrations of pure liquids and solids are omitted from the equilibrium expression since their concentrations change negligibly during the reaction. For the reaction in question, we have

$$K = \frac{[CO]^2}{[CO]^2 [O]^2}$$

since the balanced reaction is

$$2CO + O_2 \rightarrow 2CO_2$$

69. **(C)**

Carbon generally exhibits $sp^3$ bond hybridization in alkanes.

# Answer Sheets

# SAT CHEMISTRY – TEST 1

### PART A

1. Ⓐ Ⓑ Ⓒ Ⓓ Ⓔ
2. Ⓐ Ⓑ Ⓒ Ⓓ Ⓔ
3. Ⓐ Ⓑ Ⓒ Ⓓ Ⓔ
4. Ⓐ Ⓑ Ⓒ Ⓓ Ⓔ
5. Ⓐ Ⓑ Ⓒ Ⓓ Ⓔ
6. Ⓐ Ⓑ Ⓒ Ⓓ Ⓔ
7. Ⓐ Ⓑ Ⓒ Ⓓ Ⓔ
8. Ⓐ Ⓑ Ⓒ Ⓓ Ⓔ
9. Ⓐ Ⓑ Ⓒ Ⓓ Ⓔ
10. Ⓐ Ⓑ Ⓒ Ⓓ Ⓔ
11. Ⓐ Ⓑ Ⓒ Ⓓ Ⓔ
12. Ⓐ Ⓑ Ⓒ Ⓓ Ⓔ
13. Ⓐ Ⓑ Ⓒ Ⓓ Ⓔ
14. Ⓐ Ⓑ Ⓒ Ⓓ Ⓔ
15. Ⓐ Ⓑ Ⓒ Ⓓ Ⓔ
16. Ⓐ Ⓑ Ⓒ Ⓓ Ⓔ
17. Ⓐ Ⓑ Ⓒ Ⓓ Ⓔ
18. Ⓐ Ⓑ Ⓒ Ⓓ Ⓔ
19. Ⓐ Ⓑ Ⓒ Ⓓ Ⓔ
20. Ⓐ Ⓑ Ⓒ Ⓓ Ⓔ
21. Ⓐ Ⓑ Ⓒ Ⓓ Ⓔ
22. Ⓐ Ⓑ Ⓒ Ⓓ Ⓔ
23. Ⓐ Ⓑ Ⓒ Ⓓ Ⓔ

### PART B
### CHEMISTRY

|      | I     | II    | CE  |
|------|-------|-------|-----|
| 101. | Ⓣ Ⓕ | Ⓣ Ⓕ | Ⓒ Ⓔ |
| 102. | Ⓣ Ⓕ | Ⓣ Ⓕ | Ⓒ Ⓔ |
| 103. | Ⓣ Ⓕ | Ⓣ Ⓕ | Ⓒ Ⓔ |
| 104. | Ⓣ Ⓕ | Ⓣ Ⓕ | Ⓒ Ⓔ |
| 105. | Ⓣ Ⓕ | Ⓣ Ⓕ | Ⓒ Ⓔ |
| 106. | Ⓣ Ⓕ | Ⓣ Ⓕ | Ⓒ Ⓔ |
| 107. | Ⓣ Ⓕ | Ⓣ Ⓕ | Ⓒ Ⓔ |
| 108. | Ⓣ Ⓕ | Ⓣ Ⓕ | Ⓒ Ⓔ |
| 109. | Ⓣ Ⓕ | Ⓣ Ⓕ | Ⓒ Ⓔ |
| 110. | Ⓣ Ⓕ | Ⓣ Ⓕ | Ⓒ Ⓔ |
| 111. | Ⓣ Ⓕ | Ⓣ Ⓕ | Ⓒ Ⓔ |
| 112. | Ⓣ Ⓕ | Ⓣ Ⓕ | Ⓒ Ⓔ |
| 113. | Ⓣ Ⓕ | Ⓣ Ⓕ | Ⓒ Ⓔ |
| 114. | Ⓣ Ⓕ | Ⓣ Ⓕ | Ⓒ Ⓔ |
| 115. | Ⓣ Ⓕ | Ⓣ Ⓕ | Ⓒ Ⓔ |
| 116. | Ⓣ Ⓕ | Ⓣ Ⓕ | Ⓒ Ⓔ |

### PART C

24. Ⓐ Ⓑ Ⓒ Ⓓ Ⓔ
25. Ⓐ Ⓑ Ⓒ Ⓓ Ⓔ
26. Ⓐ Ⓑ Ⓒ Ⓓ Ⓔ
27. Ⓐ Ⓑ Ⓒ Ⓓ Ⓔ
28. Ⓐ Ⓑ Ⓒ Ⓓ Ⓔ
29. Ⓐ Ⓑ Ⓒ Ⓓ Ⓔ
30. Ⓐ Ⓑ Ⓒ Ⓓ Ⓔ
31. Ⓐ Ⓑ Ⓒ Ⓓ Ⓔ
32. Ⓐ Ⓑ Ⓒ Ⓓ Ⓔ
33. Ⓐ Ⓑ Ⓒ Ⓓ Ⓔ
34. Ⓐ Ⓑ Ⓒ Ⓓ Ⓔ
35. Ⓐ Ⓑ Ⓒ Ⓓ Ⓔ
36. Ⓐ Ⓑ Ⓒ Ⓓ Ⓔ
37. Ⓐ Ⓑ Ⓒ Ⓓ Ⓔ
38. Ⓐ Ⓑ Ⓒ Ⓓ Ⓔ
39. Ⓐ Ⓑ Ⓒ Ⓓ Ⓔ
40. Ⓐ Ⓑ Ⓒ Ⓓ Ⓔ
41. Ⓐ Ⓑ Ⓒ Ⓓ Ⓔ
42. Ⓐ Ⓑ Ⓒ Ⓓ Ⓔ
43. Ⓐ Ⓑ Ⓒ Ⓓ Ⓔ
44. Ⓐ Ⓑ Ⓒ Ⓓ Ⓔ
45. Ⓐ Ⓑ Ⓒ Ⓓ Ⓔ
46. Ⓐ Ⓑ Ⓒ Ⓓ Ⓔ
47. Ⓐ Ⓑ Ⓒ Ⓓ Ⓔ
48. Ⓐ Ⓑ Ⓒ Ⓓ Ⓔ
49. Ⓐ Ⓑ Ⓒ Ⓓ Ⓔ
50. Ⓐ Ⓑ Ⓒ Ⓓ Ⓔ
51. Ⓐ Ⓑ Ⓒ Ⓓ Ⓔ
52. Ⓐ Ⓑ Ⓒ Ⓓ Ⓔ
53. Ⓐ Ⓑ Ⓒ Ⓓ Ⓔ
54. Ⓐ Ⓑ Ⓒ Ⓓ Ⓔ
55. Ⓐ Ⓑ Ⓒ Ⓓ Ⓔ
56. Ⓐ Ⓑ Ⓒ Ⓓ Ⓔ
57. Ⓐ Ⓑ Ⓒ Ⓓ Ⓔ
58. Ⓐ Ⓑ Ⓒ Ⓓ Ⓔ
59. Ⓐ Ⓑ Ⓒ Ⓓ Ⓔ
60. Ⓐ Ⓑ Ⓒ Ⓓ Ⓔ
61. Ⓐ Ⓑ Ⓒ Ⓓ Ⓔ
62. Ⓐ Ⓑ Ⓒ Ⓓ Ⓔ
63. Ⓐ Ⓑ Ⓒ Ⓓ Ⓔ
64. Ⓐ Ⓑ Ⓒ Ⓓ Ⓔ
65. Ⓐ Ⓑ Ⓒ Ⓓ Ⓔ
66. Ⓐ Ⓑ Ⓒ Ⓓ Ⓔ
67. Ⓐ Ⓑ Ⓒ Ⓓ Ⓔ
68. Ⓐ Ⓑ Ⓒ Ⓓ Ⓔ
69. Ⓐ Ⓑ Ⓒ Ⓓ Ⓔ

# SAT CHEMISTRY – TEST 2

## PART A

1. Ⓐ Ⓑ Ⓒ Ⓓ Ⓔ
2. Ⓐ Ⓑ Ⓒ Ⓓ Ⓔ
3. Ⓐ Ⓑ Ⓒ Ⓓ Ⓔ
4. Ⓐ Ⓑ Ⓒ Ⓓ Ⓔ
5. Ⓐ Ⓑ Ⓒ Ⓓ Ⓔ
6. Ⓐ Ⓑ Ⓒ Ⓓ Ⓔ
7. Ⓐ Ⓑ Ⓒ Ⓓ Ⓔ
8. Ⓐ Ⓑ Ⓒ Ⓓ Ⓔ
9. Ⓐ Ⓑ Ⓒ Ⓓ Ⓔ
10. Ⓐ Ⓑ Ⓒ Ⓓ Ⓔ
11. Ⓐ Ⓑ Ⓒ Ⓓ Ⓔ
12. Ⓐ Ⓑ Ⓒ Ⓓ Ⓔ
13. Ⓐ Ⓑ Ⓒ Ⓓ Ⓔ
14. Ⓐ Ⓑ Ⓒ Ⓓ Ⓔ
15. Ⓐ Ⓑ Ⓒ Ⓓ Ⓔ
16. Ⓐ Ⓑ Ⓒ Ⓓ Ⓔ
17. Ⓐ Ⓑ Ⓒ Ⓓ Ⓔ
18. Ⓐ Ⓑ Ⓒ Ⓓ Ⓔ
19. Ⓐ Ⓑ Ⓒ Ⓓ Ⓔ
20. Ⓐ Ⓑ Ⓒ Ⓓ Ⓔ
21. Ⓐ Ⓑ Ⓒ Ⓓ Ⓔ
22. Ⓐ Ⓑ Ⓒ Ⓓ Ⓔ
23. Ⓐ Ⓑ Ⓒ Ⓓ Ⓔ

## PART B
## CHEMISTRY

|      | I     | II    | CE  |
|------|-------|-------|-----|
| 101. | Ⓣ Ⓕ | Ⓣ Ⓕ | Ⓒ Ⓔ |
| 102. | Ⓣ Ⓕ | Ⓣ Ⓕ | Ⓒ Ⓔ |
| 103. | Ⓣ Ⓕ | Ⓣ Ⓕ | Ⓒ Ⓔ |
| 104. | Ⓣ Ⓕ | Ⓣ Ⓕ | Ⓒ Ⓔ |
| 105. | Ⓣ Ⓕ | Ⓣ Ⓕ | Ⓒ Ⓔ |
| 106. | Ⓣ Ⓕ | Ⓣ Ⓕ | Ⓒ Ⓔ |
| 107. | Ⓣ Ⓕ | Ⓣ Ⓕ | Ⓒ Ⓔ |
| 108. | Ⓣ Ⓕ | Ⓣ Ⓕ | Ⓒ Ⓔ |
| 109. | Ⓣ Ⓕ | Ⓣ Ⓕ | Ⓒ Ⓔ |
| 110. | Ⓣ Ⓕ | Ⓣ Ⓕ | Ⓒ Ⓔ |
| 111. | Ⓣ Ⓕ | Ⓣ Ⓕ | Ⓒ Ⓔ |
| 112. | Ⓣ Ⓕ | Ⓣ Ⓕ | Ⓒ Ⓔ |
| 113. | Ⓣ Ⓕ | Ⓣ Ⓕ | Ⓒ Ⓔ |
| 114. | Ⓣ Ⓕ | Ⓣ Ⓕ | Ⓒ Ⓔ |
| 115. | Ⓣ Ⓕ | Ⓣ Ⓕ | Ⓒ Ⓔ |
| 116. | Ⓣ Ⓕ | Ⓣ Ⓕ | Ⓒ Ⓔ |

## PART C

24. Ⓐ Ⓑ Ⓒ Ⓓ Ⓔ
25. Ⓐ Ⓑ Ⓒ Ⓓ Ⓔ
26. Ⓐ Ⓑ Ⓒ Ⓓ Ⓔ
27. Ⓐ Ⓑ Ⓒ Ⓓ Ⓔ
28. Ⓐ Ⓑ Ⓒ Ⓓ Ⓔ
29. Ⓐ Ⓑ Ⓒ Ⓓ Ⓔ
30. Ⓐ Ⓑ Ⓒ Ⓓ Ⓔ
31. Ⓐ Ⓑ Ⓒ Ⓓ Ⓔ
32. Ⓐ Ⓑ Ⓒ Ⓓ Ⓔ
33. Ⓐ Ⓑ Ⓒ Ⓓ Ⓔ
34. Ⓐ Ⓑ Ⓒ Ⓓ Ⓔ
35. Ⓐ Ⓑ Ⓒ Ⓓ Ⓔ
36. Ⓐ Ⓑ Ⓒ Ⓓ Ⓔ
37. Ⓐ Ⓑ Ⓒ Ⓓ Ⓔ
38. Ⓐ Ⓑ Ⓒ Ⓓ Ⓔ
39. Ⓐ Ⓑ Ⓒ Ⓓ Ⓔ
40. Ⓐ Ⓑ Ⓒ Ⓓ Ⓔ
41. Ⓐ Ⓑ Ⓒ Ⓓ Ⓔ
42. Ⓐ Ⓑ Ⓒ Ⓓ Ⓔ
43. Ⓐ Ⓑ Ⓒ Ⓓ Ⓔ
44. Ⓐ Ⓑ Ⓒ Ⓓ Ⓔ
45. Ⓐ Ⓑ Ⓒ Ⓓ Ⓔ
46. Ⓐ Ⓑ Ⓒ Ⓓ Ⓔ
47. Ⓐ Ⓑ Ⓒ Ⓓ Ⓔ
48. Ⓐ Ⓑ Ⓒ Ⓓ Ⓔ
49. Ⓐ Ⓑ Ⓒ Ⓓ Ⓔ
50. Ⓐ Ⓑ Ⓒ Ⓓ Ⓔ
51. Ⓐ Ⓑ Ⓒ Ⓓ Ⓔ
52. Ⓐ Ⓑ Ⓒ Ⓓ Ⓔ
53. Ⓐ Ⓑ Ⓒ Ⓓ Ⓔ
54. Ⓐ Ⓑ Ⓒ Ⓓ Ⓔ
55. Ⓐ Ⓑ Ⓒ Ⓓ Ⓔ
56. Ⓐ Ⓑ Ⓒ Ⓓ Ⓔ
57. Ⓐ Ⓑ Ⓒ Ⓓ Ⓔ
58. Ⓐ Ⓑ Ⓒ Ⓓ Ⓔ
59. Ⓐ Ⓑ Ⓒ Ⓓ Ⓔ
60. Ⓐ Ⓑ Ⓒ Ⓓ Ⓔ
61. Ⓐ Ⓑ Ⓒ Ⓓ Ⓔ
62. Ⓐ Ⓑ Ⓒ Ⓓ Ⓔ
63. Ⓐ Ⓑ Ⓒ Ⓓ Ⓔ
64. Ⓐ Ⓑ Ⓒ Ⓓ Ⓔ
65. Ⓐ Ⓑ Ⓒ Ⓓ Ⓔ
66. Ⓐ Ⓑ Ⓒ Ⓓ Ⓔ
67. Ⓐ Ⓑ Ⓒ Ⓓ Ⓔ
68. Ⓐ Ⓑ Ⓒ Ⓓ Ⓔ
69. Ⓐ Ⓑ Ⓒ Ⓓ Ⓔ

# SAT CHEMISTRY – TEST 3

### PART A

1. Ⓐ Ⓑ Ⓒ Ⓓ Ⓔ
2. Ⓐ Ⓑ Ⓒ Ⓓ Ⓔ
3. Ⓐ Ⓑ Ⓒ Ⓓ Ⓔ
4. Ⓐ Ⓑ Ⓒ Ⓓ Ⓔ
5. Ⓐ Ⓑ Ⓒ Ⓓ Ⓔ
6. Ⓐ Ⓑ Ⓒ Ⓓ Ⓔ
7. Ⓐ Ⓑ Ⓒ Ⓓ Ⓔ
8. Ⓐ Ⓑ Ⓒ Ⓓ Ⓔ
9. Ⓐ Ⓑ Ⓒ Ⓓ Ⓔ
10. Ⓐ Ⓑ Ⓒ Ⓓ Ⓔ
11. Ⓐ Ⓑ Ⓒ Ⓓ Ⓔ
12. Ⓐ Ⓑ Ⓒ Ⓓ Ⓔ
13. Ⓐ Ⓑ Ⓒ Ⓓ Ⓔ
14. Ⓐ Ⓑ Ⓒ Ⓓ Ⓔ
15. Ⓐ Ⓑ Ⓒ Ⓓ Ⓔ
16. Ⓐ Ⓑ Ⓒ Ⓓ Ⓔ
17. Ⓐ Ⓑ Ⓒ Ⓓ Ⓔ
18. Ⓐ Ⓑ Ⓒ Ⓓ Ⓔ
19. Ⓐ Ⓑ Ⓒ Ⓓ Ⓔ
20. Ⓐ Ⓑ Ⓒ Ⓓ Ⓔ
21. Ⓐ Ⓑ Ⓒ Ⓓ Ⓔ
22. Ⓐ Ⓑ Ⓒ Ⓓ Ⓔ
23. Ⓐ Ⓑ Ⓒ Ⓓ Ⓔ

### PART B
### CHEMISTRY

|      | I | II | CE |
|------|-----|-----|-----|
| 101. | Ⓣ Ⓕ | Ⓣ Ⓕ | ⒸⒺ |
| 102. | Ⓣ Ⓕ | Ⓣ Ⓕ | ⒸⒺ |
| 103. | Ⓣ Ⓕ | Ⓣ Ⓕ | ⒸⒺ |
| 104. | Ⓣ Ⓕ | Ⓣ Ⓕ | ⒸⒺ |
| 105. | Ⓣ Ⓕ | Ⓣ Ⓕ | ⒸⒺ |
| 106. | Ⓣ Ⓕ | Ⓣ Ⓕ | ⒸⒺ |
| 107. | Ⓣ Ⓕ | Ⓣ Ⓕ | ⒸⒺ |
| 108. | Ⓣ Ⓕ | Ⓣ Ⓕ | ⒸⒺ |
| 109. | Ⓣ Ⓕ | Ⓣ Ⓕ | ⒸⒺ |
| 110. | Ⓣ Ⓕ | Ⓣ Ⓕ | ⒸⒺ |
| 111. | Ⓣ Ⓕ | Ⓣ Ⓕ | ⒸⒺ |
| 112. | Ⓣ Ⓕ | Ⓣ Ⓕ | ⒸⒺ |
| 113. | Ⓣ Ⓕ | Ⓣ Ⓕ | ⒸⒺ |
| 114. | Ⓣ Ⓕ | Ⓣ Ⓕ | ⒸⒺ |
| 115. | Ⓣ Ⓕ | Ⓣ Ⓕ | ⒸⒺ |
| 116. | Ⓣ Ⓕ | Ⓣ Ⓕ | ⒸⒺ |

### PART C

24. Ⓐ Ⓑ Ⓒ Ⓓ Ⓔ
25. Ⓐ Ⓑ Ⓒ Ⓓ Ⓔ
26. Ⓐ Ⓑ Ⓒ Ⓓ Ⓔ
27. Ⓐ Ⓑ Ⓒ Ⓓ Ⓔ
28. Ⓐ Ⓑ Ⓒ Ⓓ Ⓔ
29. Ⓐ Ⓑ Ⓒ Ⓓ Ⓔ
30. Ⓐ Ⓑ Ⓒ Ⓓ Ⓔ
31. Ⓐ Ⓑ Ⓒ Ⓓ Ⓔ
32. Ⓐ Ⓑ Ⓒ Ⓓ Ⓔ
33. Ⓐ Ⓑ Ⓒ Ⓓ Ⓔ
34. Ⓐ Ⓑ Ⓒ Ⓓ Ⓔ
35. Ⓐ Ⓑ Ⓒ Ⓓ Ⓔ
36. Ⓐ Ⓑ Ⓒ Ⓓ Ⓔ
37. Ⓐ Ⓑ Ⓒ Ⓓ Ⓔ
38. Ⓐ Ⓑ Ⓒ Ⓓ Ⓔ
39. Ⓐ Ⓑ Ⓒ Ⓓ Ⓔ
40. Ⓐ Ⓑ Ⓒ Ⓓ Ⓔ
41. Ⓐ Ⓑ Ⓒ Ⓓ Ⓔ
42. Ⓐ Ⓑ Ⓒ Ⓓ Ⓔ
43. Ⓐ Ⓑ Ⓒ Ⓓ Ⓔ
44. Ⓐ Ⓑ Ⓒ Ⓓ Ⓔ
45. Ⓐ Ⓑ Ⓒ Ⓓ Ⓔ
46. Ⓐ Ⓑ Ⓒ Ⓓ Ⓔ
47. Ⓐ Ⓑ Ⓒ Ⓓ Ⓔ
48. Ⓐ Ⓑ Ⓒ Ⓓ Ⓔ
49. Ⓐ Ⓑ Ⓒ Ⓓ Ⓔ
50. Ⓐ Ⓑ Ⓒ Ⓓ Ⓔ
51. Ⓐ Ⓑ Ⓒ Ⓓ Ⓔ
52. Ⓐ Ⓑ Ⓒ Ⓓ Ⓔ
53. Ⓐ Ⓑ Ⓒ Ⓓ Ⓔ
54. Ⓐ Ⓑ Ⓒ Ⓓ Ⓔ
55. Ⓐ Ⓑ Ⓒ Ⓓ Ⓔ
56. Ⓐ Ⓑ Ⓒ Ⓓ Ⓔ
57. Ⓐ Ⓑ Ⓒ Ⓓ Ⓔ
58. Ⓐ Ⓑ Ⓒ Ⓓ Ⓔ
59. Ⓐ Ⓑ Ⓒ Ⓓ Ⓔ
60. Ⓐ Ⓑ Ⓒ Ⓓ Ⓔ
61. Ⓐ Ⓑ Ⓒ Ⓓ Ⓔ
62. Ⓐ Ⓑ Ⓒ Ⓓ Ⓔ
63. Ⓐ Ⓑ Ⓒ Ⓓ Ⓔ
64. Ⓐ Ⓑ Ⓒ Ⓓ Ⓔ
65. Ⓐ Ⓑ Ⓒ Ⓓ Ⓔ
66. Ⓐ Ⓑ Ⓒ Ⓓ Ⓔ
67. Ⓐ Ⓑ Ⓒ Ⓓ Ⓔ
68. Ⓐ Ⓑ Ⓒ Ⓓ Ⓔ
69. Ⓐ Ⓑ Ⓒ Ⓓ Ⓔ

# SAT CHEMISTRY – TEST 4

## PART A

1. Ⓐ Ⓑ Ⓒ Ⓓ Ⓔ
2. Ⓐ Ⓑ Ⓒ Ⓓ Ⓔ
3. Ⓐ Ⓑ Ⓒ Ⓓ Ⓔ
4. Ⓐ Ⓑ Ⓒ Ⓓ Ⓔ
5. Ⓐ Ⓑ Ⓒ Ⓓ Ⓔ
6. Ⓐ Ⓑ Ⓒ Ⓓ Ⓔ
7. Ⓐ Ⓑ Ⓒ Ⓓ Ⓔ
8. Ⓐ Ⓑ Ⓒ Ⓓ Ⓔ
9. Ⓐ Ⓑ Ⓒ Ⓓ Ⓔ
10. Ⓐ Ⓑ Ⓒ Ⓓ Ⓔ
11. Ⓐ Ⓑ Ⓒ Ⓓ Ⓔ
12. Ⓐ Ⓑ Ⓒ Ⓓ Ⓔ
13. Ⓐ Ⓑ Ⓒ Ⓓ Ⓔ
14. Ⓐ Ⓑ Ⓒ Ⓓ Ⓔ
15. Ⓐ Ⓑ Ⓒ Ⓓ Ⓔ
16. Ⓐ Ⓑ Ⓒ Ⓓ Ⓔ
17. Ⓐ Ⓑ Ⓒ Ⓓ Ⓔ
18. Ⓐ Ⓑ Ⓒ Ⓓ Ⓔ
19. Ⓐ Ⓑ Ⓒ Ⓓ Ⓔ
20. Ⓐ Ⓑ Ⓒ Ⓓ Ⓔ
21. Ⓐ Ⓑ Ⓒ Ⓓ Ⓔ
22. Ⓐ Ⓑ Ⓒ Ⓓ Ⓔ
23. Ⓐ Ⓑ Ⓒ Ⓓ Ⓔ

## PART B
## CHEMISTRY

|       | I     | II    | CE  |
|-------|-------|-------|-----|
| 101.  | Ⓣ Ⓕ | Ⓣ Ⓕ | ⒸⒺ |
| 102.  | Ⓣ Ⓕ | Ⓣ Ⓕ | ⒸⒺ |
| 103.  | Ⓣ Ⓕ | Ⓣ Ⓕ | ⒸⒺ |
| 104.  | Ⓣ Ⓕ | Ⓣ Ⓕ | ⒸⒺ |
| 105.  | Ⓣ Ⓕ | Ⓣ Ⓕ | ⒸⒺ |
| 106.  | Ⓣ Ⓕ | Ⓣ Ⓕ | ⒸⒺ |
| 107.  | Ⓣ Ⓕ | Ⓣ Ⓕ | ⒸⒺ |
| 108.  | Ⓣ Ⓕ | Ⓣ Ⓕ | ⒸⒺ |
| 109.  | Ⓣ Ⓕ | Ⓣ Ⓕ | ⒸⒺ |
| 110.  | Ⓣ Ⓕ | Ⓣ Ⓕ | ⒸⒺ |
| 111.  | Ⓣ Ⓕ | Ⓣ Ⓕ | ⒸⒺ |
| 112.  | Ⓣ Ⓕ | Ⓣ Ⓕ | ⒸⒺ |
| 113.  | Ⓣ Ⓕ | Ⓣ Ⓕ | ⒸⒺ |
| 114.  | Ⓣ Ⓕ | Ⓣ Ⓕ | ⒸⒺ |
| 115.  | Ⓣ Ⓕ | Ⓣ Ⓕ | ⒸⒺ |
| 116.  | Ⓣ Ⓕ | Ⓣ Ⓕ | ⒸⒺ |

## PART C

24. Ⓐ Ⓑ Ⓒ Ⓓ Ⓔ
25. Ⓐ Ⓑ Ⓒ Ⓓ Ⓔ
26. Ⓐ Ⓑ Ⓒ Ⓓ Ⓔ
27. Ⓐ Ⓑ Ⓒ Ⓓ Ⓔ
28. Ⓐ Ⓑ Ⓒ Ⓓ Ⓔ
29. Ⓐ Ⓑ Ⓒ Ⓓ Ⓔ
30. Ⓐ Ⓑ Ⓒ Ⓓ Ⓔ
31. Ⓐ Ⓑ Ⓒ Ⓓ Ⓔ
32. Ⓐ Ⓑ Ⓒ Ⓓ Ⓔ
33. Ⓐ Ⓑ Ⓒ Ⓓ Ⓔ
34. Ⓐ Ⓑ Ⓒ Ⓓ Ⓔ
35. Ⓐ Ⓑ Ⓒ Ⓓ Ⓔ
36. Ⓐ Ⓑ Ⓒ Ⓓ Ⓔ
37. Ⓐ Ⓑ Ⓒ Ⓓ Ⓔ
38. Ⓐ Ⓑ Ⓒ Ⓓ Ⓔ
39. Ⓐ Ⓑ Ⓒ Ⓓ Ⓔ
40. Ⓐ Ⓑ Ⓒ Ⓓ Ⓔ
41. Ⓐ Ⓑ Ⓒ Ⓓ Ⓔ
42. Ⓐ Ⓑ Ⓒ Ⓓ Ⓔ
43. Ⓐ Ⓑ Ⓒ Ⓓ Ⓔ
44. Ⓐ Ⓑ Ⓒ Ⓓ Ⓔ
45. Ⓐ Ⓑ Ⓒ Ⓓ Ⓔ
46. Ⓐ Ⓑ Ⓒ Ⓓ Ⓔ
47. Ⓐ Ⓑ Ⓒ Ⓓ Ⓔ
48. Ⓐ Ⓑ Ⓒ Ⓓ Ⓔ
49. Ⓐ Ⓑ Ⓒ Ⓓ Ⓔ
50. Ⓐ Ⓑ Ⓒ Ⓓ Ⓔ
51. Ⓐ Ⓑ Ⓒ Ⓓ Ⓔ
52. Ⓐ Ⓑ Ⓒ Ⓓ Ⓔ
53. Ⓐ Ⓑ Ⓒ Ⓓ Ⓔ
54. Ⓐ Ⓑ Ⓒ Ⓓ Ⓔ
55. Ⓐ Ⓑ Ⓒ Ⓓ Ⓔ
56. Ⓐ Ⓑ Ⓒ Ⓓ Ⓔ
57. Ⓐ Ⓑ Ⓒ Ⓓ Ⓔ
58. Ⓐ Ⓑ Ⓒ Ⓓ Ⓔ
59. Ⓐ Ⓑ Ⓒ Ⓓ Ⓔ
60. Ⓐ Ⓑ Ⓒ Ⓓ Ⓔ
61. Ⓐ Ⓑ Ⓒ Ⓓ Ⓔ
62. Ⓐ Ⓑ Ⓒ Ⓓ Ⓔ
63. Ⓐ Ⓑ Ⓒ Ⓓ Ⓔ
64. Ⓐ Ⓑ Ⓒ Ⓓ Ⓔ
65. Ⓐ Ⓑ Ⓒ Ⓓ Ⓔ
66. Ⓐ Ⓑ Ⓒ Ⓓ Ⓔ
67. Ⓐ Ⓑ Ⓒ Ⓓ Ⓔ
68. Ⓐ Ⓑ Ⓒ Ⓓ Ⓔ
69. Ⓐ Ⓑ Ⓒ Ⓓ Ⓔ

# SAT CHEMISTRY – TEST 5

## PART A

1. Ⓐ Ⓑ Ⓒ Ⓓ Ⓔ
2. Ⓐ Ⓑ Ⓒ Ⓓ Ⓔ
3. Ⓐ Ⓑ Ⓒ Ⓓ Ⓔ
4. Ⓐ Ⓑ Ⓒ Ⓓ Ⓔ
5. Ⓐ Ⓑ Ⓒ Ⓓ Ⓔ
6. Ⓐ Ⓑ Ⓒ Ⓓ Ⓔ
7. Ⓐ Ⓑ Ⓒ Ⓓ Ⓔ
8. Ⓐ Ⓑ Ⓒ Ⓓ Ⓔ
9. Ⓐ Ⓑ Ⓒ Ⓓ Ⓔ
10. Ⓐ Ⓑ Ⓒ Ⓓ Ⓔ
11. Ⓐ Ⓑ Ⓒ Ⓓ Ⓔ
12. Ⓐ Ⓑ Ⓒ Ⓓ Ⓔ
13. Ⓐ Ⓑ Ⓒ Ⓓ Ⓔ
14. Ⓐ Ⓑ Ⓒ Ⓓ Ⓔ
15. Ⓐ Ⓑ Ⓒ Ⓓ Ⓔ
16. Ⓐ Ⓑ Ⓒ Ⓓ Ⓔ
17. Ⓐ Ⓑ Ⓒ Ⓓ Ⓔ
18. Ⓐ Ⓑ Ⓒ Ⓓ Ⓔ
19. Ⓐ Ⓑ Ⓒ Ⓓ Ⓔ
20. Ⓐ Ⓑ Ⓒ Ⓓ Ⓔ
21. Ⓐ Ⓑ Ⓒ Ⓓ Ⓔ
22. Ⓐ Ⓑ Ⓒ Ⓓ Ⓔ
23. Ⓐ Ⓑ Ⓒ Ⓓ Ⓔ

## PART B
## CHEMISTRY

|      | I        | II       | CE   |
|------|----------|----------|------|
| 101. | Ⓣ Ⓕ | Ⓣ Ⓕ | ⒸⒺ |
| 102. | Ⓣ Ⓕ | Ⓣ Ⓕ | ⒸⒺ |
| 103. | Ⓣ Ⓕ | Ⓣ Ⓕ | ⒸⒺ |
| 104. | Ⓣ Ⓕ | Ⓣ Ⓕ | ⒸⒺ |
| 105. | Ⓣ Ⓕ | Ⓣ Ⓕ | ⒸⒺ |
| 106. | Ⓣ Ⓕ | Ⓣ Ⓕ | ⒸⒺ |
| 107. | Ⓣ Ⓕ | Ⓣ Ⓕ | ⒸⒺ |
| 108. | Ⓣ Ⓕ | Ⓣ Ⓕ | ⒸⒺ |
| 109. | Ⓣ Ⓕ | Ⓣ Ⓕ | ⒸⒺ |
| 110. | Ⓣ Ⓕ | Ⓣ Ⓕ | ⒸⒺ |
| 111. | Ⓣ Ⓕ | Ⓣ Ⓕ | ⒸⒺ |
| 112. | Ⓣ Ⓕ | Ⓣ Ⓕ | ⒸⒺ |
| 113. | Ⓣ Ⓕ | Ⓣ Ⓕ | ⒸⒺ |
| 114. | Ⓣ Ⓕ | Ⓣ Ⓕ | ⒸⒺ |
| 115. | Ⓣ Ⓕ | Ⓣ Ⓕ | ⒸⒺ |
| 116. | Ⓣ Ⓕ | Ⓣ Ⓕ | ⒸⒺ |

## PART C

24. Ⓐ Ⓑ Ⓒ Ⓓ Ⓔ
25. Ⓐ Ⓑ Ⓒ Ⓓ Ⓔ
26. Ⓐ Ⓑ Ⓒ Ⓓ Ⓔ
27. Ⓐ Ⓑ Ⓒ Ⓓ Ⓔ
28. Ⓐ Ⓑ Ⓒ Ⓓ Ⓔ
29. Ⓐ Ⓑ Ⓒ Ⓓ Ⓔ
30. Ⓐ Ⓑ Ⓒ Ⓓ Ⓔ
31. Ⓐ Ⓑ Ⓒ Ⓓ Ⓔ
32. Ⓐ Ⓑ Ⓒ Ⓓ Ⓔ
33. Ⓐ Ⓑ Ⓒ Ⓓ Ⓔ
34. Ⓐ Ⓑ Ⓒ Ⓓ Ⓔ
35. Ⓐ Ⓑ Ⓒ Ⓓ Ⓔ
36. Ⓐ Ⓑ Ⓒ Ⓓ Ⓔ
37. Ⓐ Ⓑ Ⓒ Ⓓ Ⓔ
38. Ⓐ Ⓑ Ⓒ Ⓓ Ⓔ
39. Ⓐ Ⓑ Ⓒ Ⓓ Ⓔ
40. Ⓐ Ⓑ Ⓒ Ⓓ Ⓔ
41. Ⓐ Ⓑ Ⓒ Ⓓ Ⓔ
42. Ⓐ Ⓑ Ⓒ Ⓓ Ⓔ
43. Ⓐ Ⓑ Ⓒ Ⓓ Ⓔ
44. Ⓐ Ⓑ Ⓒ Ⓓ Ⓔ
45. Ⓐ Ⓑ Ⓒ Ⓓ Ⓔ
46. Ⓐ Ⓑ Ⓒ Ⓓ Ⓔ
47. Ⓐ Ⓑ Ⓒ Ⓓ Ⓔ
48. Ⓐ Ⓑ Ⓒ Ⓓ Ⓔ
49. Ⓐ Ⓑ Ⓒ Ⓓ Ⓔ
50. Ⓐ Ⓑ Ⓒ Ⓓ Ⓔ
51. Ⓐ Ⓑ Ⓒ Ⓓ Ⓔ
52. Ⓐ Ⓑ Ⓒ Ⓓ Ⓔ
53. Ⓐ Ⓑ Ⓒ Ⓓ Ⓔ
54. Ⓐ Ⓑ Ⓒ Ⓓ Ⓔ
55. Ⓐ Ⓑ Ⓒ Ⓓ Ⓔ
56. Ⓐ Ⓑ Ⓒ Ⓓ Ⓔ
57. Ⓐ Ⓑ Ⓒ Ⓓ Ⓔ
58. Ⓐ Ⓑ Ⓒ Ⓓ Ⓔ
59. Ⓐ Ⓑ Ⓒ Ⓓ Ⓔ
60. Ⓐ Ⓑ Ⓒ Ⓓ Ⓔ
61. Ⓐ Ⓑ Ⓒ Ⓓ Ⓔ
62. Ⓐ Ⓑ Ⓒ Ⓓ Ⓔ
63. Ⓐ Ⓑ Ⓒ Ⓓ Ⓔ
64. Ⓐ Ⓑ Ⓒ Ⓓ Ⓔ
65. Ⓐ Ⓑ Ⓒ Ⓓ Ⓔ
66. Ⓐ Ⓑ Ⓒ Ⓓ Ⓔ
67. Ⓐ Ⓑ Ⓒ Ⓓ Ⓔ
68. Ⓐ Ⓑ Ⓒ Ⓓ Ⓔ
69. Ⓐ Ⓑ Ⓒ Ⓓ Ⓔ